The Prentice Hall Florida Exit Test Study Guide for Writing

Patti Levine-Brown
Suzanne Hughes
Kathleen Cíez-Volz

Taken from:
The Prentice Hall Florida Exit Test Study Guide for Writing
by Patti Levine-Brown, Suzanne Hughes and Kathleen Cíez-Volz

Custom Publishing

New York Boston San Francisco
London Toronto Sydney Tokyo Singapore Madrid
Mexico City Munich Paris Cape Town Hong Kong Montreal

Cover Art: Coral Panorama, by Alisa Harding Stein

Taken from:

The Prentice Hall Florida Exit Text Study Guide for Writing
by Patti Levine-Brown, Suzanne Hughes, Kathleen Cíez-Volz
Copyright © 2004 by Pearson Education, Inc.
Published by Prentice Hall
Upper Saddle River, New Jersey 07458

This special edition published in cooperation with Pearson Custom Publishing.

Printed in the United States of America

11

2009240371

MT

**Pearson
Custom Publishing**
is a division of

PEARSON

www.pearsonhighered.com   ISBN 10: 0-558-38301-7
ISBN 13: 978-0-558-38301-5

Table of Contents

To help students prepare for the Florida College Basic Skills Exit Test for writing, Prentice Hall is providing a study guide that will reinforce the skills you must demonstrate on the state's exit exam.

Most Florida colleges require college preparatory students to pass a paragraph or five-paragraph essay exam as well as an English language exit exam before they can progress to English composition classes.

Adequate preparation for these exams is important to your college career, so a comprehensive pretest and post-test are available. Taking both will enable you to test your knowledge of grammar and writing skills before and after receiving classroom instruction. There are explanations and examples of prewriting strategies and a plan detailing the steps in putting a paragraph and essay together. We also have included samples of student work and analyses of their writing, as well as scoring criteria used in the exams.

Students needing remediation should spend additional time working on the skills that will be tested on the state exams. This guide will clarify what specific skills are expected and how they relate. It is designed to introduce each skill separately and to gradually move through the process, adding more detail.

Students taking any test should be given every advantage to prepare. Learning how to take advantage of strengths and compensate for weaknesses will help ease any fear or anxiety. In addition, this guide uses exercises similar to items students will see on the test.

Passages in this guide are taken from textbooks used in college classrooms nationwide, representing a variety of content areas. Even though you are presently taking a college preparatory class in English, all college courses require reading.

To help monitor your progress, comprehensive answer keys are available in the back of the guide. In order to get a true measure of the skills you have, and the ones you will acquire, work through the exercises and the tests on your own and then check the answers in the back of the book.

These courses are designed to give you a review of basic skill areas and insight into how to organize and structure your time. The skills you learn in preparatory classes and review in this guide are ones you will use when you read texts, write papers, compose essays, take tests, and decipher directions.

Acknowledgments:

We wish to thank our colleagues and dear friends Betsy Griffey, Arnold Wood, Gail Hubbard, Pat Wiseman, Cindy Gray, Nancy Banks, Shiela Kerr, Nancy Smith, Terry Getz, and Joe McClure for their support and encouragement. We are also grateful to Craig Campanella, acquisitions editor, and Joan Polk, editorial assistant at Prentice Hall for all the suggestions and attention they have given to us. Their help certainly improved the content of this guide. We especially want to express our appreciation to our family members: Noah, Gabriel, Devin, Sarah, Amanda, Don, Lloyd, James, Scott, and Nat. A special thank you goes to Patti's brother, Mark Levine, for his advice and counsel. Without the support of our families, we would never have been able to complete this project. Additionally, we wish to say thank you to the many students who have cheered us on.

Dedication:

For Kathleen's grandmother, Irene Majeius, Patti's mother, Dee Pagonis, and Suzanne's mother and father, Betty Bartholomaei and Cliff Pride, who encouraged us to follow our dreams.

FOREWORD

Just as masters of any art, professors Patti Levine-Brown, Kathleen Ciez-Volz, and Suzanne Pride-Hughes have provided a clear and compelling path for college preparatory English students. The work provides clarity by being built upon a logical intellectual framework that moves students along a well-articulated continuum from lower to higher levels of writing complexity. In addition, by using actual student writing samples as models, the authors ensure at each stage in the process a special connection from the student perspective.

The work is compelling because it is written with a key understanding of the intimate relationship between reading and writing. As students progress through the workbook, they will, for the first time in their lives, begin to read inquisitively. Furthermore, they will write with the understanding that the reader will be inquisitive.

This work is much more than a writer's guide; it is a guide to overall student growth. I urge all college prep teachers to look closely at its key ingredients: logical/systematic progression of skill development, consistency of applicable evaluation and feedback, modeling emphasis, high standards, and an underlying current of a passionate belief in the ability of our students to make quality thought visible – to write.

Dr. Donald W. Green
Author - __The Buddha and the Bandaid: A First Aid Kit for Leaders__

Part One: The Pretests

Writing Pretest

Directions: Choose the most effective word or phrase within the context suggested by the sentence(s).

1. Although Jennifer mailed the gift several weeks ago, Tyler never _____ it.

    A.   retrieved
    B.   received
    C.   redeemed

2. Showing a great deal of _____, the award-winning author humbly thanked his fans for their support.

    A.   vanity
    B.   uncertainty
    C.   modesty

Directions: Choose the option that corrects an error in an underlined portion. If no error exists, choose "No change is necessary."

3. The <u>weather</u> in the state <u>capital</u> is usually <u>ideal</u> at this time of year.
        A   B   C

    A.   whether
    B.   capitol
    C.   idea
    D.   No change is necessary.

Directions: Choose the sentence in which the modifiers are correctly placed.

4.
    A.   Desmond devoured a juicy porterhouse steak grilled on Grandpa's stove.

    B.   Grilled on Grandpa's stove, Desmond devoured a juicy porterhouse steak.

    C.   Desmond, grilled on Grandpa's stove, devoured a juicy porterhouse steak.

5.

    A. Struggling to fly the dragon-shaped kite, a strong gust of wind carried it off into the branches of an old oak tree.

    B. A strong gust of wind carried off the dragon-shaped kite into the branches of an old oak tree struggling to fly it.

    C. As two young boys struggled to fly the dragon-shaped kite, a strong gust of wind carried it off into the branches of an old oak tree.

Directions: Choose the most effective word or phrase within the context suggested by the sentence(s).

6. The Olympic swimmer trained eight hours a day for several months; _____, she felt very confident about her upcoming performance.

    A. nevertheless
    B. besides
    C. similarly
    D. consequently

Directions: Choose the sentence that most clearly expresses the thought without errors in sentence structure.

7.

    A. In order that our family loves to read books, we visit the public library once a week.

    B. Because our family loves to read books, we visit the public library once a week.

    C. Even though our family loves to read books, we visit the public library once a week.

Directions: Choose the sentence that has no errors in structure.

8.

    A. In order to win the grand prize, a child must sell one hundred boxes of cookies and to volunteer twenty hours of community service.

    B. In order to win the grand prize, a child must sell one hundred boxes of cookies and volunteering twenty hours of community service.

    C. In order to win the grand prize, a child must sell one hundred boxes of cookies and volunteer twenty hours of community service.

Directions: Choose the correct word or phrase within the context suggested by the sentence.

9. On summer afternoons, the children enjoy running through the sprinkler, diving into the pool, and _____in their fort.

    A.   play
    B.   playing
    C.   to play
    D.   and they play

Directions: For each of the questions in this section, choose the option that corrects an error in the underlined part(s) of the following sentences. If no error exists, choose "No change is necessary."

10.   When the rain stopped <u>falling and</u> the sun once again <u>emerged. A</u>
                          A   B
rainbow <u>appeared and</u> produced magnificent colors in the sky.
               C

    A.   falling. And
    B.   emerged, a
    C.   appeared. And
    D.   No change is necessary.

11. Although Justin is only twelve years <u>old, he</u> helps his family a great <u>deal by</u>
                                   A   B
dusting and vacuuming the <u>house. Also</u> watches over his younger
                               C
brothers.

    A.   old. He
    B.   deal by
    C.   house. He also
    D.   No change is necessary.

12. The elderly couple walk five miles a <u>day, they</u> are in better shape than many people half their age.

    A.   day they
    B.   day so, they
    C.   day; they
    D.   No change is necessary.

13. At his mother's <u>request, Ian</u> wears a helmet whenever he rides his motorized
    A
<u>scooter it</u> can go as fast as fifteen miles per <u>hour, so</u> he travels carefully
    B   C
on it.

    A.   request. Ian
    B.   scooter; it
    C.   hour so
    D.   No change is necessary.

14. The little girl accidentally <u>ran</u> into the ottoman that she and her older brother
    A
<u>had broken</u> yesterday during a game of tag; fortunately, she did not <u>get</u> hurt.
    B   C

    A.   run
    B.   had broke
    C.   got
    D.   No change is necessary.

15. When Mom <u>come</u> home from work, I <u>ran</u> up to her and <u>gave</u> her a big hug.
    A   B   C

    A.   came
    B.   run
    C.   given
    D.   No change is necessary.

16. Since its 1936 publication, *Gone with the Wind* <u>captivated</u> the interest of generations of
    readers.

    A.   captivates
    B.   was captivating
    C.   has captivated
    D.   No change is necessary.

17. In the 1980s, rock groups like Bon Jovi and White Snake <u>play</u> at sold-out
    A
concerts; these days, such groups, which some radio stations <u>call</u> "big hair
    B
bands," <u>are experiencing</u> a revival in their popularity.
    C

    A.   played
    B.   called
    C.   were experiencing
    D.   No change is necessary.

18. Either the tortoise or the hare <u>win</u> the long, challenging race.

    A.   are winning
    B.   were winning
    C.   wins
    D.   No change is necessary.

19. One of the puppies <u>look</u> smaller than the others; interestingly, every litter <u>has</u>
                        A   B
    a runt that often <u>captures</u> the hearts of both children and adults.
                        C

    A.   looks
    B.   have
    C.   capture
    D.   No change is necessary.

20. Each of the museum visitors <u>appears</u> surprised to discover that there <u>is</u> one
                                  A   B
    dragonfly and several butterflies in the painting that <u>portrays</u> city life.
                                                            C

    A.   appear
    B.   are
    C.   portray
    D.   No change is necessary.

21. The little boy enjoyed the circus thoroughly, but <u>he</u> especially loved the
                                                       A
    elephants because <u>they</u> performed amazing stunts for <u>him</u> and all the other
                       B   C
    children.

    A.   they
    B.   it
    C.   her
    D.   No change is necessary.

22. Many of <u>us</u> have lived in this neighborhood since <u>we</u> graduated from college
             A   B
    and started <u>their</u> families.
                 C

    A.   them
    B.   you
    C.   our
    D.   No change is necessary.

23. While preparing dinner, Darla listened to the CD <u>her</u> brothers had given her
                                                        A

when <u>you</u> visited <u>them</u> in Maine.
          B   C

    A.   my
    B.   she
    C.   us
    D.   No change is necessary.

24. Mr. Avery told Devin, <u>his</u> apprentice, that <u>he</u> needed to finish the
                           A   B

repair of the switch and check that <u>it</u> performed correctly.
                                     C

    A.   their
    B.   he, Devin,
    C.   they
    D.   No change is necessary.

25. The boys and <u>her</u> love visiting the beach; <u>they</u> enjoy swimming, surfing, and
                  A   B

tanning because such activities are fun and inexpensive for <u>them</u> to
                                                             C

experience.

    A.   she
    B.   them
    C.   they
    D.   No change is necessary.

26. The <u>quietly</u> <u>elegant</u> essay <u>profound</u> touched the audience and won first
        A   B   C

prize in the student literary contest.

    A.   quiet
    B.   elegantly
    C.   profoundly
    D.   No change is necessary.

27. Josh is the <u>powerfullest</u> of all the speakers on the debate team.

    A.   more powerful
    B.   most powerful
    C.   most powerfullest
    D.   No change is necessary.

28. The <u>committee</u> <u>succeeded</u> in electing a <u>different</u> leader for next year.
            A   B   C

    A.   comittee
    B.   suceeded
    C.   diferent
    D.   No change is necessary.

29. <u>Although Heather</u> wanted to attend her friend's baby <u>shower she</u> could not
          A   B

do <u>so because</u> she had to work.
    C

    A.   Although, Heather
    B.   shower, she
    C.   so, because
    D.   No change is necessary.

30. We enjoy listening to the news <u>programs and</u> classical music on the public
                                 A

radio <u>station, so</u> we are going to make a contribution during the <u>next, fund-</u>
          B   C

<u>raising</u> campaign.

    A.   programs, and
    B.   station so
    C.   next fund-raising
    D.   No change is necessary.

31. I love snacking on <u>cold, sweet,</u> juicy <u>watermelon, surprisingly,</u> I even enjoy
                        A   B

searching for the black <u>seeds that</u> other people find annoying.
                        C

    A.   cold sweet
    B.   watermelon; surprisingly,
    C.   seeds, that
    D.   No change is necessary.

32. Having come from the <u>Philippines,</u> Amancia speaks a variety of languages,
                        A

including <u>English,</u> and she is looking forward to practicing her writing skills
          B

this <u>Fall</u>.
    C

    A.   philippines
    B.   english
    C.   fall
    D.   No change is necessary.

Directions: <u>Read</u> the entire <u>passage</u> and then <u>answer</u> the <u>questions</u>. (Note: Intentional errors may have been included in this passage.)

1. _____. 2. The earliest tales about mermaids date back to the eighth century B.C. 3. Throughout the centuries, sailors have told stories of beautiful creatures with the upper body of a young woman and the lower body of a fish. 4. Curiously, "mermaid" contains two syllables that reveal the word's meaning: "mer" means "sea" and "maid" refers to a young woman. 5. Therefore, the term "mermaid" can be translated as "fish-like woman." 6. The two-part appearance of mermaids reflects their conflicting inner qualities. 7. On the one hand, they look friendly; on the other hand, they often behave unkindly and harm the humans whom they encounter. 8. In European folklore, mermaids are usually associated with danger, causing floods, drowning deaths among sailors, as well as shipwrecks. 9. One of the most famous mermaids in mythology is Lorelei, who reportedly dwells in the Rhine River near Germany and has lured many sailors to their deaths. 10. Indeed, for thousands of years, human beings have created myths like that of the mermaid to explain events that are difficult to understand, such as a natural disaster or a tragic accident. 11. Disney made a film titled *The Little Mermaid*. 12. Through mythology, people attempt to make sense of the world around them. 13. With its tales about Earth's mysterious waters, the myth of mermaids continues to intrigue human beings. *Some information in this passage has been paraphrased from the following sources: The History of "Mermaids," 11 May 2002 <http://rubens.anu.edu.au/student.projects/mermaids/homepage.html>. "Mermaids - Spirits or Goddesses?" 11 May 2002.*

33. Which of the following sentences, when inserted in the blank labeled number 1, is the best main idea or topic sentence for the passage?

    A.   The myth of mermaids has fascinated human beings for ages, perhaps because it helps to explain the unexplainable.

    B.   With their beautiful, mysterious appearance, mermaids attempt to lure sailors to their deaths.

    C.   Lorelei is a famous mermaid who supposedly lives in the Rhine River near Germany.

    D.   Mermaid mythology can be traced back to the eighth century B.C.

34. Which sentence provides the specific support for sentence 6 in the passage?

   A.   The earliest tales about mermaids date back to the eighth century B.C.
        (sentence 2).

   B.   On the one hand, they look friendly; on the other hand, they often behave
        unkindly and harm the humans whom they encounter (sentence 7).

   C.   Indeed, for thousands of years, human beings have created myths like that of the
        mermaid to explain events that are difficult to understand, such as a natural
        disaster or a tragic accident (sentence 10).

   D.   Disney made a film titled *The Little Mermaid* (sentence 11).

35. Select the arrangement of sentences 3, 4, and 5 that provides the most logical sequence of
    ideas and supporting details in the paragraph. If no change is needed, select option A.

   A.   Throughout the centuries, sailors have told stories of beautiful creatures with the
        upper body of a young woman and the lower body of a fish. Curiously,
        "mermaid" contains two syllables that reveal the word's meaning: "mer" means
        "sea" and "maid" refers to a young woman. Therefore, the term "mermaid" can
        be translated as "fish-like woman."

   B.   Curiously, "mermaid" contains two syllables that reveal the word's meaning:
        "mer" means "sea" and "maid" refers to a young woman. Throughout the
        centuries, sailors have told stories of beautiful creatures with the upper body of a
        young woman and the lower body of a fish. Therefore, the term "mermaid" can be
        translated as "fish-like woman."

   C.   Therefore, the term "mermaid" can be translated as "fish-like woman." Curiously,
        "mermaid" contains two syllables that reveal the word's meaning: "mer" means
        "sea" and "maid" refers to a young woman. Throughout the centuries, sailors
        have told stories of beautiful creatures with the upper body of a young woman
        and the lower body of a fish.

   D.   Therefore, the term "mermaid" can be translated as "fish-like woman."
        Throughout the centuries, sailors have told stories of beautiful creatures with the
        upper body of a young woman and the lower body of a fish. Curiously,
        "mermaid" contains two syllables that reveal the word's meaning: "mer" means
        "sea" and "maid" refers to a young woman.

36. Which numbered sentence is least relevant to the passage?

   A.   sentence 2
   B.   sentence 5
   C.   sentence 9
   D.   sentence 11

Directions: <u>Read</u> the entire <u>passage</u> carefully and then <u>answer</u> the <u>questions</u>. (Note: Intentional errors may have been included in this passage.)

1. _____. 2. Whereas the traditional artists of the eighteenth century portrayed idealized versions of people and places, the impressionists painted human subjects and landscapes in a natural, unstudied way. 3. Some key elements of impressionism include the following: theme, nature, color, and brushstrokes, all of which differed sharply from those of traditional art. 4. To begin, impressionist themes concern everyday, slice-of-life subjects, not the grand historical, religious, and mythological subjects of traditional art. 5. _____, Impressionist artists depicted nature more realistically and less dramatically than did the traditional artists. 6. The impressionists, moreover, used light, vibrant colors as opposed to the darker shades of traditional art. 7. When painting, impressionists applied quick brushstrokes that produced a spontaneous look as opposed to the precise, detailed appearance of a traditional canvas. 8. Famous French impressionists include Claude Monet, Pierre Auguste Renoir, and Edgar Degas. 9. Although these impressionists differed in terms of their backgrounds, beliefs, and artistic styles, they shared the goal of creating a different way of viewing life and reflecting it on canvas. 10. Their paintings are now displayed in a few exclusive hotels. 11. Indeed, these artists, whose nontraditional style of painting developed in nineteenth-century France, have left a lasting impression on the art world. *Information in this paragraph has been paraphrased from the following source: "Impressionism." 11 May 2002 <http://www.impressionism.org>.*

37. Which sentence, if inserted in the blank labeled 1, is the **best** main idea or topic sentence of the passage?

    A.   Unlike traditional artists, impressionists portrayed everyday subjects.

    B.   Impressionists painted with light colors instead of dark ones.

    C.   Important features of impressionism include its theme, nature, color, and brushstrokes.

    D.   Impressionism, a nontraditional style of painting that emerged in nineteenth-century France, strongly influenced the art world.

38. Select the arrangement of sentences 2, 3, and 4 that provides the most logical sequence of ideas and supporting details in the paragraph. If no change is needed, select option A.

A. Whereas the traditional artists of the eighteenth century portrayed idealized versions of people and places, the impressionists painted human subjects and landscapes in a natural, unstudied way. Some key elements of impressionism include the following: theme, nature, color, and brushstrokes, all of which differed sharply from those of traditional art. To begin, impressionist themes concern everyday, slice-of-life subjects, not the grand historical, religious, and mythological subjects of traditional art.

B. Whereas the traditional artists of the eighteenth century portrayed idealized versions of people and places, the impressionists painted human subjects and landscapes in a natural, unstudied way. To begin, impressionist themes concern everyday, slice-of-life subjects, not the grand historical, religious, and mythological subjects of traditional art. Some key elements of impressionism include the following: theme, nature, color, and brushstrokes, which differed sharply from those of traditional art.

C. To begin, impressionist themes concern everyday, slice-of-life subjects, not the grand historical, religious, and mythological subjects of traditional art. Some key elements of impressionism include the following: theme, nature, color, and brushstrokes, which differed sharply from those of traditional art. Whereas the traditional artists of the eighteenth century portrayed idealized versions of people and places, the impressionists painted human subjects and landscapes in a natural, unstudied way.

D. Some key elements of impressionism include the following: theme, nature, color, and brushstrokes, which differed sharply from those of traditional art. Whereas the traditional artists of the eighteenth century portrayed idealized versions of people and places, the impressionists painted human subjects and landscapes in a natural, unstudied way. To begin, impressionist themes concern everyday, slice-of-life subjects, not the grand historical, religious, and mythological subjects of traditional art.

39. Which numbered sentence is **least** relevant to the passage?

A. sentence 6
B. sentence 8
C. sentence 10
D. sentence 11

40. Which word or phrase, if inserted in the blank in sentence 5, would make the relationship of ideas in sentences 4 and 5 clearer?

A. However
B. Finally
C. On the other hand
D. In addition

11

Diagnostic Paragraph Pretest

Directions: On a separate sheet of paper or on the computer, write a practice paragraph according to the guidelines below. When you have completed the paragraph, submit it to your teacher for feedback.

You will have 50 minutes to plan, write, and proofread a paragraph on one of the topics below.

TOPIC 1   A person who has had a significant impact on your life

TOPIC 2   Your favorite style of music

In your writing, you should do the following:

- Establish your main idea clearly.
- Develop your main idea with adequate and relevant support.
- Organize your ideas logically and coherently.
- Make effective choices in vocabulary and sentence structure.
- Observe the conventions of standard American English grammar, spelling, capitalization, and punctuation.

Take a few minutes to think about what you want to say before you start writing. Leave yourself a few minutes at the end of the period to proofread and make corrections.

You may cross out or add information as necessary, but you should write or type as legibly as possible so that your teacher can easily read your paragraph.

Part Two: Testing and Study Tips

Most instructors giving the state exam have access to practice exams for a grammar portion of the test. If your instructor decides to give the class a practice exam, it is important for you to take advantage of this opportunity. The following information on testing and study tips will be helpful in preparing you for the state exam, but you will also find it helpful in preparing for other testing situations.

Preparing for the Test

Academic Preparation:

1. **Find out which skills and material will be included on the test.** Ask your professor about the questions that will be on the test.

   a. What skills and/or information will be included in the test?
   b. How will the questions be phrased?

   Request sample questions. Review the skills and material that will be included on the test. Look at the questions carefully to see how they are phrased.

2. **Practice.**
   a. When you want to learn a skill, it is important to practice the skill over and over until you have learned it. Just like athletes or actors improve their skills by rehearsing, you will improve your testing skills by practicing the material you need to know. You not only want to learn the skill; you want to become confident in your ability to get it right.

   b. Plan a schedule for studying the skills and doing practice exercises and tests. Do practice tests when you are offered them. They will help you know your strengths and weaknesses. When you miss a question, look at the right answer. Try to figure out why it was right and why yours was wrong. Your practice test will also let you know if you need to manage your time in a more efficient manner.

   c. Look for additional information and practice opportunities. If your school offers practice exams and workshops, attend them. Completing this book should help you practice the skills you will need for the state test.

3. **Find out how the test will be scored.** You need to know if all the questions have the same point value. Ask if some questions are more difficult or complicated than others. Find out about the time limitations on the test.

4. **Learn about the organization of the test.** Some tests have multiple parts in one section while others only address one subject at a time. Some tests mix the types of questions throughout the test. Ask your teacher the following questions.

   a. How will this test be presented?
   b. What is the style of the test?
   c. What type of language does it use?

   Most tests use a more formal language style than we use in our daily lives. Be prepared to deal with the more formal style.

5. **Self test**. Ask for practice exercises and tests. Do them and then check your answers. Look at the questions you missed. Why did you miss them? If you do not know, ask your teacher or a lab tutor.

Physical Preparation:

1. **Get enough sleep the night before the test**. Sleep about 8–12 hours the night before the test. Do not sleep an excessive amount because this can make you sleepy and slow thinking. Ideally, you should try to get enough sleep for a few nights before the test.

2. **Eat a breakfast or lunch with protein before the test**. Protein is found in eggs, meat, and nuts. Try to stay away from a meal high in carbohydrates (breads, potatoes, crackers). They have a tendency to make you sleepy. Do not drink too much before you go into the test. You may not be allowed to leave the room during the test.

3. **Try to get some light exercise before the test**. This provides oxygen to your brain, which helps you think. It also helps control tension. A brisk walk from the parking lot would probably improve your ability to think while you are taking the test.

4. **Try to arrive at the testing location a little early**. Pick a good seat. If you want to avoid distractions, choose one of the corner seats, preferably away from the door.

5. **Bring a watch with you**. Not all classrooms have a clock, so it is important to have a watch so you can pace yourself.

6. **Dress in layers**. Because the testing rooms may be cold or hot, wear light clothing and bring a sweatshirt or jacket. You need to be prepared so the temperature does not interfere with your concentration.

Emotional preparation:

1. **Be prepared**. Knowing that you have the skills to deal with the test helps you build your confidence, so you can complete the test successfully.

2. **Think positively**. You have passed many tests in your lifetime, and you can pass this one too. Psych yourself by telling yourself about the work, practice, and tests you have successfully completed.

3. **Learn some calming methods.**
   a. Visualize yourself passing the test. See yourself completing the questions accurately and efficiently.

   b. Think of a comfortable, peaceful place other than your bed. Visualize yourself in that place for a few moments before the test starts. An example would be to picture being on the beach watching the waves come in to the shore.

   c. Use deep breathing to calm your body and to allow oxygen to reach your brain. Place one hand on your chest and one on your abdomen. Practice breathing deeply until your breathing raises the hand on your abdomen before it raises the hand on your chest.

4. **Try to clear your mind**. If you have other thoughts crowding your mind, take a minute before the test to write them down, so you do not worry about them during the test.

Taking the Test

Multiple Choice Examinations

The grammar portion of the state exit exam is multiple choice. The following guidelines will help plan test-taking strategies that may help you improve your score.

1. **One of the *major considerations* to think about when you plan how to complete a test is the amount of time you are given for completion of the test.** If you are going to have difficulty completing the test in the time given, you need to consider which of the following methods is best to use for the test. A technique that can help you to decide is to try each method on one of the practice tests. See which one works the best for you.

   a. **Some educators say to do the test in order.** This method makes you positive that you do not forget any questions. It also makes it easier to put the answer in the correct space. The problem with this method is that you often spend too much time on questions that are difficult, and then you may not have enough time to complete the easier questions.

b. **Other educators say to do the questions first that you easily understand; then go back to complete the ones that are more difficult.** In a timed situation in which each question is given the same number of points doing the easier questions first helps you get the most points in the shortest amount of time. The problem with this method is that some students write the answers next to the wrong numbers because they forget they have skipped a question.

2. **Find out how the test is scored.** If the test only counts the correct answers, it is essential to answer each question. On the Florida State Test each answer counts, so it is important to have an answer for each question. Do not leave any questions blank. If you run into confusing questions that are taking too much time, choose the best answer, note the number and return to the question if you have time. Do not spend too much time on any one question.

3. **Read the question and all the answers carefully before you choose one.** Sometimes an answer may seem appropriate, but there may be a better answer below it. If you get to the point where you are not sure, go with your initial feeling or choice.

4. **A statement used in a multiple-choice answer has to be all true, or you should eliminate it.** If you use this method, you must be careful because the first part of some statements may sound as if they are true, but the second part may be false. If any part of an answer is false, that choice should be eliminated.

5. **Look for qualifying words.** Are the words absolute or do they allow for some flexibility? Answers that use absolute words such as always, never, must, all, or no should be considered carefully because few ideas in life are unchangeable or definite. These words often suggest an answer is incorrect. Words that qualify such as many, most, much, often, perhaps, and some are more likely to be the correct answer.

6. **If two answers are synonymous, eliminate them as choices.** If two answers mean the same, neither one is the best choice unless the test question gives you the option to choose more than one answer.

7. **Pay attention to grammatical clues.** If the question asks which people did the action, the test is giving you a clue that at least two people must be named in the answer. If the word *an* is used, it indicates the answer must start with a vowel. Look for other clues.

8. **When the question asks you to choose the best answer, it is often best to consider what the answer should be before you look at the choices.** For some people this helps lessen the confusion presented by the alternatives. You should still read all of the choices to make certain that there is not a better answer.

If you try to use many of these suggestions, you should find test taking to be a little less stressful. One of the best methods to help test anxiety is to be prepared. Some of these methods may seem silly such as wearing layered clothing, but if you are overheated, it can make you sleepy and less attentive. Each of the ideas should be considered as you plan to take the test.

Part Three: Conceptual and Organizational Skills

Chapter 1: The Topic Sentence

When you have to identify a topic for a paragraph, you must first ask yourself, "Who or what is this paragraph about?" Next, you must decide if there are limiting factors that restrict the topic. For example, the following paragraph is about a young man, not men in general. What part of the man's life is the paragraph about? That information would be the limiting factor.

John is an eighteen-year-old young man who cannot make up his mind about the path he needs to take after he graduates high school. One day he wants to go to college, and the next day he wants to get a job and forget about teachers and assignments. No career attracts him because the only ones that seem the least bit exciting require a four or six year degree program. His parents have told him to enlist in the armed forces, but he does not wish to execute people, or to get killed. The idea of boot camp and barking sergeants commanding him to get up before sunrise, to run twenty-five miles, to police his area, and to clean latrines nauseates him. He has to decide almost immediately because graduation is next month, and his parents are threatening to kick him out if he is not employed or registered for a higher education program of study.

If the paragraph is about one person, your topic should name that person, or state the topic as one person. The topic for this paragraph would be John's career decision, not teenage boys' career decisions or young men's career decisions. It would be about John's career choice not his whole life.

Sometimes a paragraph can have a compound subject. This is commonly found in comparison or contrast paragraphs. This can mean that the paragraph is about two or more people, concepts, or objects, but it can also be about two aspects of a person, place, or thing. An example would be the good and bad aspects of the use of diet drugs.

Process and time order paragraphs have some similarities, but there are also differences. The paragraphs both list items in the order they happen, and they both use many of the same transitions, but there are small differences. Process paragraphs are usually found in expository paragraphs that list steps for directions in the sequence in which they must occur, or that list stages in the chronological order in which they typically happen. The steps, or stages, are very similar each time they occur, though there might be small differences. Time order paragraphs are paragraphs that sequentially list activities, or events, that have taken place. Time order paragraphs are found in narratives and in expository text, such as history books, or biographies.

*Some of the paragraphs used by the authors have been altered to fit the patterns used by the Florida State Exit Test.

The subjects in this paragraph are time order paragraphs and process paragraphs. Because there are two subjects, we call this a compound subject. What is the limiting factor? This paragraph addresses the similarities and differences between the two types of paragraphs. It does not state how to write them or when to use them. There are clue words that should help you find the method of organization for the paragraph. These words are similarities, differences, and both.

Topic sentences

The topic sentence should include the topic (subject) and the main point the author is trying to make about the topic. The topic sentence must provide the reader with clues about how the paragraph is organized. It may also include key words or transitions to help the reader to know the direction the author will take. The organization of the paragraph, the arrangement of the sentences, may also help you to figure out which is the topic sentence. The sentences in the paragraph should provide details or support for the main idea, and they should relate to the topic sentence. The topic sentence should not just list a fact, but it should provide us with a more general idea that can be expanded with details and support. The specific details are the examples, reasons, facts, and particulars, such as information that answers when, where, what, when, and how.

Read the following paragraph and find the main idea.

Some colleges have stringent entrance requirements for students. For example, most entering freshman at these colleges are required to have Scholastic Achievement Test scores of one thousand two hundred or higher. The student must have a grade point average of three point two five or higher, and the student must have completed a certain number of classes in each of the following areas: mathematics, English, foreign language, history, and science. Incoming freshmen must have participated in at least one community volunteer experience. Students who have been involved in clubs, sports, or school organizations have a better chance of being accepted into the college of their choice than those who have not been active in extra-curricular activities.

How do the sentences relate to one another? They are all stating stringent entrance requirements for acceptance to certain colleges. Which statement groups the ideas in the other sentences? The first sentence is the most general. Each of the other sentences names a specific factor or a set of factors that would be needed in order to be considered for a program in a certain college.

The first sentence of this paragraph is the topic sentence. It is general enough to cover each of the ideas in the following sentences. The details that follow the topic sentence are examples of the main idea in the topic sentence. Many writers write the topic sentence first, but others place the topic sentence in other positions in the paragraph.

Read this paragraph and try to locate the topic sentence.

Dormitory living can be pleasurable because you do not have to get into a vehicle and drive to your classes, so you can sleep later. Food service provides all your meals, as a result you do not have to spend time preparing your food and

*Some of the paragraphs used by the authors have been altered to fit the patterns used by the Florida State Exit Test.

cleaning the kitchen after you eat. Laundry facilities are placed in each dormitory, which makes it unnecessary to travel, and you often have others to talk with while your laundry is getting clean. There is always someone to ask if you have trouble with your assignments, and the computer labs and the library are readily available most anytime you need them. **Even though there are advantages to dormitory living, there are also disadvantages.** One drawback is that you may not like your roommate or suitemates. Another of the major problems with dormitory living is the lack of privacy. On most floors there is always someone up and making noise, so when you want to sleep, or to study, it is very difficult. When you want to entertain, you must make arrangements with your roommate or your suitemates. It can become very frustrating if you want to spend time alone because sometimes it is hard to find a place where you can be by yourself.

In this paragraph the topic sentence is in the middle of the paragraph. The author listed all the benefits of dormitory living in the first half of the paragraph, and then listed all the weaknesses in the second half. Since the topic sentence included both ideas, it was placed in the center to divide the two sections.

Sometimes the topic sentence is listed at the end of the paragraph.

Freshmen fail classes because they do not attend class the required number of times. They have difficulty managing their time because they want to socialize and to enjoy their college experience. Since freshman are accepted into a college because of their high school work and test scores, you would predict that they would be able to cope with the academic demands in the classroom, but many have not been prepared to do the considerable amount of studying that is mandatory to achieve good grades. Naïve, new college students procrastinate with many of the demands made by their professors, and as a result, their work is tardy and receives a lower grade. Many college students eat an unbalanced diet and sleep less than the amount needed to replenish the body's energy, so they are often fatigued and unable to think clearly. **To prevent these problems from occurring, colleges should offer a mandatory course for freshmen to prepare them for the demands of college life.**

Here the author lists the causes at the beginning of the paragraph. Then the author writes a final generalized statement about the causes and suggests a solution to help the problems listed before the solution. A topic sentence can occur in various positions in a paragraph, but it is most commonly found as the first sentence.

Remember, topic sentences have to be general enough to cover specific details, but they also have to be focused enough to eliminate material that is not covered by the paragraph.

Ex.   A.   Hurricane Floyd was in the Atlantic Ocean east of Florida on September 14, 1999.

       B.   Hurricane Floyd had many characteristics, which frightened many people.

*Some of the paragraphs used by the authors have been altered to fit the patterns used by the Florida State Exit Test.

Sentence A is too specific to cover any additional ideas, whereas sentence B is general enough to cover additional ideas such as the unique features of this hurricane.

Ex.   A.   My sister's wedding had many funny mishaps.

    B.   At my sister's wedding a waitress tripped and poured beer all over one of the guests.

Sentence B is too specific to cover any additional ideas, whereas sentence A is general enough to cover additional ideas such as the different funny events at the wedding.

Note: Topic sentences may also be called main idea sentences or thesis statements.

Exercises:

Read the passages and answer the question for each passage. (Note: Intentional errors may have been included in these passages.)

Passage 1

[1] _____. [2]Charismatics have unique personal talents that can change a group of people into supporters. [3] In the process they may create their own rules and regulations and challenge the established governing bodies. [4]_____, in 1917, Vladimir Lenin directed the overthrow of Russia's imperial government and later convinced many of the Russian people to fight for a government that would consider the needs of the workers and peasants instead of the wealthy. [5]After World War II Mahatma Gandhi inspired the struggle to free India from British colonialism. [6]He convinced many of his countrymen to use passive resistance methods such as protests and fasts. [7]Soon after, Martin Luther King, Jr. organized and encouraged the civil rights movement in the United States. [8]His moving speeches and his leadership of African-American nonviolent confrontations protesting and boycotting injustices made him a recognized leader. [9]His first job was in Montgomery, Alabama. [10]As a result of his efforts, many social changes were made in the United States. [11]Similarly, Mother Teresa asked the world to take care of its poverty and spent her life ministering to the poor in Calcutta, India. *(Some of the information and ideas in this paragraph have been adapted some ideas from Macionis, John J. Sociology. 9th ed. Upper Saddle River, NJ: Prentice Hall, 2003. p. 436)*

1.1 Which sentence, if inserted in the blank labeled number 1, is the **best** main idea or topic sentence for the passage

    A. Martin Luther King, Jr. and Vladimir Lenin are two example of charismatics who changed the rules that had been established in their countries.
    B. Charismatics are people who follow others into battles in order to change the government.
    C. Vladimir Lenin was a charismatic person who led the overthrow of the Russian feudal government.
    D. Charisma improves the standing of an recognized leader and makes the influence of a challenger more powerful.

*Some of the paragraphs used by the authors have been altered to fit the patterns used by the Florida State Exit Test.

20

Passage 2

[1] _____

[2]Many efficient readers learn to like reading. [3]After completing either of these previews, you should take a minute to think about your prior knowledge of the subject in order to pull the knowledge from your memory. [4]Good readers prepare to read by using one of the previewing methods before they settle down to their serious reading. [5]The first is to scan the whole chapter to get an understanding of the topic and the aspects covered in the reading, and the second is to survey specific parts of the chapter or article to find out information about topics covered in the reading. [6]Amazingly, just using one of these two methods usually doubles a person's reading speed and increases his or her understanding. [7]The third step to reading capably and quickly is to practice reading proficiently by timing your reading and setting goals to make you read just a little bit faster each time. [8]_____, after each period of reading, check your comprehension by telling someone about the material you have read or by writing notes about the reading.

1.2 Which of the following sentences, when inserted in the blank labeled number 1, would serve as the best thesis statement for the passage?

   A. Good readers open their books and start to read; when they are done, they review the material they have read.
   B. Previewing by scanning or by reading the introduction, summary, and headings will make you understand better and read faster.
   C. Reading faster can actually help you understand the material you are reading better than if you read slowly.
   D. Many people feel that reading quickly will make understanding more difficult, but if you are taught the proper methods, reading efficiently usually leads to better comprehension.

Passage 3

[1] _____

_____ [2]One of the techniques artists use in circular paintings is radial symmetry; the center of the painting is the major focal point and the other parts of the painting surround the center in a pattern like spokes on a wheel. [3] Wheels are a visual attraction for many people who use them as decorations. [4] Another method is to use the balance of the painting or the symmetry of the lines. [5]Color, light, and contrast can be used as techniques to entice the viewer's eyes to focus first on the desired section of the painting. [6]If many of the directional lines used to draw some of the elements of the painting are parallel, the focus is to follow those lines to the end. [7]_____ shades of one color are used for the background, the viewer's eyes are drawn to the element of the painting that the artist wants as the focal point. [8]By making some of the colors a strong contrast to those used in the background, a point of emphasis is established. [9]All of these methods have been used by artists. *(Some of the information and ideas in this paragraph have been adapted from Sayre, Henry. A World of Art, 3rd ed. Upper Saddle River, NJ: Prentice Hall, 2000. pp. 162-163)*

*Some of the paragraphs used by the authors have been altered to fit the patterns used by the Florida State Exit Test.

1.3 Which sentence, if inserted in the blank labeled number 1, is the **best** main idea or topic sentence for the passage?

A. When the artist makes an object a color that strongly contrasts with the background, he or she is trying to draw your eye to that part of the picture.
B. Making the central focus in the center of a painting is one way to make people look at that part of the painting.
C. There are various methods that artists employ to draw the viewer's eyes to the part of the painting they want to emphasize.
D. Artists use many techniques for many purposes when they draw or paint.

Passage 4

1 _____.

[2]In past centuries, many countries' military leaders or religious figures such as Joan of Arc were regarded as heroes. [3]During World War I and World War II in the twentieth century, members of the military in our country were viewed as heroes. [4]But as radio, movies, and television became commonplace in United States during the last hundred years, the heroes changed to entertainment and sports stars. [5]In the later part of the twentieth century and the beginning of the twenty-first century, many people looked to stars, such as Jesse Ventura or Britney Spears, to help them choose their values. [6]Children modeled their behavior after cartoon characters. [7]The Ninja Turtles, Mighty Mouse, and Power Rangers became heroes to children because they saved characters on the shows. [8]_____, something happened during the fall in 2001 that changed the type of heroes people in the United States admired. [9]After the World Trade Center was attacked last September, people began to regard firemen and policemen as heroes because they exposed their lives to danger or sacrificed their lives while they were attempting to save others. *(Some of the information and ideas in this paragraph have been adapted from Macionis, John J. Sociology. 9th ed. Upper Saddle Ridge, NJ: Prentice Hall, 2003. p. 72)*

1.4 Which of the following sentences, when inserted in the blank labeled number 1, would serve as the best thesis statement for the passage?

A. Britney Spears, Dwight D. Eisenhower, John F. Kennedy, and the Power Rangers were heroes during the past century.
B. The public's view of heroes in the United States has changed throughout the last century.
C. Over the centuries people in different countries have changed the type of people they view as heroes.
D. During the past century some people viewed cartoon characters and superstars as heroes.

*Some of the paragraphs used by the authors have been altered to fit the patterns used by the Florida State Exit Test.

Passage 5

[1] _____

[2]The major networks offered few choices of family shows with minorities, but more minorities were being included in major network shows set in employment settings. [3]Shows such as *Third Watch, Cops,* and *E.R.* had some minority characters, but they were not in the forefront of the show weekly as a major character on a sitcom might be. [4]Other shows did include minorities such as homosexuals, but the characters still followed the old stereotypes. [5]In many cartoons even the animals, such as cats, were treated stereotypically; *Tom and Jerry* was a good example of this treatment. [6]Some of the smaller networks carried some shows, like *The My Wife and Kids,* that featured minority characters in family situations that more closely depicted people in semi-realistic settings, but the major networks rarely followed their example. [7]Some of the popular shows, *Frazier* and *Friends,* rarely included minorities in their shows. [8]_____, many people thought it would be good for the major television networks to include characters from more minority groups and to have the situations in the shows represent these characters at least as realistically as others in different shows were portrayed. *(Some information and ideas in this paragraph have been adapted from Macionis, John J. Sociology, 9th ed. Upper Saddle River, NJ: Prentice Hall, 2003. p. 128)*

1.5 Which sentence, if inserted in the blank labeled number 1, is the **best** main idea or topic sentence for the passage?

   A. Minorities are not being portrayed realistically by television networks around the world.
   B. Some shows on small networks such as Fox and Warner Brothers portrayed minorities in a more realistic fashion than many shows on the United States larger television networks.
   C. Until 2002, all networks in the United State portrayed minorities in a stereotypical fashion or did not include minorities as major characters on weekly shows, and this needed to be changed.
   D. Until 2002, major television networks in the United States either portrayed minorities in a stereotypical manner or rarely included them in shows and movies, and this needed to be changed.

*Some of the paragraphs used by the authors have been altered to fit the patterns used by the Florida State Exit Test.

Chapter 2: Supporting Details

The important details of a paragraph relate to the main idea and support the ideas presented. Details will answer the six questions used by writers: who, what, when, where, why, and how. The details give reasons; examples; explanations; descriptive characteristics; events or activities; people, places and objects; and particulars about an item or situation. Some of the details are considered major support while others that are not as important are minor details.

It is important to be able to recognize which are the major details and which are the minor details. Major details connect strongly with the topic sentence, provide substantial information, and are specific. The minor details are the sentences that support the major details. If your topic sentence stated, "Three teachers in my life shaped my future," then the three major support statements would probably name a teacher and specifically state how he or she helped shape your life. The minor details would give an example, a reason, an explanation, or a particular point of information that would make that teacher's special effect on your life more clear. An example is done for you below.

[1]**Three teachers in my life shaped my future.** [2]**Mrs. Rhine, my sixth grade teacher, taught me to believe in my abilities and to be happy using them.** [3]**A new world opened up to me because of Mrs. Rhine's encouragement and her stimulating creative, student assignments.** [4]**Though I had only been an average student in the earlier grades, throughout the sixth grade my grades improved steadily, and I earned the right to be in the honors section in junior high school.** [5]**The second teacher that affected my life was Mr. Ponte because he taught me to question what people stated and to observe the world with a questioning eye.** [6]**Up to this point in my life I had accepted ideas I read in the newspaper and in books, but he taught me to weigh the evidence and the support that was presented in order to make my own decisions.** [7]**The third teacher that had an effect on me was Dr. Schillit because he taught me to set goals, to see the wonders of the world, and to challenge myself to go further.** [8]**He continuously challenged me to try new ideas and to think of the possibilities for my life.** [9]**Without the influence of these three teachers, I would not be the person I am today.**

The topic sentence is sentence one and the idea is repeated in sentence 8. The major ideas are the three sentences naming the teachers and stating the effect they had on my life (sentences 2, 5, and 7). The minor details (sentences 3, 4, 6, 8) give a little more information about the major details in order to help the reader understand more easily.

Many major details pertain to the paragraph's organization. Each paragraph organization has specific types of details that are used as major support. The particular organization of the paragraph helps point to the major specific details.

*Some of the paragraphs used by the authors have been altered to fit the patterns used by the Florida State Exit Test.

Pattern	Major Details
Time order	events and activities in the order they happen
Process	steps or stages in the order they happen
Spatial	objects in the order they are placed
Description	characteristics of people or objects
Order of importance	items, activities, or people in a hierarchical order
Cause effect	events or actions and consequences
Comparison	likenesses
Contrast	differences
Argumentation	reasons, facts, statistics
Classification	large group, small groups, characteristics to divide groups
Definition	meanings
Generalization and example	examples of idea presented in main idea

Exercises:

Read each passage and answer the question following the passage. (Note: Intentional errors may have been included in these passages.)

Passage 1

[1] _____. [2]Charismatics have unique personal talents that can change a group of people into supporters. [3] In the process they may create their own rules and regulations and challenge the established governing bodies. [4] _____, in 1917, Vladimir Lenin directed the overthrow of Russia's imperial government and later convinced many of the Russian people to fight for a government that would consider the needs of the workers and peasants instead of the wealthy. [5]After World War II Mahatma Gandhi inspired the struggle to free India from British colonialism. [6]He convinced many of his countrymen to use passive resistance methods such as protests and fasts. [7]Soon after, Martin Luther King, Jr. organized and encouraged the civil rights movement in the United States. [8]His moving speeches and his leadership of African-American nonviolent confrontations protesting and boycotting injustices made him a recognized leader. [9]His first job was in Montgomery, Alabama. [10]As a result of his efforts, many social changes were made in the United States. [11]Similarly, Mother Teresa asked the world to take care of its poverty and spent her life ministering to the poor in Calcutta, India. *(Some of the information and ideas in this paragraph have been adapted from Macionis, John J. Sociology. 9th ed. Upper Saddle River, NJ: Prentice Hall, 2003. p. 436)*

2.1 Which of the numbered sentences is not supported by sufficient specific details?

    A. sentence 3
    B. sentence 7
    C. sentence 8
    D. sentence 11

*Some of the paragraphs used by the authors have been altered to fit the patterns used by the Florida State Exit Test.

Passage 2

1 _____

[2]Many efficient readers learn to like reading. [3]After completing either of these previews, you should take a minute to think about your prior knowledge of the subject in order to pull the knowledge from your memory. [4]Good readers prepare to read by using one of the previewing methods before they settle down to their serious reading. [5]The first is to scan the whole chapter to get an understanding of the topic and the aspects covered in the reading, and the second is to survey specific parts of the chapter or article to find out information about topics covered in the reading. [6]Amazingly, just using one of these two methods usually doubles a person's reading speed and increases his or her understanding. [7]The third step to reading capably and quickly is to practice reading proficiently by timing your reading and setting goals to make you read just a little bit faster each time. [8]_____, after each period of reading, check your comprehension by telling someone about the material you have read or by writing notes about the reading.

2.2 Which sentence provides specific support for sentence 5 in the passage?

    A. Sentence 4 (Good readers prepare to read by using one of the previewing methods before they settle down to their serious reading.)
    B. Sentence 6 (Amazingly, just using one of these two methods usually doubles a person's reading speed and increases his or her understanding.)
    C. Sentence 7 (The third step to reading capably and quickly is to practice reading proficiently by timing your reading and setting goals to make you read just a little bit faster each time.)
    D. Sentence 8 (_____, after each period of reading, check your comprehension by telling someone about the material you have read or by writing notes about the reading.)

Passage 3

1 _____

_____[2]One of the techniques artists use in circular paintings is radial symmetry; the center of the painting is the major focal point and the other parts of the painting surround the center in a pattern like spokes on a wheel. [3] Wheels are a visual attraction for many people who use them as decorations. [4] Another method is to use the balance of the painting or the symmetry of the lines. [5]Color, light, and contrast can be used as techniques to entice the viewer's eyes to focus first on the desired section of the painting. [6]If many of the directional lines used to draw some of the elements of the painting are parallel, the focus is to follow those lines to the end. [7]_____ shades of one color are used for the background, the viewer's eyes are drawn to the element of the painting that the artist wants as the focal point. [8]By making some of the colors a strong contrast to those used in the background, a point of emphasis is established. [9]All of these methods have been used by artists. *(Some of the information and ideas in this paragraph have been adapted from Sayre, Henry. A World of Art. 3rd ed. Upper Saddle River, NJ: Prentice Hall, 2000. pp. 162-163)*

*Some of the paragraphs used by the authors have been altered to fit the patterns used by the Florida State Exit Test.

2.3 Which sentence provides specific support for sentence 4 in the passage?

    A. Sentence 2 (One of the techniques artists use in circular paintings is radial symmetry; the center of the painting is the major focal point and the other parts of the painting surround the center in a pattern like spokes on a wheel.)
    B. Sentence 5 (Color, light, and contrast can be used as techniques to entice the viewer's eyes to focus first on the desired section of the painting.)
    C. Sentence 6 (If many of the directional lines used to draw some of the elements of the painting are parallel, the focus is to follow those lines to the end.)
    D. Sentence 8 (By making some of the colors a strong contrast to those used in the background, a point of emphasis is established.)

Passage 4

[1]_____.

[2]In past centuries, many countries' military leaders or religious figures such as Joan of Arc were regarded as heroes. [3]During World War I and World War II in the twentieth century, members of the military in our country were viewed as heroes. [4]But as radio, movies, and television became commonplace in United States during the last hundred years, the heroes changed to entertainment and sports stars. [5]In the later part of the twentieth century and the beginning of the twenty-first century, many people looked to stars, such as Jesse Ventura or Britney Spears, to help them choose their values. [6]Children modeled their behavior after cartoon characters. [7]The Ninja Turtles, Mighty Mouse, and Power Rangers became heroes to children because they saved characters on the shows. [8]_____, something happened during the fall in 2001 that changed the type of heroes people in the United States admired. [9]After the World Trade Center was attacked last September, people began to regard firemen and policemen as heroes because they exposed their lives to danger or sacrificed their lives while they were attempting to save others. (*Some of the information and ideas in this paragraph have been adapted from Macionis, John J. Sociology. 9th ed. Upper Saddle River, NJ: Prentice Hall, 2003. p. 72*)

2.4 Which of the numbered sentences is not supported by sufficient specific details?

    A. Sentence 3
    B. Sentence 4
    C. Sentence 6
    D. Sentence 8

*Some of the paragraphs used by the authors have been altered to fit the patterns used by the Florida State Exit Test.

Passage 5

¹ _____

²The major networks offered few choices of family shows with minorities, but more minorities were being included in major network shows set in employment settings. ³Shows such as _Third Watch, Cops_, and _E.R._ had some minority characters, but they were not in the forefront of the show weekly as a major character on a sitcom might be. ⁴Other shows did include minorities such as homosexuals, but the characters still followed the old stereotypes. ⁵In many cartoons even the animals, such as cats, were treated stereotypically; _Tom and Jerry_ was a good example of this treatment. ⁶Some of the smaller networks carried some shows, like _The My Wife and Kids,_ that featured minority characters in family situations that more closely depicted people in semi-realistic settings, but the major networks rarely followed their example. ⁷Some of the popular shows, _Frazier_ and _Friends_, rarely included minorities in their shows. ⁸_____, many people thought it would be good for the major television networks to include characters from more minority groups and to have the situations in the shows represent these characters at least as realistically as others in different shows were portrayed. (_Some of the information and ideas in this paragraph have been adapted from Macionis, John J. Sociology. 9th ed. Upper Saddle River, NJ: Prentice Hall, 2003. p. 128_)

2.5 Which of the numbered sentences is not supported by sufficient specific details?

    A. Sentence 2
    B. Sentence 4
    C. Sentence 5
    D. Sentence 6

Passage 6

¹ _____.

²The weather has to follow a particular pattern in order to make the syrup flow; freezing winter nights have to precede warmer days. ³The wintry nights make it possible for the trees to convert some of the nutrients they have accumulated into a form of sugar; the warmer days convert the sugar into a liquid, which is transported by the sap that flows through the maple tree's xylem. ⁴The sap that trickles out is clear and must be processed by completing a long labor-intensive procedure in order to make "pure" maple syrup. ⁵Farmers can "tap" into this liquid by sticking spigots into holes drilled into the trees. ⁶Farmers must boil down fifty gallons of the clear syrup to make a gallon of "pure" syrup, so it is very expensive. ⁷Owners of these trees cannot count on yearly profits from this business because if the weather does not follow the needed pattern, the trees will not produce the syrup. (_Some of the information and ideas in this paragraph have been adapted from Krogh, David. Biology: a Guide for the Natural World 2nd ed. Upper Saddle River, NJ: Prentice Hall, 2002. p. 510_)

*Some of the paragraphs used by the authors have been altered to fit the patterns used by the Florida State Exit Test.

2.6 Which sentence provides specific support for sentence 2 in the passage?

    A. Sentence 3 (Farmers in New England, New York, and Eastern Canada who possess sugar maple trees are industriously occupied during March each year preparing to obtain maple syrup from their trees.)

    B. Sentence 4 (The sap that trickles out is clear and must be processed by completing a long labor-intensive procedure in order to make "pure" maple syrup.)

    C. Sentence 5 (Farmers can "tap" into this liquid by sticking spigots into holes drilled into the trees.)

    D. Sentence 6 (Farmers must boil down fifty gallons of the clear syrup to make a gallon of "pure" syrup, so it is very expensive.)

*Some of the paragraphs used by the authors have been altered to fit the patterns used by the Florida State Exit Test.

Chapter 3: Logical Patterns

Writers must organize the sentences in their paragraphs in a particular arrangement in order to have their paragraph make sense and to help the reader understand how the ideas in the paragraph relate to one another. The order should follow a logical pattern in order for the reader to understand the main idea. The following patterns are patterns, which many writers use. Good writers may use more than one method in a paragraph.

Argumentation

- tries to persuade someone to believe a particular belief or to do something
- presents one or more sides to a dispute
- lists reasons or support for the side of the dispute they want you to believe
- sometimes lists reasons or support for the other side in hope that you will find the reasoning to be ridiculous and therefore take the side that was not addressed as thoroughly.

Example:

School uniforms have become mandatory in many schools in recent years. Many people think that they will reduce some of the distractions created by students' clothing styles. They must not have observed the clothing in the high school where I work. The girls unbutton their shirts to show cleavage and hike up their skirts to a miniskirt length by rolling up the waistband. Additionally, some people believe that students would not know other students' social status because the students would all be dressed alike. I'm not sure that this assertion is true because last week I heard a group of students in my class discussing other students' clothing styles. These students could tell if the uniforms were from a discount store, a department store, or a designer store by the way they fit, the waistbands in the pants, and the variance in color. The uniforms had not solved the problems that had created the mandate because students were still judging others by where they shopped.

Cause & Effect

- list ideas as reasons and results may be many causes for one result, or one cause with many results or one cause creates an effect that then becomes a cause for another effect (a domino effect)

Example:

When I was working as a volunteer in the local hospital providing transportation to the treatment rooms for patients, I had a life-changing experience. A high-pitched, terrifying scream from one of the patient's rooms continued without stop throughout my shift; my heart was torn by the horrifying sound. I dropped by my supervisor's office to inquire about this alarming noise that was disturbing everyone in the hospital; it was the subject of every conversation. My supervisor enlightened me and told me that a young man suffering from a "bad trip" had come into the emergency room the previous night.

*Some of the paragraphs used by the authors have been altered to fit the patterns used by the Florida State Exit Test.

The hospital personnel tried measures to soothe him, but nothing was effective. He screamed for three days though the sound grew quieter as his voice became hoarse. When I returned to work on the fourth day, it was quiet so I questioned my supervisor about him. She informed me that he had been literally "scared to death" and had a fatal heart attack. This experience made me troubled because I knew others who were experimenting with drugs that were hallucinogens, and who had offered me hallucinogenic drugs. But, as a result of my experience, I was never tempted to try drugs.

Chronological order listing–Narration (shares transitions with process) may also be labeled time order, or sequential listing
- contains a chronological listing, or a listing in time order, of activities or events that have happened in someone's life
- is developed by the activities and events being presented logically in sequential order in the paragraph.

Example:

When Ramon got out of bed this morning, he had no idea that the events of the day would change his life forever. Ramon donned his clothes, grabbed his school paraphernalia, and headed out the door. As he slammed the door, he heard a screech and a horrendous crash. There was silence for a moment, and then he heard a barely audible voice crying for assistance. He jogged down the street and scrutinized the crash scene. A car had slammed so hard into a light pole that it was split into two sections. Ramon ran to the car and saw a little child who held out her arms, and said," Up." Ramon broke the window to get the child out, removed her from the vehicle, placed her on the grass, and applied pressure above her bleeding head wound. After the ambulance arrived, and the emergency technicians connected the petite girl to the equipment that would sustain her until she arrived at the hospital, one of the technicians walked over to Ramon and told him that the little girl would not have survived without his intervention.

Classification
- divides a large group into smaller groups by using certain characteristics.
- should include a large group, the number or name of the small groups, and the characteristics used to divide the groups

Example:

College students can be divided into four groups. One of the most common groups is the "young undecided" group. This group of students is coming to college because it is expected of them. The students are not sure why they are there, but they are willing to be there because their parents are paying the bills as long as they pass. The second group is the "oldies but goodies" group. People in this group have gone out into the working world and have made the decision to come back to school to improve their lives. This group is very focused on achieving and learning. These students want

*Some of the paragraphs used by the authors have been altered to fit the patterns used by the Florida State Exit Test.

a four point average, so they do all the work assigned and complete any extra credit assignments. The third group is the "focused young people" group. The students in this group have recently graduated from high school and know where they want to go and what they want to do. They are attentive and toil rigorously to achieve their goals. The fourth group, the "ghosts and confused" group, is the group that worries professors the most. The "ghosts" are the people teachers never see, and the "confused" are the people who think that completing assignments, attending class, passing tests, and participating in class activities are unnecessary to pass the class.

Comparison
- lists likenesses or similarities between two objects, or people
- usually has a compound subject

Example:

John Belushi and Chris Farley were two humorous actors who were alike in many ways. John and Chris were both cast members of the television show **Saturday Night Live** who acted in successful movies; Belushi had a major role in *The Blues Brothers* which was extremely profitable at the box office, and Farley had one of the lead roles in *Tommy Boy*, which was also a lucrative movie. Regrettably the two men were at the height of their careers when they died due to misadventure. John died from a cocaine overdose, and Chris died because he had a massive quantity of drugs and alcohol in his system. These two exceptional actors were similar in many ways including the unfortunate manner in which they died.

Contrast
- lists differences, may list the differences between two objects or people, may list the difference in a single object or person in a variety of situations or at various times
- usually has a compound subject.

Example:

College is different from high school in many aspects. In high school you have to have a pass if you wanted to leave the room, whereas in college you can leave whenever you choose. In college you have a variety of classes and careers from which you can choose, but in high school you had to take specific courses. In college few of the professors will remind you when you have assignments or exams to make up because they consider you to be capable of keeping track of your required work. If you have a problem in a college class, the instructor will often wait for you to make an appointment to discuss your difficulties, unlike the high school instructor who would keep you after class to go over the areas in which you had problems. The mind-set of college professors is in sharp contrast with high school teachers' attitudes because the professors feel that you are a conscientious adult who can make your own choices and who can live with the results.

*Some of the paragraphs used by the authors have been altered to fit the patterns used by the Florida State Exit Test.

Comparison and Contrast
- lists the good and bad points to an issue or object,
- or lists the similarities and differences between two or more objects

Definition
- lists the meaning or meanings for a certain word or phrase
- or develops a meaning for a word or phrase to make it more understandable.

Example:
> The word bomb has many meanings. The most common usage for bomb is an explosive device that is detonated when it hits something or someone and that damages items around it. There are also cherry and smoke bombs in which case bomb means a type of firework with a fuse and the ability to make a deafening blast or quantities of smoke. A bomb in terms used by football commentators defines a ball that is thrown with great force; the ball is expected to gain numerous yards for the team throwing the ball. There are also slang meanings for the word. If you own a "bomb," you probably own a vehicle that is old and rusty whereas if you own "the bomb" the slang meaning is a desirable automobile.

Description
- creates a sensory picture of a scene or an object
- usually has few distinctive transitions
- contains many adjectives

Example:
> Yuri's appearance was extremely interesting. His skin was the color of highly polished, blonde oak wood. His long, auburn curls swirled around his face as the wind blew across the mountainside. The crayon green of his eyes made his eyes brilliantly contrast with the stark, white color of the snow on the trees behind him. The pink of his nose, cheeks, and lips was the color of a woman's blush due to the extremely frosty temperatures. The white, one-piece snowsuit he was wearing made his body blend into the snowy environment, which gave him the almost surrealistic appearance of a beautiful head floating in the air.

Enumeration/Addition
- stresses providing supplementary information
- has transitional words to let you know that part of the passage has already been presented.

Example:
> The second point is that you must be prepared when you take a final exam. Studying throughout the term and completing your work on time is definitely helpful. This balances the work on the material, so you do not have to cram at the end of the term. Passing your tests throughout the term can also help you gain confidence in your ability

*Some of the paragraphs used by the authors have been altered to fit the patterns used by the Florida State Exit Test.

to be successful on a major test. Having the right supplies and helping your body to be able to cope with the demands of the exam time can be factors to consider. It is helpful to get a good night's sleep and to eat a well-balanced breakfast that is not heavy on the carbohydrates because they can make you sleepy.

Illustration and example
- contains a generalization, or a broad statement, and examples.

Example:

There are many good examples of students with excellent academic habits in my nine o'clock class. Brittany always comes to class on time, and she is prepared to work. Anthony is also punctual, ready to listen and participate, and completes his homework before the due date. Sally is never late, completes her work efficiently, asks questions about the lesson, and studies the material presented in class within twenty-four hours in order to remember it longer. All of these students exemplify the behaviors that professors expect college students to exhibit.

Process (shares transitions with time/chronological order)
- lists the steps or stages for a course of action in sequential order.
  directions for a task
  or a development progression that an animal or human follows
  as it grows
- can be repeated and similar results will occur

Example:

To set someone up to go on a blind date you must follow these steps. First, you must find two people that seem compatible and who are not dating someone steadily. Secondly, you must make him or her receptive to the idea by telling him or her about friends that have been on successful blind dates. Next you must present the idea as a thought that just occurred to you, and then tell him or her everything appealing about the other person. If they ask any questions about the other person that you do not want to answer, you must say, "Oh, I just thought of another amazing attribute that I forgot to tell you about him or her." The final step is to offer to double date with the couple on their first date and to go to someplace that would appeal to both of the blind daters.

Order of Importance/ Emphasis
- lists the items, actions, or people in the from most important to the least important
- or lists the least important to the most important
- or separates one item as the most important
- or lists information from a hierarchy

*Some of the paragraphs used by the authors have been altered to fit the patterns used by the Florida State Exit Test.

Example:
        The hierarchy of the government of the Brownell College is very confusing to new employees. The employees all think that President Smith is the most important person in the Brownell College, but in reality President Smith cannot make very many decisions without approval from the Board of Trustees or his advisors. The Board of Trustees is the most important authority at the college; President Smith reports to the board and he must take any major decisions to the board. The deans hold the administrative rank below the president and above the faculty.

Spatial Order
- lists the details in the order they are placed
    - middle of a circle to the outer parts of the circle
    - or top to bottom or bottom to top
    - or left to right or right to left
    - or back to front or front to back
- lists many prepositions to show direction

Example:
        Mike's entertainment center was every teen's dream. In the top half of the right section of the center was a huge stereo with components for various discs and tapes. The bottom half of the right section had four huge speakers. The middle section contained an enormous television set. The right half of the left section of the center was overflowing with game paraphernalia, and the left half of the section held a new computer and oversized speakers.

Summary
- goes over the main points presented in an article or passage
- group ideas much as possible.

Example:
        In short, to prepare for a test you should do your work throughout the semester, study and do well on tests to gain confidence, sleep well the night before, and eat right the morning of the test. These are all methods to use to help you be successful on a final exam.

*Some of the paragraphs used by the authors have been altered to fit the patterns used by the Florida State Exit Test.

Exercises:

Read each passage and answer the question below the passage. (Note: Intentional errors may have been included in these passages.)

Passage 1

[1] _____. [2]Charismatics have unique personal talents that can change a group of people into supporters. [3] In the process they may create their own rules and regulations and challenge the established governing bodies. [4] _____, in 1917, Vladimir Lenin directed the overthrow of Russia's imperial government and later convinced many of the Russian people to fight for a government that would consider the needs of the workers and peasants instead of the wealthy. [5]After World War II Mahatma Gandhi inspired the struggle to free India from British colonialism. [6]He convinced many of his countrymen to use passive resistance methods such as protests and fasts. [7]Soon after, Martin Luther King, Jr. organized and encouraged the civil rights movement in the United States. [8]His moving speeches and his leadership of African-American nonviolent confrontations protesting and boycotting injustices made him a recognized leader. [9]His first job was in Montgomery, Alabama. [10]As a result of his efforts, many social changes were made in the United States. [11]Similarly, Mother Teresa asked the world to take care of its poverty and spent her life ministering to the poor in Calcutta, India. *(Some of the information and ideas in this paragraph have been adapted from Macionis, John J. Sociology. 9th ed. Upper Saddle River, NJ: Prentice Hall, 2003. p. 436)*

3.1 Which is the best placement for the sentence below to make the sequence of ideas in the paragraph clearer?

At different times Gandhi advocated a boycott of Britain's products, nonpayment of British taxes, and nonsupport of Britain's part in the war.

A. before sentence 8
B. before sentence 6
C. before sentence 4
D. before sentence 2

Passage 2

[1] _____

[2]Many efficient readers learn to like reading. [3]After completing either of these previews, you should take a minute to think about your prior knowledge of the subject in order to pull the knowledge from your memory. [4]Good readers prepare to read by using one of the previewing methods before they settle down to their serious reading. [5] The first is to scan the whole chapter to get an understanding of the topic and the aspects covered in the reading, and the second is to survey specific parts of the chapter or article to find out information about topics covered in the reading. [6]Amazingly, just using one of these two methods usually doubles a person's reading speed and increases his or her understanding. [7]The third step to reading

*Some of the paragraphs used by the authors have been altered to fit the patterns used by the Florida State Exit Test.

capably and quickly is to practice reading proficiently by timing your reading and setting goals to make you read just a little bit faster each time. [8]_____, after each period of reading, check your comprehension by telling someone about the material you have read or by writing notes about the reading.

3.2 Select the arrangement of sentences 3, 4, and 5 that provides the most logical sequence of ideas and supporting details in the paragraph. If no change is needed, select answer A.

A. After completing either of these previews, you should take a minute to think about your prior knowledge of the subject in order to pull the knowledge from your memory. Good readers prepare to read by using one of the previewing methods before they settle down to their serious reading. The first is to scan the whole chapter to get an understanding of the topic and the aspects covered in the reading, and the second is to survey specific parts of the chapter or article to find out information about topics covered in the reading.

B. Good readers prepare to read by using one of the previewing methods before they settle down to their serious reading. The first is to scan the whole chapter to get an understanding of the topic and the aspects covered in the reading, and the second is to survey specific parts of the chapter or article to find out information about topics covered in the reading. After completing either of these previews, you should take a minute to think about your prior knowledge of the subject in order to pull the knowledge from your memory.

C. After completing either of these previews, you should take a minute to think about your prior knowledge of the subject in order to pull the knowledge from your memory. The first is to scan the whole chapter to get an understanding of the topic and the aspects covered in the reading, and the second is to survey specific parts of the chapter or article to find out information about topics covered in the reading. Good readers prepare to read by using one of the previewing methods before they settle down to their serious reading.

D. Good readers prepare to read by using one of the previewing methods before they settle down to their serious reading. After completing either of these previews, you should take a minute to think about your prior knowledge of the subject in order to pull the knowledge from your memory. The first is to scan the whole chapter to get an understanding of the topic and the aspects covered in the reading, and the second is to survey specific parts of the chapter or article to find out information about topics covered in the reading.

Passage 3

[1]
_____

_____[2]One of the techniques artists use in circular paintings is radial symmetry; the center of the painting is the major focal point and the other parts of the painting surround the center in a pattern like spokes on a wheel. [3] Wheels are a visual attraction for many people who use them as decorations. [4] Another method is to use the balance of the painting or the symmetry of the lines. [5]Color, light, and contrast can be used as techniques to entice the

*Some of the paragraphs used by the authors have been altered to fit the patterns used by the Florida State Exit Test.

37

viewer's eyes to focus first on the desired section of the painting. [6]If many of the directional lines used to draw some of the elements of the painting are parallel, the focus is to follow those lines to the end. [7]_____ shades of one color are used for the background, the viewer's eyes are drawn to the element of the painting that the artist wants as the focal point. [8]By making some of the colors a strong contrast to those used in the background, a point of emphasis is established. [9]All of these methods have been used by artists. *(Some of the information and ideas in this paragraph have been adapted from Sayre, Henry. A World of Art. 3rd ed. Upper Saddle River, NJ: Prentice Hall, 2000. pp. 162-163)*

3.3 Select the arrangement of sentences 4, 5, and 6 that provides the most logical sequence of ideas and supporting details in the paragraph. If no change is needed, select answer A.

A. Another method is to use the balance of the painting or the symmetry of the lines. Color, light, and contrast can be used as techniques to entice the viewer's eyes to focus first on the desired section of the painting. If many of the directional lines used to draw some of the elements of the painting are parallel, the focus is to follow those lines to the end.

B. Another method is to use the balance of the painting or the symmetry of the lines. If many of the directional lines used to draw some of the elements of the painting are parallel, the focus is to follow those lines to the end. Color, light, and contrast can be used as techniques to entice the viewer's eyes to focus first on the desired section of the painting.

C. If many of the directional lines used to draw some of the elements of the painting are parallel, the focus is to follow those lines to the end. Color, light, and contrast can be used as techniques to entice the viewer's eyes to focus first on the desired section of the painting. Another method is to use the balance of the painting or the symmetry of the lines.

D. Color, light, and contrast can be used as techniques to entice the viewer's eyes to focus first on the desired section of the painting. If many of the directional lines used to draw some of the elements of the painting are parallel, the focus is to follow those lines to the end. Another method is to use the balance of the painting or the symmetry of the lines.

Passage 4

[1]_____.

[2]In past centuries, many countries' military leaders or religious figures such as Joan of Arc were regarded as heroes. [3]During World War I and World War II in the twentieth century, members of the military in our country were viewed as heroes. [4]But as radio, movies, and television became commonplace in United States during the last hundred years, the heroes changed to entertainment and sports stars. [5]In the later part of the twentieth century and the beginning of the twenty-first century, many people looked to stars, such as Jesse Ventura or Britney Spears, to help them choose their values. [6]Children modeled their behavior after cartoon characters.

*Some of the paragraphs used by the authors have been altered to fit the patterns used by the Florida State Exit Test.

[7]The Ninja Turtles, Mighty Mouse, and Power Rangers became heroes to children because they saved characters on the shows. [8]_____, something happened during the fall in 2001 that changed the type of heroes people in the United States admired. [9]After the World Trade Center was attacked last September, people began to regard firemen and policemen as heroes because they exposed their lives to danger or sacrificed their lives while they were attempting to save others. *(Some of the information and ideas in this paragraph have been adapted from Macionis, John J. Sociology. 9th ed. Upper Saddle River, NJ: Prentice Hall, 2003. p. 72)*

3.4 Which is the best placement for the sentence below to make the sequence of ideas in the paragraph clearer?

General Eisenhower and John Kennedy, two of the presidents in the twentieth century, were both viewed as special leaders because of their military service.

A. before sentence 8
B. before sentence 6
C. before sentence 4
D. before sentence 2

Passage 5

[1]
_____

[2]The major networks offered few choices of family shows with minorities, but more minorities were being included in major network shows set in employment settings. [3]Shows such as *Third Watch, Cops,* and *E.R.* had some minority characters, but they were not in the forefront of the show weekly as a major character on a sitcom might be. [4]Other shows did include minorities such as homosexuals, but the characters still followed the old stereotypes. [5]In many cartoons even the animals, such as cats, were treated stereotypically; *Tom and Jerry* was a good example of this treatment. [6]Some of the smaller networks carried some shows, like *The My Wife and Kids,* that featured minority characters in family situations that more closely depicted people in semi-realistic settings, but the major networks rarely followed their example. [7]Some of the popular shows, *Frazier* and *Friends*, rarely included minorities in their shows. [8]_____, many people thought it would be good for the major television networks to include characters from more minority groups and to have the situations in the shows represent these characters at least as realistically as others in different shows were portrayed. *(Some of the information and ideas in this paragraph have been adapted from Macionis, John J. Sociology. 9th ed. Upper Saddle River, NJ: Prentice Hall, 2003. p. 128)*

3.5 Which is the best placement for the sentence below to make the sequence of ideas in the paragraph clearer?

Will and Grace was a show in which homosexuals were depicted stereotypically.

A. after sentence 2
B. after sentence 3
C. after sentence 4
D. after sentence 6

*Some of the paragraphs used by the authors have been altered to fit the patterns used by the Florida State Exit Test.

Passage 6

¹ _____ .

²The weather has to follow a particular pattern in order to make the syrup flow; freezing winter nights have to precede warmer days. ³The wintry nights make it possible for the trees to convert some of the nutrients they have accumulated into a form of sugar; the warmer days convert the sugar into a liquid, which is transported by the sap that flows through the maple tree's xylem. ⁴The sap that trickles out is clear and must be processed by completing a long labor-intensive procedure in order to make "pure" maple syrup. ⁵ Farmers can "tap" into this liquid by sticking spigots into holes drilled into the trees. ⁶Farmers must boil down fifty gallons of the clear syrup to make a gallon of "pure" syrup, so it is very expensive. ⁷Owners of these trees cannot count on yearly profits from this business because if the weather does not follow the needed pattern, the trees will not produce the syrup. *(Some of the information and ideas in this paragraph have been adapted from Krogh, David. Biology: A Guide for the Natural World. 2ⁿᵈ ed. Upper Saddle River, NJ: Prentice Hall, 2002. p. 510)*

3.6 Select the arrangement of sentences 4, 5, and 6 that provides the most logical sequence of ideas and supporting details in the paragraph. If no change is needed, select answer A.

A. The sap that trickles out is clear and must be processed by completing a long labor-intensive procedure in order to make "pure" maple syrup. Farmers can "tap" into this liquid by sticking spigots into holes drilled into the trees. Farmers must boil down fifty gallons of the clear syrup to make a gallon of "pure" syrup, so it is very expensive.

B. Farmers can "tap" into this liquid by sticking spigots into holes drilled into the trees. The sap that trickles out is clear and must be processed by completing a long labor-intensive procedure in order to make "pure" maple syrup. Farmers must boil down fifty gallons of the clear syrup to make a gallon of "pure" syrup, so it is very expensive.

C. Farmers can "tap" into this liquid by sticking spigots into holes drilled into the trees. Farmers must boil down fifty gallons of the clear syrup to make a gallon of "pure" syrup, so it is very expensive. The sap that trickles out is clear and must be processed by completing a long labor-intensive procedure in order to make "pure" maple syrup.

D. The sap that trickles out is clear and must be processed by completing a long labor-intensive procedure in order to make "pure" maple syrup. Farmers must boil down fifty gallons of the clear syrup to make a gallon of "pure" syrup, so it is very expensive. Farmers can "tap" into this liquid by sticking spigots into holes drilled into the trees.

*Some of the paragraphs used by the authors have been altered to fit the patterns used by the Florida State Exit Test.

Chapter 4: Relevant Details

It is important to be able to recognize relevant (pertaining to the subject) and irrelevant (unrelated) details. When you are reading and trying to discern which details are important to remember, it is necessary to be able to determine the relevancy of details the author includes. It is also important to be able to determine the relevancy of details in your own writing, so you can decide if the inclusion of a sentence is important to the reader's understanding, or if the sentence should be eliminated.

To determine relevancy, you should look at several factors.

- Is the sentence the topic sentence, conclusion, or major specific detail? If it is any of the above, it should be relevant.
- Does the sentence support the message the author is stating in the topic sentence or main idea? Does it relate to the topic?
- Does this sentence give important information that helps you understand the major specific detail? Does it explain a point made in the detail?
- Does the sentence fit into the organizational plan for the paragraph? Remember how each paragraph organizational pattern has a plan to follow. Does this sentence address that plan?
- Does the sentence use an additional plan? Does it relate to a different topic?

For example, if the paragraph were about the classifications of small dogs, the details should relate to the large group (small dogs), the smaller groups the large group can be divided into (dachshund or poodle), and the characteristics of those types of small dogs. A sentence should not relate to large dogs, other animals, or funny tricks the small dog next door has been taught to do.

It is very important to judge the relevancy of materials you write. By including too many irrelevant details, you may confuse your readers, and they may end up not understanding the point you set out to make. As a reader, you want to be able to make a decision about the importance of the details to the main idea or topic sentence so you can understand what is important to know in order to understand the concepts.

In the exercises in this section, you will be asked to identify the sentence, which is the least relevant to the paragraph. Remember to think whether the sentence relates to the topic, the organization, the point the author is making about the topic, or the major details. Does it give reasons; examples; explanations; descriptive characteristics; events or activities; people, places, and objects; and particulars about an item or situation that relate to the topic?

---

*Some of the paragraphs used by the authors have been altered to fit the patterns used by the Florida State Exit Test.

Exercises:

Read each passage and answer the question. (Note: Intentional errors may have been included in these passages.)

Passage 1

[1] _____. [2]Charismatics have unique personal talents that can change a group of people into supporters. [3] In the process they may create their own rules and regulations and challenge the established governing bodies. [4] _____, in 1917, Vladimir Lenin directed the overthrow of Russia's imperial government and later convinced many of the Russian people to fight for a government that would consider the needs of the workers and peasants instead of the wealthy. [5]After World War II Mahatma Gandhi inspired the struggle to free India from British colonialism. [6]He convinced many of his countrymen to use passive resistance methods such as protests and fasts. [7]Soon after, Martin Luther King, Jr. organized and encouraged the civil rights movement in the United States. [8]His moving speeches and his leadership of African-American nonviolent confrontations protesting and boycotting injustices made him a recognized leader. [9]His first job was in Montgomery, Alabama. [10]As a result of his efforts, many social changes were made in the United States. [11]Similarly, Mother Teresa asked the world to take care of its poverty and spent her life ministering to the poor in Calcutta, India. *(Some of the information and ideas in this paragraph have been adapted from Macionis, John J. Sociology. 9th ed. Upper Saddle River, NJ: Prentice Hall, 2003. p. 436)*

4.1 Which numbered sentence is the least relevant to the passage?

    A. sentence 4
    B. sentence 6
    C. sentence 9
    D. sentence 11

Passage 2

[1] _____

[2]Many efficient readers learn to like reading. [3]After completing either of these previews, you should take a minute to think about your prior knowledge of the subject in order to pull the knowledge from your memory. [4]Good readers prepare to read by using one of the previewing methods before they settle down to their serious reading. [5] The first is to scan the whole chapter to get an understanding of the topic and the aspects covered in the reading, and the second is to survey specific parts of the chapter or article to find out information about topics covered in the reading. [6]Amazingly, just using one of these two methods usually doubles a person's reading speed and increases his or her understanding. [7]The third step to reading capably and quickly is to practice reading proficiently by timing your reading and setting goals to make you read just a little bit faster each time. [8] _____, after each period of reading, check your comprehension by telling someone about the material you have read or by writing notes about the reading.

*Some of the paragraphs used by the authors have been altered to fit the patterns used by the Florida State Exit Test.

4.2 Which numbered sentence is the least relevant to the passage?

    A. sentence 2
    B. sentence 3
    C. sentence 4
    D. sentence 5

Passage 3

1
_____

_____ [2]One of the techniques artists use in circular paintings is radial symmetry; the center of the painting is the major focal point and the other parts of the painting surround the center in a pattern like spokes on a wheel. [3] Wheels are a visual attraction for many people who use them as decorations. [4] Another method is to use the balance of the painting or the symmetry of the lines. [5]Color, light, and contrast can be used as techniques to entice the viewer's eyes to focus first on the desired section of the painting. [6]If many of the directional lines used to draw some of the elements of the painting are parallel, the focus is to follow those lines to the end. [7]_____ shades of one color are used for the background, the viewer's eyes are drawn to the element of the painting that the artist wants as the focal point. [8]By making some of the colors a strong contrast to those used in the background, a point of emphasis is established. [9]All of these methods have been used by artists. *(Some of the information and ideas in this paragraph have been adapted from Sayre, Henry. A World of Art. 3rd ed. Upper Saddle River, NJ: Prentice Hall, 2000. pp. 162-163)*

4.3 Which numbered sentence is the least relevant to the passage?

    A. sentence 5
    B. sentence 4
    C. sentence 3
    D. sentence 2

Passage 4

1
_____.

[2]In past centuries, many countries' military leaders or religious figures such as Joan of Arc were regarded as heroes. [3]During World War I and World War II in the twentieth century, members of the military in our country were viewed as heroes. [4]But as radio, movies, and television became commonplace in United States during the last hundred years, the heroes changed to entertainment and sports stars. [5]In the later part of the twentieth century and the beginning of the twenty-first century, many people looked to stars, such as Jesse Ventura or Britney Spears, to help them choose their values. [6]Children modeled their behavior after cartoon characters. [7]The Ninja Turtles, Mighty Mouse, and Power Rangers became heroes to children because they saved characters on the shows. [8]_____, something happened during the fall in 2001 that changed the type of heroes people in the United States admired. [9]After the World Trade Center

*Some of the paragraphs used by the authors have been altered to fit the patterns used by the Florida State Exit Test.

was attacked last September, people began to regard firemen and policemen as heroes because they exposed their lives to danger or sacrificed their lives while they were attempting to save others. *(Some of the information and ideas in this paragraph have been adapted from Macionis, John J. Sociology. 9th ed. Upper Saddle River, NJ: Prentice Hall, 2003. p. 72)*

4.4 Which numbered sentence is the least relevant to the passage?

    A. sentence 2
    B. sentence 3
    C. sentence 4
    D. sentence 5

Passage 5

1 _____

[2]The major networks offered few choices of family shows with minorities, but more minorities were being included in major network shows set in employment settings. [3]Shows such as *Third Watch, Cops,* and *E.R.* had some minority characters, but they were not in the forefront of the show weekly as a major character on a sitcom might be. [4]Other shows did include minorities such as homosexuals, but the characters still followed the old stereotypes. [5]In many cartoons even the animals, such as cats, were treated stereotypically; *Tom and Jerry* was a good example of this treatment. [6]Some of the smaller networks carried some shows, like *The My Wife and Kids,* that featured minority characters in family situations that more closely depicted people in semi-realistic settings, but the major networks rarely followed their example. [7]Some of the popular shows, *Frazier* and *Friends*, rarely included minorities in their shows.
[8]_____, many people thought it would be good for the major television networks to include characters from more minority groups and to have the situations in the shows represent these characters at least as realistically as others in different shows were portrayed. *(Some of the information and ideas in this paragraph have been adapted from Macionis, John J. Sociology. 9th ed. Upper Saddle River, NJ: Prentice Hall, 2003. p. 128)*

4.5 Which numbered sentence is the least relevant to the passage?

    A. sentence 7
    B. sentence 5
    C. sentence 3
    D. sentence 2

*Some of the paragraphs used by the authors have been altered to fit the patterns used by the Florida State Exit Test.

Chapter 5: Transitional Devices

Transitions are words or phrases that a writer uses to help the reader understand the logical relationships between parts of a sentence or parts of a passage. It helps the reader determine the purpose of the writing and the main idea. This section tests your ability to figure out the relationship between the ideas being presented and to choose the proper transitional word.

Addition–*stress on providing additional information*

additionally	and	finally	moreover
also	besides	furthermore	
another	equally important	in addition	

Argumentation–*lists reasons or support for sides of a disputed idea*

certainly
surely
undeniably

Cause Effect/ Result–*names reasons (conditions) and effects (consequences)*

accordingly	hence	thus
as a result	so	
consequently	therefore	

Chronological Order/Narration–*lists activities or events*

after	finally	now	until
as	first	often	when
before	later	soon	while
during	next	then	

Comparison–*lists similarities*

in the same way
likewise
similarly

Contrast–*lists differences*

alternatively	however	on the other hand
although	in contrast	on the contrary
but	nevertheless	still
conversely	nonetheless	yet
despite	on one hand	

*Some of the paragraphs used by the authors have been altered to fit the patterns used by the Florida State Exit Test.

Classification–*divides a large group into smaller groups by using specific characteristics*

    category   group   kind   type

Description–*creates a sensory picture of an object, person, or scene by appealing to the senses: smell, sight, taste, touch, sound*

here
there

Illustration and Example–*contains a general statement and examples*

for example	in particular
for instance	specifically
in general	thus

Order of Importance–*lists ideas, people, or objects in the order of value*

the most important	principal	major
the least important	chief	

Process–*lists steps or stages*

after	finally	now	until
as	first	often	when
before	later	soon	while
during	next	then	

Spatial–*lists the details in the order they are placed*

above	between	far	south
adjacent to	beyond	farther	to the left
behind	closer to	near	to the right
below	down from	over there	west

Summary–*reiterates the material in a brief form*

finally	in summary
in conclusion	lastly
in short	to summarize

*Some of the paragraphs used by the authors have been altered to fit the patterns used by the Florida State Exit Test.

Exercises:

Read each paragraph and choose the word that should replace the blank in the paragraph.   (Note: Intentional errors may have been included in these passages.)

Passage 1

[1] _____. [2]Charismatics have unique personal talents that can change a group of people into supporters. [3] In the process they may create their own rules and regulations and challenge the established governing bodies. [4] _____, in 1917, Vladimir Lenin directed the overthrow of Russia's imperial government and later convinced many of the Russian people to fight for a government that would consider the needs of the workers and peasants instead of the wealthy. [5]After World War II Mahatma Gandhi inspired the struggle to free India from British colonialism. [6]He convinced many of his countrymen to use passive resistance methods such as protests and fasts. [7]Soon after, Martin Luther King, Jr. organized and encouraged the civil rights movement in the United States. [8]His moving speeches and his leadership of African-American nonviolent confrontations protesting and boycotting injustices made him a recognized leader. [9]His first job was in Montgomery, Alabama. [10]As a result of his efforts, many social changes were made in the United States. [11]Similarly, Mother Teresa asked the world to take care of its poverty and spent her life ministering to the poor in Calcutta, India. *(Some of the information and ideas in this paragraph have been adapted from Macionis, John J. Sociology. 9th ed. Upper Saddle River, NJ: Prentice Hall, 2003. p. 436)*

5.1 Which word or phrase, if inserted in the blank in sentence 4, would make the relationship of the ideas between sentence 3 and sentence 4 clearer?

    A. Therefore
    B. For example
    C. Similarly
    D Because

Passage 2

[1] _____
[2]Many efficient readers learn to like reading. [3]After completing either of these previews, you should take a minute to think about your prior knowledge of the subject in order to pull the knowledge from your memory. [4]Good readers prepare to read by using one of the previewing methods before they settle down to their serious reading. [5] The first is to scan the whole chapter to get an understanding of the topic and the aspects covered in the reading, and the second is to survey specific parts of the chapter or article to find out information about topics covered in the reading. [6]Amazingly, just using one of these two methods usually doubles a person's reading speed and increases his or her understanding. [7]The third step to reading

*Some of the paragraphs used by the authors have been altered to fit the patterns used by the Florida State Exit Test.

capably and quickly is to practice reading proficiently by timing your reading and setting goals to make you read just a little bit faster each time. [8]_____, after each period of reading, check your comprehension by telling someone about the material you have read or by writing notes about the reading.

5.2 Which word or phrase, if inserted in the blank in sentence 8, would make the

    A. In front of
    B. In contrast
    C. Likewise
    D. Finally

Passage 3

[1]_____

_____ [2]One of the techniques artists use in circular paintings is radial symmetry; the center of the painting is the major focal point and the other parts of the painting surround the center in a pattern like spokes on a wheel. [3] Wheels are a visual attraction for many people who use them as decorations. [4] Another method is to use the balance of the painting or the symmetry of the lines. [5]Color, light, and contrast can be used as techniques to entice the viewer's eyes to focus first on the desired section of the painting. [6]If many of the directional lines used to draw some of the elements of the painting are parallel, the focus is to follow those lines to the end. [7] _____ shades of one color are used for the background, then the viewer's eyes are drawn to the element of the painting that the artist wants as the focal point. [8]By making some of the colors a strong contrast to those used in the background, a point of emphasis is established. [9]All of these methods have been used by artists. *(Some of the information and ideas in this paragraph have been adapted from Sayre, Henry. A World of Art. 3rd ed. Upper Saddle River, NJ: Prentice Hall, 2000. pp. 162-163)*

5.3 Which word or phrase, if inserted in the blank in sentence 7, would make the
    relationship of the ideas between sentence 6 and sentence 7 clearer?

    A. To summarize
    B. Because
    C. Despite
    D. Similarly

Passage 4

[1]_____.

[2]In past centuries, many countries' military leaders or religious figures such as Joan of Arc were regarded as heroes. [3]During World War I and World War II in the twentieth century, members of the military in our country were viewed as heroes. [4]But as radio, movies, and television became commonplace in United States during the last hundred years, the heroes changed to entertainment and sports stars. [5]In the later part of the twentieth century and the beginning of

*Some of the paragraphs used by the authors have been altered to fit the patterns used by the Florida State Exit Test.

the twenty-first century, many people looked to stars, such as Jesse Ventura or Britney Spears, to help them choose their values. [6]Children modeled their behavior after cartoon characters. [7]The Ninja Turtles, Mighty Mouse, and Power Rangers became heroes to children because they saved characters on the shows. [8]_____, something happened during the fall in 2001 that changed the type of heroes people in the United States admired. [9]After the World Trade Center was attacked last September, people began to regard firemen and policemen as heroes because they exposed their lives to danger or sacrificed their lives while they were attempting to save others. *(Some of the information and ideas in this paragraph have been adapted from Macionis, John J. Sociology. 9th ed. Upper Saddle River, NJ: Prentice Hall, 2003.p. 72)*

5.4 Which word or phrase, if inserted in the blank in sentence 5, would make the relationship of the ideas between sentence 4 and sentence 5 clearer?

    A. Similarly
    B. For instance
    C. Finally
    D. However

Passage 5

[1]
_____

[2]The major networks offered few choices of family shows with minorities, but more minorities were being included in major network shows set in employment settings. [3]Shows such as *Third Watch, Cops*, and *E.R.* had some minority characters, but they were not in the forefront of the show weekly as a major character on a sitcom might be. [4]Other shows did include minorities such as homosexuals, but the characters still followed the old stereotypes. [5]In many cartoons even the animals, such as cats, were treated stereotypically; *Tom and Jerry* was a good example of this treatment. [6]Some of the smaller networks carried some shows, like *The My Wife and Kids,* that featured minority characters in family situations that more closely depicted people in semi-realistic settings, but the major networks rarely followed their example. [7]Some of the popular shows, *Frazier* and *Friends*, rarely included minorities in their shows. [8]_____, many people thought it would be good for the major television networks to include characters from more minority groups and to have the situations in the shows represent these characters at least as realistically as others in different shows were portrayed. *(Some of the information and ideas in this paragraph have been adapted from Macionis, John J. Sociology. 9th ed. Upper Saddle River, NJ: Prentice Hall, 2003. p. 128)*

5.5 Which word or phrase, if inserted in the blank in sentence 8, would make the relationship of the ideas between sentence 7 and sentence 8 clearer?

    A. In the same way
    B. Specifically
    C. As a result
    D. Yet

*Some of the paragraphs used by the authors have been altered to fit the patterns used by the Florida State Exit Test.

Chapter 6: Putting the Parts Together–Ten Test Paragraphs

Read each paragraph and answer the questions. (Note: Intentional errors may have been included in these passages.)

Passage 1

1 _____

[2]When the study of United States college students was conducted, women and men were quite discriminating about the satisfactory characteristics required for future marriage partners. [3]One of the characteristics that both men and women looked for in a marriage partner was education. [4]For males the criteria for some character traits were lower for casual sex partners than for future marriage prospects. [5]The difference between the males' criteria for marriage partners and for casual dates was significant. [6]The character traits the males lowered for casual partners were related to charm, education, independence, and generosity. [7]_____, when college women were polled, their preferred characteristics for marriage partners were lowered only slightly when they were asked what traits they would search for in a casual sex partner. [8]Some women dated more frequently than others. *(Some of the information and ideas in this paragraph have been adapted from Krogh, David. Biology: A Guide for the Natural World. 2nd ed. Upper Saddle River, NJ: Prentice Hall, 2002. pp. 744-745)*

1. Which sentence, if inserted in the blank labeled number 1, is the **best** main idea or topic sentence for the passage?

   A. Researchers have found that men have higher standards for future wives than they do for casual dates and sex partners.
   B. Researchers have found that all men and women have different preferred traits for future marriage partners and casual dates or sex partners; women are more discriminating about the preferred candidates for casual sex partners and dates.
   C. Researchers have found that college women and men have different ideas about what characteristics are important in casual sex partners; they were both more selective about possible marriage candidates.
   D. Researchers have found that women have different preferred character traits for possible spouses and casual sex partners.

2. Which of the numbered sentences is not supported by sufficient specific details?

   A. sentence 2
   B. sentence 4
   C. sentence 5
   D. sentence 7

*Some of the paragraphs quoted by the authors have been altered to fit the patterns used by the Florida State Exit Test.

3. Select the arrangement of sentences 3, 4, and 5 that provides the most logical sequence of ideas and supporting details in the paragraph. If no change is needed, select answer A.

A. One of the characteristics that both men and women looked for in a marriage partner was education. For males the criteria for some character traits were lower for casual sex partners than for future marriage prospects. The difference between the males' criteria for marriage partners and for casual dates was significant.

B. One of the characteristics that both men and women looked for in a marriage partner was education. The difference between the males' criteria for marriage partners and for casual dates was significant. For males the criteria for some character traits were lower for casual sex partners than for future marriage prospects.

C. For males the criteria for some character traits were lower for casual sex partners than for future marriage prospects. The difference between the males' criteria for marriage partners and for casual dates was significant. One of the characteristics that both men and women looked for in a marriage partner was education.

D. The difference between the males' criteria for marriage partners and for casual dates was significant. One of the characteristics that both men and women looked for in a marriage partner was education. For males the criteria for some character traits were lower for casual sex partners than for future marriage prospects.

4. Which word or phrase, if inserted in the blank in sentence 6, would make the relationship of the ideas between sentence 5 and sentence 6 clearer?

A. For example
B. Presently
C. However
D. Similarly

5. Which numbered sentence is the least relevant to the passage?

A. sentence 4
B. sentence 5
C. sentence 6
D. sentence 8

Passage 2

1_____

[2]Some people in Asia consider this fish to be a delicious ingredient for many dishes. [3]Many Asian cookbooks have recipes to prepare this marine delicacy by frying, broiling, or baking. [4]_____ the Asians, people from other regions in Australia and North America regard this unique, exotic fish as a wonderful addition to their aquarium. [5]It is different from normal

*Some of the paragraphs quoted by the authors have been altered to fit the patterns used by the Florida State Exit Test.

aquarium fish because it must be kept in a tank by itself because it has a tendency to eat the other fish, and it must be contained securely because of its ambulatory abilities. [6]Conversely, people who fish or own fish farms in the Southeastern United States consider this ambulatory fish to be a costly nuisance. [7]Therefore, it can eat all the fish in one pond or tank, and then go to another pond in order to decimate the fish population there as well. [8]This fish is capable of moving across land from one body of water to another and has a voracious appetite. [9]Many fish farms raise fish for food and for aquariums. [10]This unique fish is viewed differently by people in several regions.

1. Which of the following sentences, when inserted in the blank labeled number 1, would serve as the best thesis statement for the passage?

    A. The "walking catfish," *Clarias batrachus,* moves by sticking its spines into the ground and bending its body in order to crawl across the ground.
    B. The "walking catfish," *Clarias batrachus,* has features that make it desired by some people and detested by others.
    C. People in many countries find the "walking catfish," Clarias batrachus, to be an interesting addition to their exotic fish collection.
    D. The "walking catfish," *Clarias batrachus,* is an appetizing food, and they make interesting unique aquarium pets.

2. Which sentence provides specific support for sentence 2 in the passage?

    A. sentence 4 (_____ the Asians, people from other regions in Australia and North America regard this unique, exotic fish as a wonderful addition to their aquarium.)
    B. sentence 3 (Many Asian cookbooks have recipes to prepare this marine delicacy by frying, broiling, or baking.)
    C. sentence 6 (Conversely, people who fish or own fish farms in the Southeastern United States consider this ambulatory fish to be a costly nuisance.)
    D. sentence 8 (This fish is capable of moving across land from one body of water to another and has a voracious appetite.)

*Some of the paragraphs quoted by the authors have been altered to fit the patterns used by the Florida State Exit Test.

3. Select the arrangement of sentences 6, 7, and 8 that provides the most logical sequence of ideas and supporting details in the paragraph. If no change is needed select answer A.

A. Conversely, people in the Southeastern United States consider this ambulatory fish to be a costly nuisance. Therefore, it can eat all the fish in one pond and then go to another pond in order to decimate the fish population there as well. This fish is capable of moving across land from one body of water to another and has a voracious appetite.

B. Conversely, people in the Southeastern United States consider this ambulatory fish to be a costly nuisance. This fish is capable of moving across land from one body of water to another and has a voracious appetite. Therefore, it can eat all the fish in one pond and then go to another pond in order to decimate the fish population there as well.

C. Therefore, it can eat all the fish in one pond and then go to another pond in order to decimate the fish population there as well. Conversely, people in the Southeastern United States consider this ambulatory fish to be a costly nuisance. This fish is capable of moving across land from one body of water to another and has a voracious appetite.

D. This fish is capable of moving across land from one body of water to another and has a voracious appetite. Therefore, it can eat all the fish in one pond and then go to another pond in order to decimate the fish population there as well. Conversely, people in the Southeastern United States consider this ambulatory fish to be a costly nuisance.

4. Which word or phrase, if inserted in the blank in sentence 4, would make the relationship of the ideas between sentence 3 and sentence 4 clearer?

A. Therefore
B. For example
C. Finally
D. Unlike

5. Which numbered sentence is the least relevant to the passage?

A. sentence 9
B. sentence 8
C. sentence 7
D. sentence 6

Passage 3

[1]In the past centuries colleges were considered a male domain; there were a few women's colleges, but many more men received higher education than women. [2]During the last part of the twentieth century women worked to gain rights and job opportunities which caused women to increase their college attendance in the United States until the women's attendance equaled

*Some of the paragraphs quoted by the authors have been altered to fit the patterns used by the Florida State Exit Test.

the men's attendance in 1980. [3]When women started to work outside their homes, they had to consider childcare. [4]_____

[5]Because men's attendance declined to forty-four per cent in 2000, many theories concerning the cause for the decline were proposed. [6]Some felt that the job opportunities offered men a sufficient means of support. [7]The salaries paid to many workers exceeded the minimum wage by a comfortable margin. [8]_____ young men may have been tempted by what they considered a decent wage. [9]Others felt that the social values of teens may have affected college attendance. [10]Young men were not encouraged to be academic by their peers, and intellectuals were often ostracized. *(Some of the information and ideas in this paragraph have been adapted from Macionis, John J. Sociology. 9th ed. Upper Saddle River, NJ: Prentice Hall, 2003. p. 537)*

1. Which sentence, if inserted in the blank labeled number 4, is the **best** main idea or topic sentence for the passage?

   A. Men's attendance at college has decreased steadily during the last part of the twentieth century and the beginning of the twenty-first century.
   B. But as the twentieth century ended a shocking change occurred; the number of women attending college increased steadily, whereas the number of men attending college decreased for many reasons.
   C. During the twentieth century women fought to earn more rights and to increase their social status so many women attended college to improve their opportunities.
   D. But as the twentieth century ended more people needed to attend college in order to improve their vocational skills and to improve their social status.

2. Which of the numbered sentences is not supported by sufficient specific details?

   A. sentence 1
   B. sentence 5
   C. sentence 6
   D. sentence 9

3. Which is the best placement for the sentence below to make the sequence of ideas in the paragraph clearer?

   Many popular music lyrics and television shows reinforced this idea.

   A. immediately before sentence 6
   B. immediately after sentence 8
   C. immediately after sentence 9
   D. immediately after sentence 10

*Some of the paragraphs quoted by the authors have been altered to fit the patterns used by the Florida State Exit Test.

4. Which word or phrase, if inserted in the blank in sentence 8, would make the relationship of the ideas between sentence 7 and sentence 8 clearer?

    A. While
    B. On the contrary
    C. As a result
    D. Likewise

5. Which numbered sentence is the least relevant to the passage?

    A. sentence 7
    B. sentence 6
    C. sentence 4
    D. sentence 3

Passage 4

[1] _____ "[2]Some choices young children can make include selecting books or stories to read before bedtime, choosing juice to drink during snack time, deciding what clothes to wear, and so on. [3]Giving children choices is an excellent way to reduce power struggles. [4]Most adults have had enough power struggles at their place of employment. [5]Of course, caregivers should limit the range of choices. [6]Caregivers frequently feel that, to be in control of children's behavior, they must resort to giving directives. [7]Sometimes directives are appropriate; however, young children who are struggling to develop their independence may respond negatively to a lack of choices, leading to a cycle of caregiver-versus-child battles. [8]_____, when we say that children may decide what to drink, the caregiver first limits the choice ("Do you want orange juice or apple juice?"). [9]In this way, mature adults remain in control while providing opportunities for children to make safe choices." *(Some of the information and ideas in this paragraph have been adapted from Mellov, Kristine. J. and Zirpoli, Thomas. J. Behavior Management. 3rd ed. Upper Saddle River, NJ: Prentice Hall, 2001. p. 434)*

1. Which of the following sentences, when inserted in the blank labeled number 1, would serve as the best thesis statement for the passage?

    A. Adults should limit the choices children make by offering them a choice between two or three objects.
    B. Children should be allowed to choose anything they want for their meals as long as all their nutritional needs are met.
    C. Children should be allowed to make choices in order to avoid battles with them.
    D. Children will learn how to make good choices if they are allowed to practice making choices from an early age.

*Some of the paragraphs quoted by the authors have been altered to fit the patterns used by the Florida State Exit Test.

2. Which sentence provides specific support for sentence 8 in the passage?

    A. sentence 3   (Giving children choices is an excellent way to reduce power struggles.)
    B. sentence 4   (Most adults have had enough power struggles at their place of employment.)
    C. sentence 7 (Sometimes directives are appropriate; however, young children who are struggling to develop their independence may respond negatively to a lack of choices, leading to a cycle of caregiver-versus-child battles.)
    D. sentence 9 (In this way, mature adults remain in control while providing opportunities for children to make safe choices.)

3. Select the arrangement of sentences 5, 6, and 7 that provides the most logical sequence of ideas and supporting details in the paragraph. If no change is needed select answer A.

    A. Caregivers frequently feel that, to be in control of children's behavior, they must resort to giving directives. Of course, caregivers should limit the range of choices. Sometimes directives are appropriate; however, young children who are struggling to develop their independence may respond negatively to a lack of choices, leading to a cycle of caregiver-versus-child battles.

    B. Caregivers frequently feel that, to be in control of children's behavior, they must resort to giving directives. Sometimes directives are appropriate; however, young children who are struggling to develop their independence may respond negatively to a lack of choices, leading to a cycle of caregiver-versus-child battles. Of course, caregivers should limit the range of choices.

    C. Sometimes directives are appropriate; however, young children who are struggling to develop their independence may respond negatively to a lack of choices, leading to a cycle of caregiver-versus-child battles. Caregivers frequently feel that, to be in control of children's behavior, they must resort to giving directives. Of course, caregivers should limit the range of choices.

    D. Of course, caregivers should limit the range of choices. Sometimes directives are appropriate; however, young children who are struggling to develop their independence may respond negatively to a lack of choices, leading to a cycle of caregiver-versus-child battles. Caregivers frequently feel that, to be in control of children's behavior, they must resort to giving directives

4. Which word or phrase, if inserted in the blank in sentence 8, would make the relationship of the ideas between sentence 7 and sentence 8 clearer?

    A. For example
    B. Whereas
    C. Equally
    D. Because

*Some of the paragraphs quoted by the authors have been altered to fit the patterns used by the Florida State Exit Test.

5. Which numbered sentence is the least relevant to the passage?

    A. sentence 2
    B. sentence 3
    C. sentence 4
    D. sentence 5

Passage 5

1 _____

[2]These viruses do not live long if they are in an exterior environment, but they are well adapted to life inside human tissue. [3]Sexually transmitted diseases can be divided into two groups. [4]The first group is caused by bacteria. [5]The second group is caused by viruses. [6]Viruses cause the sexually transmitted diseases genital herpes, human immunodeficiency virus, and genital warts. [7]_____ treatments do exist that slow down these diseases, arrest them for a period of time, and help many of the symptoms, these infections cannot be cured. [8]One other common sexually transmitted disease that has characteristics of being caused by bacteria and a virus is Chlamydia. [9]It can be cured with antibiotics if it is diagnosed in its early stages. [10]Many ministers advocate abstinence until marriage instead of promiscuity, so people do not catch these diseases. *(Some of the information and ideas in this paragraph have been adapted from Krogh, David. Biology: A Guide for the Natural World. 2nd ed. Upper Saddle River, NJ: Prentice Hall, 2002. p. 648)*

1. Which sentence, if inserted in the blank labeled number 1, is the **best** main idea or topic sentence for the passage?

    A. All sexually transmitted disease, those spread by sexual contact, can be arrested and symptoms can be helped, but the diseases cannot be cured; symptoms will continue to appear sporadically throughout the person's lifetime.
    B. There are two types of sexually transmitted diseases, which are passed from one person to another by sexual contact; both can be treated, but only one type can be cured.
    C. Sexually transmitted diseases can live outside the body for a short time, but they can live for a long time inside a human.
    D. The symptoms of the viruses that cause genital herpes, human immunodeficiency virus, and genital warts can be treated

2. Which of the numbered sentences is not supported by sufficient specific details?

    A. sentence 8
    B. sentence 5
    C. sentence 4
    D. sentence 3

*Some of the paragraphs quoted by the authors have been altered to fit the patterns used by the Florida State Exit Test.

3. Which is the best placement for the sentence below to make the sequence of ideas in the paragraph clearer?

Gonorrhea and syphilis are two types of sexually transmitted disease that are caused by bacterium and that may be curable if they are caught early and treated with antibiotics (although some antibiotic resistant strains do exist).

   A. before sentence 3
   B. immediately before sentence 5
   C. immediately before sentence 6
   D. immediately before sentence 7

4. Which word or phrase, if inserted in the blank in sentence, would make the relationship of the ideas between sentence and sentence clearer?

   A. Because
   B. Meanwhile
   C. For example
   D. Although

5. Which numbered sentence is the least relevant to the passage?

   A. sentence 10
   B. sentence 9
   C. sentence 8
   D. sentence 7

Passage 6

1 _____

[2]This massive, prominent, circular stained glass window in the south transept of the Chartres Cathedral in France is called a rose window because of its prevailing color and flowerlike form; the pictures on the window symbolize the Last Judgment. [3] It is very beautiful. [4]Seraphim are celestial beings that are considered the highest order of angels. [5]In the center of the window is Jesus, who is encircled by the symbols of the writers of the Christian Bible's New Testament's Gospels (Matthew, Mark, Luke, and John), seraphim, and angels. [6]The Apostles, who are paired, encircle the writers of the New Testament and the celestial beings in the second ring of the window. [7]_____ rings contain scenes from the New Testament of the Christian Bible. [8]The picture on the window is meant to show the Christian belief that the entire New Testament of the Christian Bible emanates from Jesus Christ in the center. [9]Each ring shows a different part of the stories about Jesus. [10]Each ring's placement relates the importance of these people and items in Jesus' life. *(Some of the information and ideas in this paragraph have been adapted from Sayre, Henry. A World of Art. 3rd ed. Upper Saddle River, NJ: Prentice Hall, 2000. pp. 161-163)*

*Some of the paragraphs quoted by the authors have been altered to fit the patterns used by the Florida State Exit Test.

1. Which of the following sentences, when inserted in the blank labeled number 1, would serve as the best thesis statement for the passage?

   A. The stained glass windows, architecture, and statues in the Chartres Cathedral in France are beautiful examples of Gothic art.
   B. The center picture in the rose window in the south transept of the Chartres Cathedral depicts Jesus; Christians believe he is their savior.
   C. One type of balance used in art is radial balance, in which everything radiates outward from a central point; an example is the rose window in the south transept of the Chartres Cathedral.
   D. The writers of the New Testament were Matthew, Mark, Luke, and John, and they are depicted in the first ring on the rose window in the south transept in the Chartres Cathedral.

2. Which sentence provides specific support for sentence 5 in the passage?

   A. sentence 2 (This massive, prominent, circular stained glass window in the south transept of the Chartres Cathedral in France is called a rose window because of its prevailing color and flowerlike form; the pictures on the window symbolize the Last Judgment) .
   B. sentence 4 (Seraphim are celestial beings that are considered the highest order of angels) .
   C. sentence 6 (The Apostles, who are paired, encircle the writers of the New Testament and the celestial beings in the second ring of the window) .
   D. sentence 8 (The picture on the window is meant to show the Christian belief that the entire New Testament of the Christian Bible emanates from Jesus Christ in the center) .

*Some of the paragraphs quoted by the authors have been altered to fit the patterns used by the Florida State Exit Test.

3. Select the arrangement of sentences 4, 5, and 6 that provides the most logical sequence of ideas and supporting details in the paragraph. If no change is needed select answer A.

A. Seraphim are celestial beings that are considered the highest order of angels. In the center of the window is Jesus, who is encircled by the symbols of the writers of the Christian Bible's New Testament's Gospels (Matthew, Mark, Luke, and John), seraphim, and angels. The Apostles, who are paired, encircle the writers of the New Testament and the celestial beings in the second ring of the window.

B. The Apostles, who are paired, encircle the writers of the New Testament and the celestial beings in the second ring of the window. In the center of the window is Jesus, who is encircled by the symbols of the writers of the Christian Bible's New Testament's Gospels (Matthew, Mark, Luke, and John), seraphim, and angels. Seraphim are celestial beings that are considered the highest order of angels.

C. The Apostles, who are paired, encircle the writers of the New Testament and the celestial beings in the second ring of the window. Seraphim are celestial beings that are considered the highest order of angels. In the center of the window is Jesus, who is encircled by the symbols of the writers of the Christian Bible's New Testament's Gospels (Matthew, Mark, Luke, and John), seraphim, and angels.

D. In the center of the window is Jesus, who is encircled by the symbols of the writers of the Christian Bible's New Testament's Gospels (Matthew, Mark, Luke, and John), seraphim, and angels. Seraphim are celestial beings that are considered the highest order of angels. The Apostles, who are paired, encircle the writers of the New Testament and the celestial beings in the second ring of the window.

4. Which word or phrase, if inserted in the blank in sentence 7, would make the relationship of the ideas between sentence 6 and sentence 7 clearer?

A. In the future
B. Likewise
C. The outer
D. Inversely

5. Which numbered sentence is the least relevant to the passage?

A. sentence 2
B. sentence 3
C. sentence 5
D. sentence 6

*Some of the paragraphs quoted by the authors have been altered to fit the patterns used by the Florida State Exit Test.

Passage 7

¹
_____

²Many teens use candy pacifiers at raves. ³ _____ a person is under the influence of Ecstasy, he or she may have difficulty with the regulation of his or her body temperature and their cardiovascular systems. ⁴ Environmental factors can exacerbate these difficulties leading to dehydration, heart problems, and death. ⁵ Recent studies by the National Institute of Drug Abuse using brain imaging have also led scientists to believe that Ecstasy has an impact on a user's brain dealing with the production of serotonin transporters and serotonin nerve endings. ⁶This damage can lead to impairments with visual and verbal memory as well as other areas of cognitive functioning. ⁷ Studies are being done with humans to determine if the brain functions improve after Ecstasy use is curtailed, but when this study was conducted with monkeys using Ecstasy, the monkeys had not regained their memory after seven years. ⁸Though Ecstasy may seem to be a drug that makes people have a pleasant experience, its unnoticed effects on the brain may be permanent. _Some of the information in this passage was obtained from the following sources: Mathias, Robert. "Ecstasy" Damages the Brain and Impairs Memory in Humans." 26 October 2002. <http:www.usdoj.gov/dea/concern/mdma/ecstacy020700.htm>._

1. Which sentence, if inserted in the blank labeled number 1, is the **best** main idea or topic sentence for the passage?

   A. The use of drugs can have negative effects on the user's physical and mental well being.
   B. The illegal drug Ecstasy that is used by many teens at "raves" can make the user feel euphoric, high, and self-confident.
   C. Damage in the part of the brain that controls serotonin transporters, which affect memory, mood, digestion, appetite, blood vessel constriction, and blood clotting can occur if a person does illegal drugs; these effects on your body and emotional well-being may be short term or permanent.
   D. Ecstasy is an illegal drug that many people use because it makes them feel euphoric and increases their self-confidence, but research has shown that there may be short term and permanent consequences that are hurtful to your physical and mental health.

2. Which of the numbered sentences is not supported by sufficient specific details?

   A. sentence 6
   B. sentence 5
   C. sentence 4
   D. sentence 3

*Some of the paragraphs quoted by the authors have been altered to fit the patterns used by the Florida State Exit Test.

3. Which is the best placement for the sentence below to make the sequence of ideas in the paragraph clearer?

Serotonin has an effect on mood, memory, appetite control, digestion, blood vessel constriction, and blood clotting.

A. immediately before sentence 6
B. immediately before sentence 5
C. immediately before sentence 4
D. immediately before sentence 3

4. Which word or phrase, if inserted in the blank in sentence 3, would make the relationship of the ideas between sentence 2 and sentence 3 clearer?

A. While
B. After
C. Before
D. For example

5. Which numbered sentence is the least relevant to the passage?

A. sentence 8
B. sentence 6
C. sentence 4
D. sentence 2

Passage 8

[1]_____

[2]After the fire, scientists investigated the pollutants in the tributary and discovered that eighty metric tons of phosphorous, a standard ingredient in laundry detergent, had been discharged into the river daily. [3]In 1969 the Cuyahoga River pollution was so extensive that the gasoline, marine engine oil, and technological waste in the river combusted and damaged two railroad bridges; while Lake Erie, into which the Cuyahoga flowed, was so full of toxic chemicals that the majority of the fish had expired. [4]Consequently, the city and the surrounding areas labored to reduce the rate of pollution in the waterways, so at present there is eighty-five percent less phosphorus in the river and Lake Erie is a freshwater fishery. [5]_____Cleveland transformed the district adjacent to the river from an unsightly manufacturing region into an entertainment area with a cruise ship, restaurants with seating on the river, and nightclubs. [6]Tourists are attracted to this area by the entertainment. [7]Cleveland's waterways still contain some noxious substances, but the pollution levels have been greatly reduced since 1969. *(Some information and ideas in this paragraph have been adapted from Krogh, David. Biology: A Guide for the Natural World. 2nd ed. Upper saddle River, NJ: Prentice Hall, 2002. p. 721)*

*Some of the paragraphs quoted by the authors have been altered to fit the patterns used by the Florida State Exit Test.

1. Which of the following sentences, when inserted in the blank labeled number 1, would serve as the best thesis statement for the passage?

   A. During the 1960s pollution created catastrophic problems in Cleveland's Cuyahoga River and Lake Erie, but Cleveland and the surrounding communities have made significant progress cleaning the waterways and the areas around them.
   B. Cleveland has a new entertainment district near the river with a cruise ship, many restaurants, and numerous nightclubs; this has become a meeting place for the city dwellers and a new tourist attraction.
   C. In 1969 Cleveland's pollution became so widespread that the gas, marine engine oil, and technological waste caught fire and burnt two railroad bridges.
   D. Pollution level in the country's rivers, lakes, ponds, and streams has been greatly reduced due to the work of environmentalists in the 1970s and 1980s.

2. Which sentence provides specific support for sentence 2 in the passage?

   A. sentence 6 (Tourists are attracted to this area by the entertainment.)
   B. sentence 5 (_____Cleveland transformed the district adjacent to the river from an unsightly manufacturing region into an entertainment area with a cruise ship, restaurants with seating on the river, and nightclubs.)
   C. sentence 4 (Consequently, the city and the surrounding areas labored to reduce the rate of pollution in the waterways, so at present there is eighty-five percent less phosphorus in the river and Lake Erie is a freshwater fishery.)
   D. sentence 3 (In 1969 the Cuyahoga River pollution was so extensive that the gasoline, marine engine oil, and technological waste in the river combusted and damaged two railroad bridges; while Lake Erie, into which the Cuyahoga flowed, was so full of toxic chemicals that the majority of the fish had expired.)

*Some of the paragraphs quoted by the authors have been altered to fit the patterns used by the Florida State Exit Test.

3. Select the arrangement of sentences 2, 3 and 4 that provides the most logical sequence of ideas and supporting details in the paragraph. If no change is needed select answer A.

A. After the fire, scientists investigated the pollutants in the tributary and discovered that eighty metric tons of phosphorous, a standard ingredient in laundry detergent, had been discharged into the river daily. In 1969 the Cuyahoga River pollution was so extensive that the gasoline, marine engine oil, and technological waste in the river combusted and damaged two railroad bridges; while Lake Erie, into which the Cuyahoga flowed, was so full of toxic chemicals that the majority of the fish had expired. Consequently, the city and the surrounding areas labored to reduce the rate of pollution in the waterways, so at present there is eighty-five percent less phosphorus in the river and Lake Erie is a freshwater fishery.

B. In 1969 the Cuyahoga River pollution was so extensive that the gasoline, marine engine oil, and technological waste in the river combusted and damaged two railroad bridges; while Lake Erie, into which the Cuyahoga flowed, was so full of toxic chemicals that the majority of the fish had expired. After the fire, scientists investigated the pollutants in the tributary and discovered that eighty metric tons of phosphorous, a standard ingredient in laundry detergent, had been discharged into the river daily. Consequently, the city and the surrounding areas labored to reduce the rate of pollution in the waterways, so at present there is eighty-five percent less phosphorus in the river and Lake Erie is a freshwater fishery.

C. Consequently, the city and the surrounding areas labored to reduce the rate of pollution in the waterways, so at present there is eighty-five percent less phosphorus in the river and Lake Erie is a freshwater fishery. In 1969 the Cuyahoga River pollution was so extensive that the gasoline, marine engine oil, and technological waste in the river combusted and damaged two railroad bridges; while Lake Erie, into which the Cuyahoga flowed, was so full of toxic chemicals that the majority of the fish had expired. After the fire, scientists investigated the pollutants in the tributary and discovered that eighty metric tons of phosphorous, a standard ingredient in laundry detergent, had been discharged into the river daily.

D. After the fire, scientists investigated the pollutants in the tributary and discovered that eighty metric tons of phosphorous, a standard ingredient in laundry detergent, had been discharged into the river daily. Consequently, the city and the surrounding areas labored to reduce the rate of pollution in the waterways, so at present there is eighty-five percent less phosphorus in the river and Lake Erie is a freshwater fishery. In 1969 the Cuyahoga River pollution was so extensive that the gasoline, marine engine oil, and technological waste in the river combusted and damaged two railroad bridges; while Lake Erie, into which the Cuyahoga flowed, was so full of toxic chemicals that the majority of the fish had expired.

*Some of the paragraphs quoted by the authors have been altered to fit the patterns used by the Florida State Exit Test.

64

4. Which word or phrase, if inserted in the blank in sentence 5, would make the relationship of the ideas between sentence 4 and sentence 5 clearer?

   A. Consequently
   B. Meanwhile
   C. For example
   D. Similarly

5. Which numbered sentence is the least relevant to the passage?

   A. sentence 4
   B. sentence 5
   C. sentence 6
   D. sentence 7

Passage 9

"[1]No human disease has yet been cured with stem cells; so far, these cells have demonstrated therapeutic benefits mostly in mice. [2] Some people have protested against using mice for lab experiments.[3]_____ _____ _____[4]Stem cells stand to alleviate or cure altogether: Parkinson's disease, heart disease, arthritis, Alzheimer's disease, multiple sclerosis, osteoporosis, and diabetes. [5]_____, people who suffer from "Type 1" diabetes have lost the capacity to produce the hormone insulin, which moves blood sugar into cells. [6]They have lost this capacity because the cells in their pancreas that produce insulin have been destroyed. [7]As a result, they have to inject themselves with insulin each day to keep their blood sugar from building up to toxic levels. [8]Even with this, they suffer from a host of diabetes-related afflictions, particularly as they get older. [9]In 2001, researchers announced that embryonic stems they had received from mice had begun secreting insulin when transplanted back into diabetic mice. [10]Imagine a diabetic child being treated not with lifelong insulin injections, but with a similar cell transplant. " *(Some of the information and ideas in this paragraph have been adapted from Krogh, David. Biology: A Guide for the Natural World. 2nd ed. Upper Saddle River, NJ: Prentice Hall, 2002. p. 631)*

1. Which sentence, if inserted in the blank labeled number 3, is the **best** main idea or topic sentence for the passage?

   A. Stem cells may help children with diabetes to produce insulin, instead of having injections.
   B. Nevertheless, scientists seem to agree that stem cells hold out enormous potential to help people with diseases, conditions, and damaged spinal cord injuries.
   C. Diabetic mice that have had embryonic stems they received from mice implanted into their body have started to produce insulin again thereby stopping their need for daily injections.
   D. Stem cell research may help people with spinal cord injuries to regain the use of their limbs and body parts.

*Some of the paragraphs quoted by the authors have been altered to fit the patterns used by the Florida State Exit Test.

65

2. Which sentence provides specific support for sentence 5 in the passage?

    A. sentence 2   (Some people have protested against using mice for lab experiments.)
    B. sentence 6 (They have lost this capacity because the cells in their pancreas that produce insulin have been destroyed.)
    C. sentence 7 (As a result, they have to inject themselves with insulin each day to keep their blood sugar from building up to toxic levels.)
    D. sentence 9 (In 2001, researchers announced that embryonic stems they had received from mice had begun secreting insulin when transplanted back into diabetic mice)

3. Which is the best placement for the sentence below to make the sequence of ideas in the paragraph clearer?

Some of the life-threatening complications are blindness, kidney failure, and heart disease.

    A. immediately before sentence 2
    B. immediately before sentence 5
    C. immediately before sentence 6
    D. immediately before sentence 9

4. Which word or phrase, if inserted in the blank in sentence 5, would make the relationship of the ideas between sentence 4 and sentence 5 clearer?

    A. Similarly
    B. Meanwhile
    C. For instance
    D. As a result

5. Which numbered sentence is the least relevant to the passage?

    A. sentence 2
    B. sentence 5
    C. sentence 6
    D. sentence 9

Passage 10

[1]Fort Clinch, located on Amelia Island in northern Florida, was incomplete when the Civil War started. [2] The fort has now been restored and enactments are presented. [3]Shortly after the Civil War was initiated the Confederate Army took over occupation of the fort. [4]The Union decided to gain control of the fort because they felt it would be important to the Southern cause; the South could use the fortress to take delivery of provisions from captains of ships willing to break through the blockade that had been established by the Northern army. [5]_____ the fort was only partially completed and almost impossible to defend, so the Southern general Robert

*Some of the paragraphs quoted by the authors have been altered to fit the patterns used by the Florida State Exit Test.

E. Lee ordered the fort to be evacuated. [6]When the Northern soldiers arrived to capture the fort, the fort was almost abandoned, so the Northern soldiers chased away the few remaining Southern soldiers and the North took over occupancy. [7]This was recorded as a victory for the North. [8]The fort became a strategic port for the Northern army ships in the blockade because it was located in the area being patrolled. [9]_____

_____

1. Which of the following sentences, when inserted in the blank labeled number 9, would serve as the best thesis statement for the passage?

   A. Robert E. Lee ordered the confederate troops to abandon the unfinished Fort Clinch, on Amelia Island, even though the fort might have been used for a place for blockade runners to deliver goods to the Southern people who were desperate for supplies.
   B. Fort Clinch, on Amelia Island, was taken over by the Union troops after they scared away the Confederate soldiers.
   C. Fort Clinch, on Amelia Island, played a small part in the Civil War because it became a port for the Northern army to use while enforcing the blockade against the South, and the takeover was considered a northern victory.
   D. Capturing forts was one of the major objectives of the Union soldiers and of the Confederate troops during the United States Civil War, which took place in the middle of the nineteenth century.

2. Which of the numbered sentences is not supported by sufficient specific details?

   A. sentence 2
   B. sentence 3
   C. sentence 5
   D. sentence 7

3. Which is the best placement for the sentence below to make the sequence of ideas in the paragraph clearer?

   Fort Clinch's location was a helpful area from which to take part in the blockade because it was close to the southern shorelines and the Gulf of Mexico, so both areas of water could be observed.

   A. immediately before sentence 9
   B. immediately before sentence 7
   C. immediately before sentence 5
   D. immediately before sentence 3

4. Which word or phrase, if inserted in the blank in sentence 5, would make the relationship of the ideas between sentence 4 and sentence 5 clearer?

   A. Similarly
   B. But
   C. For example
   D. Therefore

5. Which numbered sentence is the least relevant to the passage?

   A. sentence 1
   B. sentence 2
   C. sentence 3
   D. sentence 4

*Some of the paragraphs quoted by the authors have been altered to fit the patterns used by the Florida State Exit Test.

Paragraph and Essay Writing Skills

In addition to The Florida State Exit Exam in English, many community colleges also require college preparatory students to take and pass a writing test. If you have to take a writing test, you will be given at least two different topics and asked to choose one on which to write a paragraph or essay. These paragraphs or essays are then scored by group of professors.

Several community colleges require that students pass both the writing and English language (grammar) exams before they are permitted to exit college preparatory classes. In order to pass the writing portion of the test, you must demonstrate that you can write either a well-developed paragraph or essay. Let's start by talking about the paragraph. A paragraph is a collection of sentences that, when put together, make a point.

The first step in planning a paragraph is to choose a topic, or subject. A topic is a word, or phrase, that identifies a general subject. The topic names the who or what you will be writing about in the paragraph, but it does not describe the details of the paragraph's subject matter. The topic should be specific enough to block out any ideas that you will not discuss, but general enough to cover the details you will discuss.

For example, if you are writing about one thing, name it or qualify it by stating the type or limiting factors. Let's say you decide to write about Hurricane Andrew. Begin by naming it instead of using the topic "hurricanes" as your subject. Next, think about what might be true about Hurricane Andrew and what might not be true of all hurricanes. If you are writing a paragraph, the idea is to zero in on one subject so your supporting sentences are specific enough that the reader can tell what you think is important.

As you move through the writing process, a paragraph needs to become more specific and detailed, but in the beginning stages the main thrust is to get started by putting something down on paper. Once a topic is chosen, organizing your thoughts, using what is referred to as prewriting strategies, can help generate ideas for developing a good paragraph.

There are several prewriting techniques you can use to help generate ideas on what you want to say about your topic. Some of the most widely used are: brainstorming, freewriting and clustering, also known as mapping.

Brainstorming involves listing any ideas you have about your topic. To do this, write as quickly as you can, without stopping, for at least five minuets. Afterward, look over your list to get ideas that will help you narrow your topic. After you are done, you may want to label the major details and the points that go with each detail. The following is an example of brainstorming using the topic: **A pet that is unusual.**

Brainstorming Activity—Timed at Five Minutes

*Remember brainstorming is a listing of ideas on a particular topic.

<u>Dog</u>
Noel
walks sideways
walks into walls
chases tail in a circle
stinks because she plays in the St. Johns River
Smells like fish .... why?
spends a lot of time cleaning herself
chews on my favorite dolls
high-pitched bark
dances when music plays
snores when she sleeps
howls when she wants to go out
sits on floor and turns in circles
attacks the sliding glass door in the early morning hours
refuses to eat when anyone is standing near her
likes cat food
complains if not served milk with her food
thinks all baby kittens belong to her
looks right at me when she barks
makes me think she is talking to me
acts as if she understands every word I say
social organizer of the others dogs in our neighborhood
has never met a dog she did not like
greets newcomers by prancing
always gives other dogs nuzzles
sits on the bench near window to see which dogs walk by

Freewriting Activity—Timed at Five Minutes

Freewriting is similar to brainstorming, but instead of listing ideas, you simply start writing anything and everything you can think of about your topic. Write continuously for at least five minutes. Don't concern yourself with using correct grammar or spelling; just write. The following is an example of freewriting using the previous topic: **A pet that is unusual.**

*Remember, the goal of freewriting is to get ideas down on paper. Do not worry about grammar, punctuation, or sentence structure – just write uninterrupted for a few minutes. The goal is to get ideas down on paper.

My dog, Noel is very unusual. She is very funny to watch. She moves like no other dog I have ever seen. For example, Noel walks sideways and has been known to walk into walls. She also dances anytime I play my U2 CDs. **However, she seems to like other kind of music as well**. The other day my dad put on a big band CD and she started turning in circles and hopping up and down. Noel also has this prancing act she performs whenever she meets a new dog in our neighborhood. She also has an interesting way of interacting with dogs and people. When she greets a dog she will prance around, sniff them and then nuzzels them. Our neighbors say she is the social organizer for all of the dogs in our neighborhood. Noel also makes unusual noises. She snores when she sleeps and howls when she wants to go outside. **When she is inside she sits on a bench near the windows and watches which dogs walk by always making what sound like little gunts**. It is almost as if she is sending some kind of secret code. In addition to unusual sounds, movements, and interactions with others, she also has unusual characteristics. For instance, she has some very unusual habits when she eats. She refuses to eat when anyone is near her. She also loves cat food and complains when we don't serve her milk with her food. She also takes on a real attitude and sometimes I even get the feeling that she is human. **At least I think she may have more human characteristics**. Like when she looks directly at me when she barks or when she acts as if she understands every word I say. **Also at times she makes me think she is talking to me. But one of the most unusual things about Noel is her likeness of kittens**. We had two litters at once and she tried to take on all 11 as if they were her own. When the mother of the kittens comes inside Noel acts as if she is an outsider. She will grawl at her sometimes and turn her nose up and walk away. I feel all of these behaviors and characteristics make Noel truly unusual.

Note:
In the freewriting above you can see that the ideas have not been separated into paragraphs. It also contains some misspelled words (nuzzles, grunts, and growls are misspelled and an *s* has been left off the word "turn"), errors in punctuation, and fragmented and fused sentences.

Clustering Activity

Clustering, or mapping, is a visual way of listing ideas about a topic. To start, write your topic on a blank sheet of paper and draw a circle around it. Then begin writing down whatever comes to you. Link the ideas by connecting them to the circled topic or to the details that they support. The following is an example of clustering using the previous topic: **A pet that is unusual.**

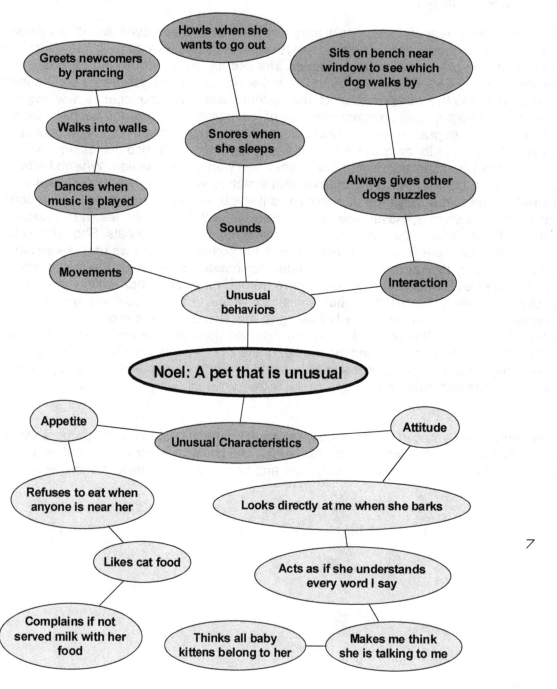

Now that you have looked at ways to both generate ideas and limit a topic for a paragraph, let's look at starting a paragraph.

A paragraph is a collection of sentences that, when put together, make a logical point. This point, referred to as the topic sentence, is what the writer wants to get across to the reader about a certain topic. A clearly stated topic sentence is the key to writing a good paragraph. Looking back at your prewriting exercises and search for an idea that makes a strong statement that clearly states the aspect of the topic you will be writing about in your paragraph. Avoid starting your paragraph with a sentence like "This paragraph is about."

Look at the following example from the practice exercises on prewriting.

A topic sentence expresses the focal point of the paragraph. This sentence, which incorporates the topic you have chosen to write about, is often the first sentence of the paragraph; however, a topic sentence may appear anywhere in the paragraph.

The body of the paragraph explains and supports the focal point. It typically contains five to eight sentences that contain facts and details which all support the focal point. The body of the paragraph for the state test should include at least five major details and a support statement for each detail. The concluding sentence refers back to the focal point and helps the reader recall the main point of the paragraph.

Now that you have decided on a main idea for your paragraph, let's review the format necessary for writing a good paragraph. The paragraph includes three parts–a main point, a body, and a concluding sentence. Each of these parts has a specific purpose.

The following is a paragraph using the original topic: **A pet that is unusual.**

Paragraph Model

     My dog, Noel, is an unusual pet. She is very funny to watch because she moves like no other dog I have ever seen. For example, Noel walks sideways and has been known to walk into walls. She also dances anytime I play my U2 CDs. However, I have also discovered that she likes other kinds of music as well. The other day my dad put on a big band CD and she started turning in circles. Noel also has this prancing act that she does whenever she meets a new dog in our neighborhood. After she finishes her prancing act, she takes a moment to nuzzle up to the dog and then she moves on to her next destination. In addition to her unusual movements, she also makes odd noises. For example, she snores when she sleeps and howls when she wants to go outside. She also sits on the bench we have in front of the window on our sun porch and makes grunting sounds when other dogs walk down the street. In addition to the unusual sounds, movements and interactions she has with others, she also has some very unusual characteristics. For instance, she loves cat food and will make a whiney noise if we don't serve her milk with her food. Also, she refuses to eat when anyone is standing near her. We always have to leave the kitchen after putting her food on the floor. Otherwise, she will simply walk into another room and wait until everyone has left the area. While all of these behaviors and characteristics are unusual, the one thing that I feel distinguishes Noel from all of the rest of my pets is her attitude. Recently, we had two cats that each had a litter of kittens. Noel tried to claim all 11 of the kittens for herself. When the mothers of the kittens would come inside to feed their babies, Noel made it clear that they were treading on her territory by growling, turning up her nose and walking away. When anyone would walk over to the boxes where the kittens were sleeping, she would follow behind to make sure they did not move them. If either of the mother cats moved any of the kittens, Noel would look directly at me and bark. My reply would always be, "Don't worry baby, everything is fine." She would then look at me with those dark, soulful eyes and act as if she understood every word I said. Noel's quirky characteristics and comical ways have certainly endeared her to my family. While her unusual behaviors and characteristics are a little annoying at times, we are pleased that she is part of our lives. She has become a wonderful companion and a faithful friend.

Scoring Criteria and Writing Samples for the Exit Paragraph

On the exit exam, you will be asked to write a well-organized, thoughtfully developed, and carefully edited paragraph or essay. Teachers will score your paragraph or essay, using a 1 through 6 scale. To understand what each score means, review the following Scoring Criteria for the Florida College Basic Skills Exit Test.

SCORING CRITERIA FOR THE FLORIDA COLLEGE BASIC SKILLS EXIT TEST

SCORE of 6 The paragraph or essay has a clearly established main idea that the writer has fully developed with specific details and examples. The organization of the paragraph or essay is logical and coherent. The vocabulary and sentence structure within the paragraph or essay is varied and effective. Errors in sentence structure, usage, and mechanics are few and minor.

SCORE of 5 The paragraph or essay has a clearly established main idea that is adequately developed and recognizable through specific details and/or examples. The organization of the paragraph or essay follows a logical and coherent pattern. The vocabulary and sentence structure within the paragraph or essay is mostly varied and effective. The paragraph or essay contains some errors in sentence structure, usage, and mechanics, but those errors do not get in the way of the writer's ability to communicate.

SCORE of 4 The paragraph or essay has an adequately stated main idea that is developed with some specific details and examples. The supporting ideas in the paragraph or essay are presented mostly in a logical and coherent manner. The vocabulary and sentence structure within the paragraph or essay is somewhat varied and effective. The paragraph or essay contains some errors in sentence structure, usage, and mechanics that may get in the way of the writer's ability to communicate.

SCORE of 3 The paragraph or essay has a stated main idea that is developed with generalizations or lists. The essay or paragraph main contain some lapses in logic and coherence and is mechanical in its structure. The vocabulary and sentence structure within the paragraph or essay is repetitious and often ineffective. The paragraph or essay contains a variety of errors in sentence structure, usage, and mechanics that sometimes get in the way of the writer's ability to communicate.

SCORE of 2 The paragraph or essay presents an incomplete or unclear main idea. Supporting details for the main idea are developed with generalizations and lists. The organization of the paragraph or essay is mechanical. The paragraph or essay contains lapses in logic and coherence. The vocabulary in the paragraph or essay is simple and the sentence structure is disjointed. The paragraph or essay contains errors in sentence structure, usage, and mechanics that frequently get in the way of the writer's ability to communicate.

SCORE of 1   The paragraph or essay has no evident main idea and its supporting points are inadequate and/or irrelevant. The organization of the paragraph or essay is illogical and/or incoherent. The vocabulary and sentence structure within the paragraph or essay are garbled and confusing. The paragraph or essay contains significant and numerous errors in sentence structure, usage, and mechanics that get in the way of the writer's ability to communicate.

After studying the scoring criteria, examine the six paragraphs below. Each one illustrates a specific score and is followed by a paragraph analysis to help you understand the strengths and weaknesses of the writing sample.

*These scoring standards have been adapted from the scoring criteria guidelines established by the state of Florida.

Scored Writing Samples

The 1 Paragraph

Topic: A game that is physically or intellectually challenging

A game that is physically challenging. i play baseball a lot. Usually the position of catcher. When i was a kid and my dad taught me how to play. Now i like being on the field the thrill of hitting the ball amazes me. There was several leagues that i use to play for. They coaches help me to do my best. Id rather be on the baseball field then anywhere else. Its physically challenging.

Paragraph Analysis:

Although this paragraph expresses a main idea about baseball, the supporting points are neither adequately developed nor logically organized. The paragraph is very disjointed; it does not flow logically and coherently. The sentence structure is also confusing and difficult to read. Furthermore, the paragraph contains many serious errors in usage and mechanics that inhibit the writer's ability to communicate. As a result, this paper scores a 1.

The 2 Paragraph

Topic: A hobby that you love to participate in

A hobby that I love to participate in is Art's and Crafts. Whenever, I start to work with my hands I feel that I am using one of the tools that God gave me to work with. He said whatever your hands find to do, do it well, and that's what I try to do every opportunity I get. For instance, I'm always doing something, like flower arrangements, once, my sister and I decided to take a craft class making adoption dolls. We decided that I was better at painting on the faces than she. Although I could do all of it well. We came to an agreement that we could accomplish more if she worked on the other parts of the dolls. That year we made 1,000.00 each, so we tried it again the next year. The manufacturers of that fabric saw that a lot of people were profiting from this hobby. This hurt the doll making business too. It went to the point of not being able to find the doll fabric any more. These are just a few of the things that I like to do. I have made macramai hanging planters too. In conclusion, I made an arrangement for someone that was interviewed by the. News Media and it was shown on their table in the newspaper. I love doing things with my hands.

Paragraph Analysis:

This paragraph presents an idea about arts and crafts that the writer does not coherently develop. The paragraph contains lapses in logic and coherence, for it addresses a number of different topics like flower arrangements, adoption dolls, and a specific fabric that do not seem to relate to one another. The paragraph also contains many errors in sentence structure, usage, and mechanics that interfere with the writer's ability to communicate. Consequently, this piece scores a 2.

The 3 Paragraph

Topic: Your favorite hobby

One of my favorite hobbies is going to the beach with my friends. We all cannot wait for the weekend, so we can pack up and head for the beach. I especially love to layout in the hot sun, and catch up with the latest about my friends. The beach is such a relaxing atmosphere, with the waves, and the children playing. I also enjoy just listening to the waves and the seagulls as they fly overhead. Going to the beach gives me a chance to put my worries behind me, and just have a good time with my friends. It is nice to have a day of relaxation, after a full week of school and work. The beach is a peaceful and fun place where I like to go in my free time. The beach is one of my favorite hobbies that I share with my friends.

Paragraph Analysis:

This paragraph about the beach states a main idea that is developed with generalizations. The paragraph is mechanical in its structure, moving from one idea to another without adequate support and transitions. The vocabulary and sentence structure within the paragraph are somewhat weak and repetitious. The paper also contains a number of errors in sentence structure, usage, and mechanics that occasionally interfere with the writer's ability to communicate. Nevertheless, the paragraph focuses on one main idea and does not contain gross errors; therefore, it demonstrates minimal writing proficiency and scores a 3.

The 4 Paragraph

Topic: A decision you made that has turned out well

A decision that I have made that has turned out well is not to give in to peer pressure. For example, when I was around people who smoked at high school socials, I chose not to do so. Also, at parties, I chose not to drink when everyone else did; therefore, I could be a designated driver for my friends. Additionally, I chose to attend college right after high school, whereas most of my friends decided to take a year off and just work at part time jobs. Lastly, I deal with peer pressure by not listening to my friends when it comes to my relationship with my boyfriend. For example, when they pressure me to go to a club and not tell my boyfriend, I chose not to go. Indeed, a decision that I have made that has turned out well is not to give in to peer pressure.

Paragraph Analysis:

This paragraph has an adequately stated main idea about peer pressure. The paragraph is developed with some specific examples, included being a designated driver, attending college, and visiting a club. The supporting ideas in the paragraph are presented in a logical manner through the student's use of such transitions as "for example," "additionally," and "lastly." However, the paragraph could be improved if the student were to develop some of the examples further, elaborating on her thoughts and feelings. The student could also improve the paper by varying vocabulary; the word "chose," for instance, is used four times. Lastly, some errors in sentence structure, usage, and mechanics have occurred. Nonetheless, the paper reads well overall and therefore scores a 4.

The 5 Paragraph

Topic: The use of the word "free" by some businesses

The word free has a price. FREE, in today's usage has a cost. I recently received two letters from a bank and a car dealership both claiming I could receive FREE gifts. First, the bank letter congratulated me on having been chosen to receive a FREE Visa gold card with an introductory offer of a 0% interest rate. After the letter made a point of telling me that it was a FREE card, it stated that a $49 deposit was required. Even though it also stated that the fee was refundable, they offered to conveniently bill my account for the total cost. Additionally, a letter I received from a car dealership, started the same way. After congratulating me for being selected to win FREE car, they gave asked that I come into the dealership and try a key they had enclosed in the envelop. I guess the letter caught me off guard because I thought they were telling me I had won a car. When I reread the letter, I realized they were congratulating me for being selected to enter a drawing, not winning a car. My next thought was, when did anyone ever have to be selected to enter a free drawing? The two examples demonstrate that we all need to be careful when we see the word FREE because it can carry a price when it is used by some businesses.

Paragraph Analysis:

This paragraph has a clearly established main idea about the word "free." The paragraph, moreover, is adequately developed through specific details about a free credit card and a free drawing. By using transitions like "first" and "additionally," the student organizes the paragraph well. For the most part, the vocabulary and sentence structure within the paragraph are varied and effective. Although the paragraph does contain a few errors in sentence structure, usage, and mechanics, these errors do not interfere with the writer's ability to express the main idea. Thus, this paper scores a 5.

The 6 Paragraph

Topic: The inconvenience(s) of modern technology

Most modern technology is invented in the hopes of making one's life easier, but I have found that some of today's technology can be quite an inconvenience. One new invention that truly bothers me is the automated phone service. When dialing 411 information or calling a large company, we can expect the automated phone service to answer. Unfortunately, we find ourselves pressing any button on the phone in the hopes of talking to a real person. Not only is this service an inconvenience, but it also replaces jobs in the workforce. In addition to the automated phone service, I have found that a self-serve gas station with computerized gas pumps can be a real nuisance. I used to detest visiting full service gas stations because the full service gas attendant always wanted to look under my car's hood. I found this aspect of gas stations to be cumbersome and time-consuming. Unfortunately, now that the computerized gas pump has been invented, my windows are dirty and my tires are flat. Despite these complaints, I do enjoy many modern conveniences. Heaven knows, I do not want to be beating my clothes on a rock. Nevertheless, I sometimes find myself feeling very frustrated with some of today's technologies.

Paragraph Analysis:

This paragraph has a clearly established main idea about the inconvenience of modern technology. The student fully develops the paragraph with specific details about the automated phone service and self-serve gas stations. In addition, the organization of the paragraph is logical and coherent: the student uses a variety of transitions such as "unfortunately," "in addition," and "also" to help the paragraph read smoothly. Vocabulary words like "automated," "computerized," and "inconvenient" effectively support the topic sentence. Furthermore, the student varies sentence structure through coordination and subordination. Lastly, the grammar, punctuation, and spelling of the paper reflect careful editing. This paper, therefore, scores a 6.

After reviewing how to plan and write a paragraph as well as studying various writing samples, you are ready to write your own paragraph. Throughout the course, practice writing paragraphs on the topics below. To get started on your writing, consider using the organizational and planning sheets located in the Appendix of this book. When you finish the paragraph, share it with your teacher for feedback.

Topics for Paragraph Practice Writing

Directions: Write well-organized and thoughtfully developed paragraphs on the topics below. Be sure to edit and proofread your writing carefully.

1. A first impression that turned out to be *either* right *or* wrong

2. An important event that changed your life

3. A place where you can go to relax

4. An invention that people cannot live without

5. A problem that needs to be solved in your community

6. Necessary skills for being a successful student

7. A memorable vacation experience that you had

8. A possession that has special meaning to you

9. A valuable lesson you learned from participating in a sport *or* hobby

10. The importance of writing clearly and effectively

11. A family pet that you love

12. A celebrity who sets a positive *or* negative example for youth

Tips for Time Management: The 10-30-10 Plan

You will have fifty minutes to plan and write your timed exit paragraph. Writing under such time constraints can make you feel rushed and uncomfortable. However, you can manage this fifty-minute period well by applying the **10-30-10 Plan**. Below are suggestions for how to use your time effectively.

Ten Minutes at the Beginning: Rather than start writing your paragraph immediately, take ten minutes at the beginning of the session to experiment with a prewriting technique, such as brainstorming, freewriting, or clustering. Then, jot down a brief outline of your paragraph, including a topic sentence, supporting details, and concluding sentence.

Thirty Minutes in the Middle: Devote thirty minutes in the middle of the session to writing a well-organized and thoughtfully developed paragraph. Focus on constructing clear and effective sentences as you express your thoughts and feelings.

Ten Minutes at the End: Take ten minutes at the end of the session to proofread your paragraph for grammar, punctuation, and spelling. By following the 10-30-10 Plan, you can manage time effectively rather than feel pressured by it.

Tips for Writing a College Essay

Some community colleges in Florida require that students enrolled in ENC 0021 write a clear and effective essay to exit the course. The typical college essay consists of four to six paragraphs, with an introduction, a body, and a conclusion. Such an essay may contain approximately 500 to 750 words, but the length requirements may vary by school. To learn about how to compose an essay, review the brief guidelines below. Please consult your course textbook for more in-depth information about essay writing.

The Introduction

- Begin your essay with an attention grabber (a question, a quotation, an anecdote, a statistic, or a joke) in which you address the essay topic.
- Offer background information about your topic. Discuss what your topic is about, why it is worth studying, and how it touches your readers' lives.
- Develop a thesis statement in which you convey your opinion about the essay's subject. A thesis statement is usually one to two sentences long. Acting as a bridge between the opening paragraph and the body, the thesis statement is typically the last sentence of the introduction.

Body Paragraphs

- Plan on writing two to four body paragraphs in the average essay. Apply the guidelines in this section to each body paragraph that you write.
- Just as the thesis statement is the controlling idea for the entire essay, so also is a topic sentence the main idea for a particular body paragraph. Start each body paragraph with a topic sentence in which you express the main point of that paragraph.
- Apply the same strategy for writing a body paragraph in an essay as you do for writing individual paragraphs in ENC 0021. Support the topic sentence of each body paragraph with two to four general statements—namely, your explanations and observations about the subject.
- Offer two to three specific details, such as facts, examples, and experiences to support each general statement.
- Use transition words like *additionally, furthermore, then,* and *therefore* throughout the body paragraphs to help readers follow the train of your thoughts. For a complete list of transitions and clue words, please see the Appendix in the back of this study guide.
- Prepare a concluding sentence for each body paragraph in which you summarize the main idea of that paragraph and transition to the next one.

Conclusion

- Tie the ideas in your essay together.
- Re-state the thesis in fresh, original words.
- End with a clincher, or a catchy line, in which you inspire readers to think further about your essay. Try a thought-provocative question, quotation, anecdote, or another device that ties into your opening and brings a sense of closure to the essay.

Do you suffer from writer's block? Do you struggle to organize your thoughts effectively? Is it difficult for you to develop your ideas? What you need is the Paper Plan—a step-by-step worksheet for planning your essays! Please turn to the Appendix of this book to use the Paper Plan.

Sentence Structure Skills

Chapter 7: Modifiers

A modifier is a word, phrase, or clause that gives more information about other words in a sentence. To clearly understand the meaning of a sentence, modifiers should be next to, or as near as possible, to what the words are modifying.

Two mistakes often made when using modifiers involve dangling and misplaced modifiers. A dangling modifier is one that has no word or words in the sentence to modify. A misplaced modifier is one that is in the wrong place. If a modifier is left dangling or is misplaced, the reader will be confused as to who actually did what in the sentence.

This chapter of the guide will give you information on how to correctly use modifiers.

Dangling Modifiers

Example:

While driving through a wooded area outside the city, the dog began to bark.
NOTE: This sentence does not say a person was driving. The way it is worded indicates that the dog was driving through a wooded area outside the city.
Revise the sentence to read:
The dog began to bark as I drove through a wooded area outside the city.

Example:

Standing at the top of the hill, the lights of the city twinkle like tiny stars in the night sky.
NOTE: The way this sentence reads indicates that the lights were standing at the top of the hill. Lights are inanimate (nonliving) objects and they cannot stand at the top of a hill.
Revise the sentence to read:
Standing at the top of the hill, we watched the lights of the city twinkle like tiny stars in the night sky.

Misplaced Modifiers

Example:

Laura totes an old book bag to school that is torn and frayed.
NOTE: Though the writer of the sentence meant for the reader to understand that the book bag is torn and frayed, the way it is worded indicates that the school is torn and frayed.
Revise the sentence to read:
Laura totes an old book bag that is torn and frayed to school.

Example:

The tall Christmas tree captured the attention of the small children with bright lights.
NOTE: The writer of the sentence meant for the reader to understand that the Christmas tree had bright lights, but the way it is worded indicates that the children had bright lights.
Revise the sentence to read:
The tall Christmas tree, with bright lights, captured the attention of the small children.

Modifiers Exercise

In the sentences below, circle the letter next to the sentence that is written correctly.

1.
    A. I sold my old computer after I purchased a new one in a garage sale.
    B. After I purchased a new one in a garage sale, I sold my old computer.
    C. After I sold my old computer in a garage sale, I purchased a new computer.

2.
    A. Barbara went to the mall with her husband wearing her new boots.
    B. Wearing her new boots, Barbara went to the mall with her husband.
    C. Barbara went to the mall wearing her new boots with her husband.

3.
    A. We baked a homemade lasagna with freshly grated mozzarella cheese in the oven.
    B. We baked a homemade lasagna in the oven with freshly grated mozzarella cheese.
    C. With freshly grated mozzarella cheese, we baked a homemade lasagna in the oven.

4.
    A. The expectant mother exclaimed in the middle of the night the baby was coming.
    B. The expectant mother in the middle of the night exclaimed the baby was coming.
    C. In the middle of the night, the expectant mother exclaimed the baby was coming.

5.
    A. Freshly cut in the morning, Carlos gave Sandy a dozen red roses.
    B. Carlos gave Sandy a dozen red roses that were freshly cut in the morning.
    C. Carlos gave Sandy freshly cut in the morning a dozen red roses.

6.
    A. To enroll for classes, tuition must be paid by the first of the month.
    B. To enroll for classes by the first of the month, tuition must be paid.
    C. To enroll for classes, students must pay tuition by the first of the month.

7.
    A. Jogging along Lake Shore Drive in the early morning, the shoe fell off Katy's foot.
    B. Jogging along Lake Shore Drive, the shoe fell off Katy's foot in the early morning.
    C. Jogging along Lake Shore Drive in the early morning, Katy felt her shoe fall off her foot.

8.
    A. To win a courtroom trial, a lawyer must carefully prepare the client's case.
    B. To win a courtroom trial, careful preparation of a client's case must be done.
    C. To win a courtroom trial, a client's case must be carefully prepared.

9.

    A. As a working mother of three, many errands around the house are left undone.

    B. As a working mother of three around the house, many errands are left undone.

    C. As a working mother of three, Mary must leave many errands around the house undone.

10.

    A. The trunk was full after the Smiths placed the suitcases in it.

    B. The trunk was full after placing the suitcases in it.

    C. After placing the suitcases in it, the trunk was full.

Chapter 8: Parallel Structure

When sentences are written using parallel structure they are balanced and easier to read. To make sentences parallel you need to write them using words, phrases, and clauses that express like ideas.

This section of the guide will help you better understand the use of parallel structure.

Examples:

Parallel Words

Greg's favorite outdoor activities are: camping, cycling, and swimming.
(This sentence contains a balanced number of **ing** words)

George spent the first day of his new job moving shelves, packing boxes, and loading trucks.
(This sentence contains a balanced number of **verbs** with **ing** endings)

Parallel Phrases

My recent job promotion has provided me with enough money to buy a new car, to move to a larger apartment, and to pay off my outstanding credit card debts.
(This sentence contains a balanced number of **phrases** using **to verbs**: to buy, to move, to pay)

Parallel Clauses

Joan's mother said she could go to the mall after she finished cleaning her room and after she finished her homework.
(This sentence contains balanced clauses: (after she finished cleaning her room and after she finished her homework)

Parallelism Exercise

Directions: For each of the following questions, chose the sentence that has no errors in structure.

1.
    A. Janet enjoys exercising in a variety of ways, including running, to swim, and lifting weights.
    B. Janet enjoys exercising in a variety of ways, including running, swimming, and lifting weights.
    C. Janet enjoys exercising in a variety of ways, including to run, to swim, and lifting weights.

2.

    A. After Jason bought an unfinished kitchen table from the natural wood furniture store, he applied a pre-stain coating to the table, stained it with a mahogany finish, and then applied a wood sealer to it.

    B. After Jason bought an unfinished kitchen table from the natural wood furniture store, he applied a pre-stain coating to the table, staining it with a mahogany finish, and then he applied a wood sealer to it.

    C. After Jason bought an unfinished kitchen table from the natural wood furniture store, he applied a pre-stain coating to the table, staining it with a mahogany finish, and then applying a wood sealer to it.

3.

    A. During the presidential campaign, the college students gathered in their dormitory lounge to listen to the candidates on television, discuss important social issues, and to decide for whom to vote.

    B. During the presidential campaign, the college students gathered in their dormitory lounge to listen to the candidates on television, to discuss important social issues, and deciding for whom to vote.

    C. During the presidential campaign, the college students gathered in their dormitory lounge to listen to the candidates on television, to discuss important social issues, and to decide for whom to vote.

4.

    A. Each year in early spring, Grandma Eleanor digs a small hole in her garden, plants a handful of sunflower seeds, and she lovingly nurtures them until they blossom in late summer.

    B. Each year in early spring, Grandma Eleanor digs a small hole in her garden, plants a handful of sunflower seeds, and lovingly nurtures them until they blossom in late summer.

    C. Each year in early spring, Grandma Eleanor digs a small hole in her garden, planting a handful of sunflower seeds, and lovingly nurturing them until they blossom in late summer.

5.

    A. In the local public schools, children are asked to read twenty-five books a year, to write book reports about several of them, and to give oral presentations to their classmates.

    B. In the local public schools, children are asked to read twenty-five books a year, to write book reports about several of them, and give oral presentations to their classmates.

    C. In the local public schools, children are asked to read twenty-five books a year, write book reports about several of them, and they give oral presentations to their classmates.

Directions: For each of the following questions, choose the correct word or phrase within the context suggested by the sentence.

6.   When Bonnie looked up at the night sky, she saw the planets shining, the stars twinkling, and the moon _____.

        A. was beaming
        B. beams
        C. beaming
        D. that looked to be beaming

7.   After a long nap, the toddler emerged from his room and _____ that he felt hungry.

        A. announced
        B. announcing
        C. he was announcing
        D. to announce

8.   Jumping from tree to tree, playing with a beach ball, and _____, the monkeys at the zoo entertained the visitors.

        A. to grin from ear to ear
        B. grinned from ear to ear
        C. will grin from ear to ear
        D. grinning from ear to ear

9.   At the Strawberry Festival, the local townspeople enjoyed juicy strawberries, oven-fresh pie, and _____.

        A. eating refreshing shortcake
        B. refreshing shortcake
        C. they eat refreshing shortcake
        D. to eat refreshing shortcake

10.   The professor advised the students to review their notes, to re-read the textbook chapters, and _____.

        A. forming study groups
        B. they form study groups
        C. form study groups
        D. to form study groups

Chapter 9: Coordination and Subordination

Coordination

To capture and maintain the reader's interest in your writing, strive to vary your sentence structure through coordination and subordination, two techniques discussed in this chapter. Coordination is the joining of two independent clauses (or sentences) that are closely related in both their content and length. You can join two sentences by using one of the seven coordinating conjunctions; by using one of several conjunctive adverbs; or by using a semicolon.

Coordinating Conjunctions

You might remember the seven coordinating conjunctions as the FAN BOYS:

FOR

AND

NOR

BUT

OR

YET

SO

To achieve coordination, you will join two independent clauses with a comma and one of the FAN BOYS. A comma must be placed before one of the conjunctions in order to coordinate a sentence correctly. Your sentence will have the pattern modeled below.

IC,   FAN BOYS   IC

Examples:

- John went to the store, <u>but</u> he forgot to buy milk.
- Trish ate a small dinner, <u>for</u> she was saving room for dessert.

Conjunctive Adverbs

Another way to coordinate sentences is by using conjunctive adverbs. You may know these words as transitions: *consequently, meanwhile, moreover, however, nevertheless, furthermore, therefore, then, thus, otherwise, indeed, finally, as a result, on the other hand,* among others. A semicolon and a comma must be used with one of the conjunctive adverbs to coordinate a sentence correctly, as modeled in the pattern below.

IC;   TRANSITION,   IC

Examples:

- John went to the store; <u>however,</u> he forgot to buy milk.
- Trish was saving room for dessert; <u>consequently,</u> she ate a small dinner.

The Semicolon

You can also coordinate, or join, two sentences by using only a semicolon, as modeled in the pattern below.

IC   ;   IC

Examples:

- John went to the store; he forgot to buy milk.
- Trish ate a small dinner; she was saving room for dessert.

Subordination

In addition to exploring coordination, you can use subordination to vary your sentence structure. Subordination is the joining of an independent clause and a dependent clause. Recall that an independent clause is a complete sentence and a dependent clause is a group of words that cannot stand alone.

A dependent clause always starts with a subordinating conjunction. Study the list of subordinating conjunctions below.

Subordinating Conjunctions[1]

after	before	since	where
although	even if	so that	whereas
as	even though	though	while
as if	if	unless	
as though	in order that	until	
because	rather than	when	

---

[1] For a more detailed list of subordinating conjunctions, please consult your course textbook.

You can use subordination to join an independent clause and a dependent clause in one of two key ways.

1.   If a subordinating conjunction is used to form a dependent clause that is placed at the beginning of a sentence, a comma must be used to separate the dependent clause from the independent clause, as modeled in the pattern below.

DC,   IC

Examples:

- <u>Because John had studied for several hours</u>, he performed well on the test.
- <u>Although traffic was heavily congested</u>, Abby arrived at work on time.

(Note that a comma follows the dependent clauses in these examples.)

2.   If a subordinating conjunction is used to form a dependent clause in the middle of a sentence, it will normally not be preceded by a comma, as modeled in the pattern below.

IC   DC

Examples:

- John performed well on the test <u>because he had studied for several hours</u>.
- Abby arrived to work on time <u>although traffic was heavily congested</u>.

Now try the following exercise on coordination and subordination.

Coordination and Subordination Exercise

In the following exercises choose the correct coordinating or subordinating conjunction.

1. The secretary opened the office window, _____she wanted to smell the fresh air from outside.

    A.   for
    B.   and
    C.   nor
    D.   so

2. The little boy asked his mother to buy cotton candy at the circus; _____, she did not want him to eat such a sweet snack before dinner.

    A.   therefore
    B.   also
    C.   then
    D.   however

3. William Wordsworth wrote romantic poetry over one hundred and fifty years ago, _____ many of his poems are as fresh and insightful today as they were during his lifetime.

    A.   so
    B.   but
    C.   for
    D.   or

4. _____ the family had run out of gas in their car, the police officer stopped to help them.

    A.   Although
    B.   Even if
    C.   Because
    D.   Rather than

5. Noel likes to eat peanut butter and banana sandwiches for lunch, _____ Joyce prefers peanut butter and honey on crackers.

    A.   whereas
    B.   if
    C.   since
    D.   whether

6.
    A.   In order that DVDs are the latest, most technologically advanced way of recording music, James still prefers to listen to songs on old vinyl records.
    B.   Even though DVDs are the latest, most technologically advanced way of recording music, James still prefers to listen to songs on old vinyl records.
    C.   Since DVDs are the latest, most technologically advanced way of recording music, James still prefers to listen to songs on old vinyl records.

7.
    A.   Polite and respectful, Pauline always sends a hand-written thank you note to prospective employers until they interview her.
    B.   Polite and respectful, Pauline always sends a hand-written thank you note to prospective employers although they interview her.
    C.   Polite and respectful, Pauline always sends a hand-written thank you note to prospective employers after they interview her.

8.
    A.   The retired couple enjoys traveling throughout Florida and shopping at used bookstores that sell rare, first edition books about landscape architecture.
    B.   The retired couple enjoys traveling throughout Florida and shopping at used bookstores who sell rare, first edition books about landscape architecture.
    C.   The retired couple enjoys traveling throughout Florida and shopping at used bookstores whether they sell rare, first edition books about landscape architecture.

9.

  A.   Wherever Didia immigrated to West Palm Beach, Florida, from Ecuador, she
       enrolled in an English as a Second or Other Language course at the local
       community college.

  B.   Provided that Didia immigrated to West Palm Beach, Florida, from Ecuador, she
       enrolled in an English as a Second or Other Language course at the local
       community college.

  C.   After Didia immigrated to West Palm Beach, Florida, from Ecuador, she enrolled
       in an English as a Second or Other Language course at the local community
       college.

10.

  A.   If the manager quotes a reasonable price, the couple will rent the reception hall
       for their wedding.

  B.   As the manager quotes a reasonable price, the couple will rent the reception hall
       for their wedding.

  C.   Though the manager quotes a reasonable price, the couple will rent the reception
       hall for their wedding.

Chapter 10: Fragments

A sentence is a group of words that expresses a complete thought. Writing complete and correct sentences is a must in building solid paragraphs and essays. This chapter will show you how to avoid a major sentence error known as the fragment (an incomplete sentence).

Unlike sentences, fragments do not express complete thoughts. A fragmented sentence may be missing a subject, a verb, or some combination of these important sentence parts. By studying two common types of fragments, you can learn to recognize and correct them in your writing.

Dependent Word Fragments

Recall from your study of subordination that a dependent clause must be connected to an independent clause according to one of the following patterns:

IC   DC

DC,   IC

A dependent word fragment is an error that occurs when a dependent clause is not joined to an independent clause, as modeled below.

INCORRECT: Paul is a happy man. Because Linda said she would marry him.

(The underlined statement is a dependent word fragment. It starts with the dependent word "because" and cannot stand alone.)

By using the two sentence patterns from above, you can correct a dependent word fragment.

CORRECT: Paul is a happy man because Linda said she would marry him. **(IC DC)**

Because Linda said she would marry him, Paul is a happy man. **(DC, IC)**

Missing Subject Fragments

A missing subject fragment lacks a subject. The underlined statement below models this type of fragment.

INCORRECT: Mrs. Green planted colorful flowers in our neighborhood park. And painted the weather-beaten bench.

You can correct a missing subject fragment by making it a part of a nearby sentence.

CORRECT: Mrs. Green planted colorful flowers in our neighborhood park and painted the weather-beaten bench.

You can also correct a missing subject fragment by adding a subject to it and then coordinating it with a nearby sentence.

CORRECT: Mrs. Green planted colorful flowers in our neighborhood park<u>, and she painted the weather-beaten bench.</u>

Note: *A sentence could also be missing a verb. Avoid fragments by making sure your sentence contains both a subject and a complete verb, as illustrated below.*

INCORRECT: The soccer team <u>practicing</u> outside in the rain for the game.

(This sentence does not have a complete verb. If you insert the helping verb "was," the sentence becomes complete.)

CORRECT: The soccer team <u>was practicing</u> outside in the rain for the game.

Complete the following practice exercise on fragments.

Exercise: Fragments

Directions: For each of the following questions, choose the option that corrects an error in the underlined portion. If no error exists, choose "no change is necessary."

1. A day at the beach is relaxing, entertaining, and <u>inspirational. Especially</u> at
A
Jacksonville Beach, <u>Florida, where</u> our family <u>visits at least</u> once a month.
B   C

   A. inspirational, especially
   B. Florida. Where
   C. visits; at least
   D. No change is necessary.

2. Early in the morning, as the sun <u>rises, we</u> dress in our bathing <u>suits. And</u> drive to
A   B
Jacksonville <u>Beach, which</u> is about thirty miles from where we live.
C

   A. rises. We
   B. suits and
   C. Beach. Which
   D. No change is necessary.

3. When we arrive at the <u>beach. We</u> observe a <u>couple, whose</u> love-struck eyes are
                                   A   B

    as bright as the <u>sun, strolling</u> hand-in-hand along the ocean shore.
                             C

    A. beach, we
    B. couple. Whose
    C. sand; strolling
    D. No change is necessary.

4. The sun's <u>warm, radiant</u> rays brown the skin of <u>sunbathers who</u> recline leisurely
                       A   B

    in lawn <u>chairs. And</u> peer through sunglasses at passersby.
                  C

    A. warm; radiant
    B. sunbathers. Who
    C. chairs and
    D. No change is necessary.

5. Cautious mothers apply generous handfuls of <u>sun block to</u> the faces, shoulders,
                                                  A

    and backs of their <u>children. To</u> prevent them from getting a <u>sunburn while</u> they
                            B   C

    frolic in the ocean.

    A. sun block. To
    B. children to
    C. sunburn; while
    D. No change is necessary.

6. Riding piggyback on her father's shoulders as he wades into the <u>ocean, a</u> little

    girl squeals with laughter.

    A. ocean a
    B. ocean; a
    C. ocean. A
    D. No change is necessary.

7. As the sand tickles our <u>toes, we</u> look down to see footprints, both tiny and
                                    A

    <u>large, that</u> blanket the entire <u>beach. But</u> are soon washed away by the tide.
        B   C

    A. toes; we
    B. large. That
    C. beach but
    D. No change is necessary.

8. Suddenly, a yellow Labrador retriever leaps into the <u>air and</u> catches a

   A

   <u>frisbee.   Which</u> bears the colors of the American <u>flag, and</u> then proudly returns

   BC

   the frisbee to his owner.

   A. air. And
   B. frisbee, which
   C. flag; and
   D. No change is necessary.

9. Nearby, a seagull boldly <u>lands by</u> a group of volleyball players and pecks at a

   A

   discarded <u>biscuit until</u> other members of its flock <u>arrive and</u> it must share the

   BC

   precious leftovers.

   A. lands; by
   B. biscuit; until
   C. arrive; and
   D. No change is necessary.

10. As the waves wash onto the shore at Jacksonville <u>Beach and</u> then recede into

    A

    the <u>ocean, they</u> seem to carry our troubles away with <u>them. Leaving</u> us relaxed,

    BC

    entertained, and inspired.

    A. Beach. And
    B. ocean; they
    C. them, leaving
    D. No change is necessary.

Chapter 11: Run-ons (Fused Sentences and Comma Splices)

A run-on is a sentence that goes on and on because it lacks proper punctuation. One idea runs into another, often confusing the reader. Two types of run-ons occur in writing: fused sentences and comma splices.

Fused Sentences

A fused sentence is a run-on that occurs when you combine two or more independent clauses without punctuation, as illustrated below.

- John kindly took me to the <u>theater the movie</u> I really wanted to see wasn't playing.

(Two independent clauses have been incorrectly fused, or joined, in this sentence. Notice that the first independent clause ends with "theater" and the second begins with "the.")

You might want to correct this fused sentence by placing a comma between the two independent clauses. Yet if you were to add a comma between two independent clauses, you would create the second type of run-on—the comma splice.

Comma Splices

A comma splice is a run-on that occurs when you combine two independent clauses with only a comma, as modeled below.

- John kindly took me to the <u>theater, the movie</u> I really wanted to see wasn't playing.

(Two independent clauses have been incorrectly connected with only a comma.)

You can correct fused sentences and comma splices by applying the rules of effective sentence structure, most of which you studied in Chapter 9 on coordination and subordination.

Rules of Effective Sentence Structure

Rule 1: Separate two independent clauses with a period.

- John kindly took me to the <u>theater. The</u> movie I really wanted to see wasn't playing.

Rule 2: Join two independent clauses with a comma and a coordinating conjunction.

- John kindly took me to the <u>theater, but the</u> movie I really wanted to see wasn't playing.

Rule 3: Join two independent clauses with a semicolon.

- John kindly took me to the <u>theater; the</u> movie I really wanted to see wasn't playing.

Rule 4: Join two independent clauses with a semicolon, transition, and comma.

- John kindly took me to the <u>theater; however, the</u> movie I really wanted to see wasn't playing.

Rule 5: Use subordination to join a dependent clause and an independent clause.

- John kindly took me to the theater <u>although the movie I really wanted to see wasn't playing</u>.

- <u>Although the movie I really wanted to see wasn't playing</u>, John kindly took me to the theater.

After studying run-ons and the rules of effective sentence structure, you are ready to complete the following exercise.

Run-ons (Comma Splices and Fused Sentences) Exercise

Directions: For each of the following questions, choose the option that corrects an error in the underlined portion. If no error exists, choose "no change is necessary."

1. The black and tan cocker spaniel sat in its owner's lap during the ride to the veterinary <u>clinic, at the stop light,</u> the dog barked at some construction workers who were fixing a pothole in the road.

   A. clinic at the stop light
   B. clinic, at the stop light;
   C. clinic; at the stop light,
   D. No change is necessary.

2. A train with a red caboose rumbled down the <u>railroad tracks several</u> children in a nearby park waved at the engineer.

   A. railroad tracks, several
   B. railroad tracks, and several
   C. railroad; tracks several
   D. No change is necessary.

3. The clothing detergent is so powerful that it can remove stains caused by ketchup, chocolate, and <u>grease, however,</u> the detergent smells as gentle as baby powder.

   A. grease however
   B. grease, however
   C. grease; however,
   D. No change is necessary.

4. Tucked away in an old oak tree, the bird nest housed several robin <u>eggs, the</u> baby birds were beginning to hatch under their mother's watchful presence.

   A. eggs; the
   B. eggs and, the
   C. eggs the
   D. No change is necessary.

5. Jake and Suzette save newspapers, plastic bottles, and <u>glass for</u> they believe in recycling.

   A. glass for,
   B. glass, for
   C. glass; for
   D. No change is necessary.

6. Hurricane season in Florida lasts from April to <u>November during this time,</u> residents should stock up on extra food and water in case of an emergency.

   A. November, during this time,
   B. November and, during this time,
   C. November; during this time
   D. No change is necessary.

7. The aroma of barbequed ribs from Tom's grill drifted throughout the <u>neighborhood; consequently,</u> many people arrived at the cookout early.

   A. neighborhood consequently
   B. neighborhood, consequently
   C. neighborhood, consequently,
   D. No change is necessary.

8. The street musician moved the gathering crowd to sing and dance as he played the <u>saxophone, many</u> people complimented his performance and placed money in the well-worn hat beside his stool.

   A. saxophone many
   B. saxophone, in fact, many
   C. saxophone; many
   D. No change is necessary.

9. The famous author appeared at the pubic library for a book <u>signing; she</u> signed over one hundred copies of her latest novel.

   A. signing she
   B. signing, she
   C. signing, then she
   D. No change is necessary.

10. The sixty-year-old college professor participates in many bike-a-thons each <u>year he</u> often cycles more than fifty miles at a time.

   A. year, he
   B. year he;
   C. year. He
   D. No change is necessary.

Grammar, Spelling, Punctuation, and Capitalization Skills

Chapter 12: Adjectives Verses Adverbs and Degree Forms of Adjectives and Adverbs

This chapter will help you understand and recognize the difference between adjectives and adverbs and the degree forms of adjectives and adverbs. Adjectives and adverbs are words, or groups of words, that describe other words.

Adjectives describe nouns and pronouns. Adjectives usually come before the word they describe and tell which one, what kind, and how many.

Examples:
Her dog is the one that is barking. **Which** dog? Her dog.
Julie lives in the big, yellow house on the corner. **What kind** of house? The big, yellow one.
Ruby has four cats, three dogs, and two ferrets. **How many** cats, dogs, and ferrets? Four cats, three dogs, and two ferrets.

GRAMMAR TIP: Adjectives can come after forms of the verb be (are, is, was, and were).

Example: The dog is sick.

Adverbs describe verbs, adjectives, and other adverbs and tell how, how much, when, where, why, and to what extent.

Examples:
I hurt my foot, so I need to walk slowly. Walk how? Slowly.
We need to leave quickly. Leave when? Quickly.
Mark was very reluctant about investing $10,000 in his sister's boutique. To what extent was Mark reluctant? Very.

GRAMMAR TIP: A key to identifying adverbs is that many of them end in ly.
In the sentences above, slowly and quickly are both adverbs.

Exercises: Adjectives and Adverbs

Underline the correct adjective or adverb form in each of the sentences below.

1. Because Tanesa did not want to wake the baby, she walked (quite, quietly) through the room.

2. The little boy, who lost his ball on the playground, looked so (sad, sadly).

3. She wore a (blue, bluer) dress to the dance.

4. My new car is (green, greener).

5. I don't think I was treated (fair, fairly) in the deal.

6. Your pie smells wonderful; I am sure it tastes (well, good).

7. Lance treated his girlfriend (bad, badly).

8. The books are (heavy, heaviest).

9. Joey is a (nice, nicer) young man.

10. I live in the (yellow, most yellow) house on the corner.

Degrees of Adjectives and Adverbs

To use adjectives and adverbs correctly, it is important to understand how they take on various degree forms when describing other words. These degree forms fall into three categories: positive, comparative, and superlative. Additionally, most adjectives and adverbs show degrees of meaning by taking on an *er* or *est* ending or by taking on qualifying words such as better, best, least, and worst.

*The positive degree is used when nothing is being compared.

Example: Her dress is red.

* The comparative degree is used when comparing two things. Adjectives and adverbs that fall into these categories take on an *er* ending and use qualifying words such as better, worse, more, less.

Examples: Margo is taller than Morgan.
          Don is a better dancer than I.
* The superlative degree is used when comparing three or more things. Adjectives and adverbs that fall into these categories take on an *est* ending and use qualifying words such as best, worst, most, least.

Examples: She is the tallest child in her kindergarten class.
          Don is the best dancer in our class.

Grammar Tips:
- If an adjective or adverb is only one syllable, add the er ending to form the comparative and the *est* ending to form the superlative. This rule also applies to adjectives that end in *y*, however you need to change the *y* to *I* before adding the *er* or *est* ending.
- If an adjective or adverb has more than one syllable, use the word more to make the comparative and the word most to make the superlative.

Many forms of comparison for adjectives and adverbs are regular, but a few are irregular, which means their form may change entirely such as good becomes better or best. The chart below lists some examples of both the regular and irregular forms of adjectives and adverbs in the positive, comparative, and superlative categories.

Regular

Positive	Comparative	Superlative
beautiful	more beautiful	most beautiful
big	bigger	biggest
green	greener	greenest
small	smaller	smallest
young	younger	youngest

Irregular

Positive	Comparative	Superlative
good	better	best
well	better	best
bad	worse	worst
badly	worse	worst
many	more	most
much	more	most
some	more	most
little	less	least

Exercises: Degree Forms of Adjectives and Adverbs

Fill in the blanks by choosing the correct adjective and adverb forms listed below. If there is no error, select "no change is needed."

1. I am the <u>taller</u> person in my class.
   A. tall
   B. tallest
   C. most tallest
   D. No change is needed.

2. Russian is a <u>more difficult</u> language to learn than Spanish.
   A. difficult
   B. most difficult
   C. very difficult
   D. No change is needed.

3. Because I dislike hot weather, summer is the <u>bad</u> time of the year for me.
   A. more bad
   B. worse
   C. worst
   D. No change is needed.

4. It is <u>easier</u> to find a sales job during the Christmas season than any other time of the year.
   A. easy
   B. most easy
   C. more easy
   D. No change is needed.

5. I consider the time I spent in college to be the <u>best</u> years of my life.
   A. goodly
   B. better
   C. good
   D. No change is needed.

6. Jack is the <u>more generous</u> person I know.
   A. generous
   B. generously
   C. most generous
   D. No change is needed.

7. Albert will <u>likely</u> win the election and become our new class president.
   A. very likely
   B. more likely
   C. most likely
   D. No change is needed.

8. I made <u>less</u> money when I was working as a teacher than I do now working as a waitress.
   A. little
   B. very little
   C. least
   D. No change is needed.

9. Abby reads <u>fastest</u> than many of the other students in her class.
   A. faster
   B. more faster
   C. most faster
   D. No change is needed

10. Lucy's shoe size is at least two sizes <u>bigger</u> than her sister, Dawn.
    A. biggest
    B. most bigger
    C. more bigger
    D. No change is needed.

Chapter 13: Verb Forms

The information in this part of the guide will explain the correct way to use regular and irregular verb forms.

Verbs are groups of words that change form to express time. The purpose of verbs is to explain an action, an occurrence, or a state of being and give us important information about what is taking place, what has taken place, and what will take place.

Most verbs in the English language are regular verbs. These verbs can change form by adding an ending such as: talk, talks, talking, talked. Other verbs, known as irregular verbs, change form significantly which means that they will either change their spelling or even make use of different words. There are three common irregular verbs: be, have, and do.

Understanding the proper use of verb forms, regular and irregular, can help you better see how words can deliver meaning.

Each verb has four principal parts: present, past, past participle, and present participle. A participle is a verb form used to describe something. A regular verb forms its past tense and past participle by adding *d* or *ed* to its present form. Past participles are used with helping verbs such as have or had. Present participles are formed by adding *ing* to the present form of a verb.

Below are some examples of regular verbs and the changes they take on within their principle parts:

Present	**Past**	**Past Participle**	**Present Participle**
laugh	laughed	laughed	laughing
open	opened	opened	opening
walk	walked	walked	walking

Irregular verbs change form in past tense and past participle. Below is a partial list of irregular verbs:

Present	Past	Past Participle
awake	awoke or awaked	awoke or awaked
be (am, are, is)	was (were)	been
begin	began	begun
blow	blew	blown
bring	brought	brought
choose	chose	chosen
come	came	come
do	did	done
drink	drank	drunk
drive	drove	driven
eat	ate	eaten
fall	fell	fallen
feel	felt	felt
fly	flew	flown
get	got	got or gotten
give	gave	given
go (goes)	went	gone
grow	grew	grown
have (has)	had	had
hide	hid	hidden
keep	kept	kept
know	knew	known
lay	laid	laid
lead	led	led
leave	left	left
lie	lay	lain
ride	rode	ridden
ring	rang	rung
rise	rose	risen
sit	sat	sat
shake	shook	shaken
sing	sang	sung
speak	spoke	spoken
swim	swam	swum
wear	wore	worn
write	wrote	written

Below is a list of the three common irregular verbs that shows how they change form based on tense.

BE
Present Tense

I am	we are
you are	you are
he, she, it is	they are

BE
Past Tense

I was	we were
you were	you were
he, she, it was	they were

HAVE
Present Tense

I have	we have
you have	you have
he, she, it has	they have

HAVE
Past Tense

I had	we had
you had	you had
he, she, it had	they had

DO
Present Tense

I do	we do
you do	you do
he, she, it does	they do

DO
Past Tense

I did	we did
you did	you did
he, she, it did	they did

You can avoid making mistakes in the use of these verb forms when you understand verb tenses and how verbs change based on the tense in which they are used.

COMMON TENSES
(Divides time into present, past, and future)

- ❏ Present tense describes an action or state of being that is occurring now.

  Examples: Joe runs five miles a day. (action)
  Linda appears pleased with her new job. (state of being)

- ❏ Past tense describes an action or condition that has already occurred.

  Example: Lisa finished writing her research paper yesterday.

- ❏ Future tense describes an action or state of being that will occur.

  Examples: My aunt will be coming to town next week. (action)
  I will feel less stressed once I turn in my research paper tomorrow.
  (state of being)

PERFECT TENSES
(Describes actions or incidents that have already been completed or ones that will be completed before a more recent point in time. These tenses are formed by adding has, had, or have to the past participle)

- ❏ Present perfect tense explains that action begun and completed in the past, also continues into the present.

  Example: Since I started school, I have had very little time to socialize.

- ❏ Past perfect tense specifies that a past action was completed before another one took place.

  Example: She knew Lisa had won the award even before her name was announced.

- ❏ Future perfect tense specifies that an action or state of being will be finished before a certain time in the future.

  Example: Amanda will have gathered all of the information I need for the meeting by the time my flight arrives in California.

PROGRESSIVE TENSES

(Shows that an action or condition is ongoing. These tenses are formed by adding am, is, are, was, or were to the present participle)

- ❑ Present progressive tense describes something that is taking place at the time it is written or spoken about.

    Examples: I am not going to the movie today.
    You are going to the movie today.
    My friend is not going to the movie today.

- ❑ Past progressive tense describes the continuing nature of a past action.

    Example: Elaine was running down the street,
    The caterers were moving all of the tables to the back of the room.
    Future progressive specifies that a future action will continue for some time.
    Jack will be running in next week's race.

PERFECT PROGRESSIVE TENSES

(Shows that a future action will continue for a time. These tenses are formed by adding has, have, or had with been to the present participle)

- ❑ Present perfect progressive describers something ongoing in the past that will likely continue on in the future.

    Example: The stock market averages have been dropping drastically.
    The vulture has been circling the area ever since the sickly creature came into view.

- ❑ Past perfect progressive describes an ongoing condition in the past that has been ended by something states in the sentence.

    Example: Eugene had been playing baseball on the neighborhood team until he moved across town.

- ❑ Future perfect progressive describes an action or condition ongoing until a specific future time.

    Example: I will have been driving for hours by the time you get up.

STANDARD ENGLISH VERB EXERCISES
Fill in the blanks with the correct standard form of the verbs be, have, or do. Read carefully and choose both the present or past tense verb forms accordingly.

My childhood friend, John, ___ a self-made millionaire. He ___ numerous businesses located in various parts of the United States, but he ___made most of his money in the stock market. He ____ not get intimidated when it comes to taking risks. He ___ obviously made more money than he ___ lost, so any great fear he may ____ ___ in the beginning about taking a risk ____ most likely been lessened by his tremendous gains. Yesterday, we ____ watching a national news program when suddenly John appeared and ___ being asked about his thoughts on the recent drop in the stock market. We ____ excited to see him and hear what he ___ to say, but I know that while we were listening to him, we ____ all thinking about the days we spent as kids in our old neighborhood. John always told us he ___ going to be rich one day and he ___ certainly succeeded. We ___ proud of our old friend, John.

PAST TENSE ENDINGS EXERCISE
Regular verbs in past tense form need –d or –ed endings. In the sentences below mark out the incorrect verb form and write the correct past tense form above it.

1. The children jump up and down on the playground.

2. Because Priscilla and I had not seen each other in a long time, we sat up most of the night and talk about old times.

3. Jack once play the drums in the school marching band.

4. Leslie learn to play the piano when she was a child.

5. After waiting nearly an hour, the waiter finally seat us for dinner.

6. Joe call me last night, but I never got his message.

7. Last weekend we camp on the beach.

8. Lori and I walk to the store.

9. Karen was so mesmerized by the view, she just stare into the distance.

10. Linda race down the street trying to catch the dog that had escaped from its pen.

STANDARD VERB FORMS EXERCISE

In the sentences below, correct the error in the underlined section(s). If there is no error, select "no change is needed."

1. Because I was so tired, I should <u>have went</u> home to rest instead of going to the mall.

   A. had gone
   B. have gone
   C. had went
   D. No change is needed.

2. While still in high school, I <u>decided</u> I <u>want</u> to <u>become</u> a writer.
                                A   B   C

   A. decided
   B. wanted
   C. become
   D. No change is needed.

3. I should <u>have known</u> that as soon as I <u>leave</u> on vacation, my cat <u>would have</u> her kittens.
                 A   B   C

   A. have known
   B. left
   C. would have
   D. No change is needed.

4. The baby <u>fought</u> taking a nap, but as soon as I <u>lay</u> him down he <u>fell</u> asleep.
             A   B   C

   A. fought
   B. laid
   C. fell
   D. No change is needed.

5. I <u>give</u> Trina twenty dollars, but she <u>spent</u> it before she <u>got</u> to the mall.
      A   B   C

   A. gave
   B. spent
   C. got
   D. No change is needed.

6. I <u>sat</u> patiently and <u>waited</u> for the nurse to <u>call</u> my name.
     A   B   C

   A. sat
   B. waited
   C. call
   D. No change is needed.

114

7. I could not find the eggs because they <u>were hid</u> behind some other items on the shelf in the refrigerator.

   A. were hid
   B. were hidden
   C. had been hidden
   D. No change is needed.

8. Once you <u>come</u> home, the puppy <u>will stop</u> whimpering and <u>went</u> to sleep.
                 A   B   C

   A. come
   B. will stop
   C. go
   D. No change is needed.

9. I <u>did</u> not hear you <u>ask</u> me to <u>buy</u> milk at the grocery store.
      A   B   C

   A. did
   B. ask
   C. buy
   D. No change is needed

10. He could not <u>have ran</u> that far in such a short period of time.

    A. have run
    B. had ran
    C. had run
    D. no change is needed.

Chapter 14: Verb Tense

If you want to learn to write well, then you need to understand the importance of maintaining consistency in verb tense. Tense reflects time by indicating when an action, occurrence, or state of being expressed by the verb takes place. A change in verb tense changes the time element involving actions, states of being, and events. If your writing contains shifts in verb tenses, the reader could become confused as to when what you are writing about actually took place. Many times the progression of tense is established by the relationship between clauses because one incident takes place in relationship to another. This part of the guide will help you learn how to correct errors in verb tense.

Example:

My dad can <u>recalls</u> what it was like before television <u>exist</u>, but he said he was never bored. His family <u>gather</u> nightly around the radio that sat in the living room of his home much the way families gather in front of the television set today to view a favorite program or movie. He <u>remember</u> how they listened to broadcasts by such great comics such as Jack Benny and Bob Hope and <u>listen</u> intently to the sounds of the big bands including: Harry James, Glenn Miller, and Artie Shaw. His memories of these days are fond ones and I never get tired of hearing his humorous stories about how life was simpler and more enjoyable without the luxuries we have today.

Explanation:

The five underlined words are errors in verb tense. The paragraph should read as follows:

My grandad can <u>recall</u> what it was like before television <u>existed</u>, but he said he was never bored. His family <u>gathered</u> nightly around the radio that sat in the living room of his home, much the way families gather in front of the television set today to view a favorite program or movie. He <u>remembers</u> how they listened to broadcast by such great comics such as Jack Benny and Bob Hope and <u>listened</u> intently to the sounds of the big bands including: Harry James, Glenn Miller, and Artie Shaw. His memories of these days are fond ones and I never get tired of hearing his humorous stories about how life was simpler and more enjoyable without the luxuries we have today.

Exercises: Avoiding Shifts in Verb Tense
Some of the sentences below contain shifts in verb tense. Correct the errors in the underlined section(s) of the following sentences. If there is no error, select "no change is needed."

1. The memo <u>has to be written</u> before I leave work today.
   A. have to be written
   B. has to be write
   C. has to be writing
   D. No change is needed

2. Amanda <u>sung</u> in the play and surprised everyone with her beautiful voice.
   A. sang
   B. sing
   C. singing
   D. No change is needed

3. Have you <u>driven</u> the car to school yet?
   A. been driving
   B. will have driven
   C. drove
   D. No change is needed

4. She <u>leaves</u> her house keys on her desk at work.
   A. left
   B. is leaving
   C. will be leaving
   D. No change is needed

5. Because she studied hard, her grades <u>improves</u>.
   A. improves
   B. improved
   C. are improving
   D. No change is needed.

6. He <u>eats</u> a dozen eggs and two pounds of bacon for breakfast yesterday.
   A. ate
   B. is eating
   C. has eaten
   D. No change is needed.

7. Kerri <u>gave</u> Josh three pieces of cake, but he still wanted more.
   A. is giving
   B. has given
   C. will give
   D. No change is needed.

8. The baby <u>has cried</u> ever since her parents left to go to dinner.
   A. had cried
   B. will cry
   C. has been crying
   D. No change is needed.

9. The cost of college tuition <u>had been rising</u> every year.
   A. have been rising
   B. is rising
   C. has been rising
   D. No change is needed.

10. Joan left for work and then <u>stops</u> to get a doughnut and coffee from the neighborhood bakery.
    A. stopping
    B. stopped
    C. will stop
    D. No change is needed

Chapter 15: Subject-Verb Agreement

Every day we face situations in which we must reach agreement with other people about various issues. A couple planning their wedding, for instance, must agree on a place to hold the reception. A car buyer and a salesperson must agree on the price of a vehicle. Two friends taking a trip by car must agree on which radio station to play as they are traveling.

Achieving agreement is a necessary part of daily life. Writing, like life, involves agreement.   One important form of agreement, called subject-verb agreement, occurs between subjects and verbs.

Subject-verb agreement can be a tricky area in English grammar because it involves many rules, but the most important rule for subject-verb agreement is the following: <u>A subject must agree in number with its verb. In English grammar, the word "number" refers to whether a word is singular (one) or plural (more than one). Singular subjects must be paired with singular verbs. Plural subjects must be paired with plural verbs.</u>

A singular subject refers to one person, place, or object. The singular subjects below have been underlined and labeled "S."

           S   V
- <u>The teenager</u> <u>enjoys</u> reading mystery novels in her leisure time.

              S   V
- The little <u>boy</u> <u>flies</u> his red, white, and blue kite every day after school.

To make a singular subject plural, you will usually add an –s or –es. For example, to make the singular subject "teenager" plural, you should add an –s: teenagers. To make the singular subject "boy" plural, you should likewise add an –s: boys.

Now, look closely at the verbs in the above sentences. They agree in number with their singular subjects, but interestingly, <u>singular verbs end in –s</u>. The verbs in the sentences above have been underlined and labeled "V."

The subject of the following sentences is the plural noun "twins," so it requires a plural verb. Study the examples below.

                           S   V
Incorrect: Fortunately, the identical <u>twins</u> <u>wears</u> different hair styles so that their friends can distinguish them.

                         S   V
Correct: Fortunately, the identical <u>twins</u> <u>wear</u> different hair styles so that their friends can distinguish them.

In order to master subject-verb agreement, you should be aware of several other important rules.

Intervening Word Groups

When sentences are simple and clear, such as "The teenager enjoys reading mystery novels in her leisure time," it is easy to make sure that the subject and verb agree. However, problems with subject-verb agreement often occur when extra words, called <u>intervening word groups, come in between the subject and the verb</u>. Many times the words that come between the subject and the verb are prepositional phrases.

!!GRAMMAR REVIEW!! *Prepositional phrases are groups of words that contain both a preposition and an object. A preposition is a word that conveys time or place. An object is the noun or pronoun that follows the preposition.*

Below are some examples of prepositional phrases; the prepositions have been underlined.

<u>in</u> the driveway   <u>at</u> the same time   <u>behind</u> the couch

When prepositional phrases appear between the subject and verb in a sentence, they can cause confusion. You might think, for instance, that the subject of the sentence is in the prepositional phrase. Actually, <u>a subject will never be inside a prepositional phrase</u>.

!!TEST TAKING TIP!! *The best strategy to follow when taking the exit exam is to cross off any prepositional phrases in a sentence. Once crossed off, these phrases can no longer be mistaken for subjects. You will therefore be able to make your subject and verb agree.*

                                           S   Prep. Phrase   V

- The blossoming magnolia <u>trees</u> ~~in Mrs. Richards' garden~~ <u>are making</u> me sneeze.

(The subject in this sentence is the plural word "trees," not the singular word "garden" inside the prepositional phrase; therefore, you need the plural verb "are making.")

                 S   Prep. Phrase   V   Prep. Phrase

- <u>One</u> ~~of the employees~~ <u>arrives</u> ~~at work~~ half an hour early every day.

(The subject of this sentence is the word "one," not the plural word "employees" inside the prepositional phrase; thus, you need the singular verb "arrives.")

Compound Subjects

Sometimes a sentence will have a compound subject—that is, two or more subjects. Use the three rules below to make a verb agree in number with a compound subject.

Rule 1: Use a plural verb when compound subjects are joined by "and."

    S   S   V
- <u>Seth</u> and <u>Adam</u> <u>are</u> twin brothers born in the year 2000.

        S   S   V
- The <u>hostess</u> and the <u>waiter</u> <u>suggest</u> today's special—chicken pot pie.

(In these sentences, the compound subjects require a plural verb.)

Rule 2: Use a singular verb when both subjects refer to the same singular person, place, or object. In other words, if a compound subject forms a singular unit, use a singular verb.

        S   S   V
- Dan's <u>coach</u> and history <u>teacher</u> <u>is</u> Mr. McKinney.

(Although the underlined subjects above may look like two separate individuals, they represent the same person—Mr. McKinney; therefore, the compound subject forms a singular unit and takes a singular verb.)

        S   S   V
- <u>Spaghetti</u> and <u>meatballs</u> <u>provides</u> a delicious and nutritious dinner.

(In this sentence, spaghetti and meatballs are not two separate subjects but rather two parts of one dish, thus forming a singular unit and taking a singular verb.)

Rule 3: Match the verb to the closer of two subjects when compound subjects are joined with "or" or "nor."

        S   S   V
- Neither the vegetable <u>soup</u> *nor* the submarine <u>sandwiches</u> <u>have been seasoned</u> with salt.

(In the sentence above, the verb "have been seasoned" agrees in number with the closer of the two subjects, the plural subject "sandwiches.")

        S   S   V
- Either the preschool <u>children</u> or the <u>teacher</u> <u>paints</u> a picture of the sun and clouds.

(In the sentence above, the verb "paints" agrees in number with the nearer of the two subjects, the singular subject "teacher.")

Inverted Subjects

Most of the time in English, subjects come before verbs. Sometimes, however, this order is reversed. <u>When a subject follows a verb, it is called an inverted subject</u>. It may be difficult to find an inverted subject and therefore challenging to achieve subject-verb agreement. By becoming aware of two types of inverted subjects, you will be more likely to pair subjects and verbs correctly in these situations.

Sentences That Begin with "Here" and "There":

<u>The words "here" and "there" will never be the subjects of a sentence</u>. The verb will almost always be a linking verb (am, is, are, was, were). Once you identify the verb, ask who or what the sentence is about. When a sentence begins with "here" or "there," moreover, be sure to cross off any prepositional phrases that you see. By doing so, you will increase your chances of correctly matching the subject and verb in terms of number agreement.

          V   S

- Here <u>is</u> the <u>disk</u> that you lost in the computer lab.

(In this inverted sentence, the singular subject "disk" agrees with the singular verb "is.")

          V   S

- There <u>are</u> several <u>cars</u> for sale in the used car lot.

(In this inverted sentence, the plural subject "cars" agrees with the plural verb "are.")

Sentences That Begin with Questions Words (Who, What, When, Where, Why, and How)

<u>A question word will not be the subject of an inverted sentence</u>. Look for who or what the sentence is about, and then match the subject in number to the verb, as in the following examples.

          V   S

- Who <u>is</u> the <u>director</u> of the exciting, new theater production?

(In this inverted sentence, the singular subject "director" agrees with the singular verb "is.")

          V   S

- When <u>are</u> the <u>report cards</u> being mailed to students?

(In this inverted sentence, the plural subject "report cards" agrees with the plural verb "are.")

Indefinite Pronouns

Indefinite pronouns are pronouns that do not refer to any person or thing in particular. Some indefinite pronouns are always singular, whereas others are always plural. A few indefinite pronouns can be singular or plural depending on how they are used in a sentence. When an indefinite pronoun acts as the subject of a sentence, it must agree in number with its verb. Below is a list of indefinite pronouns.

A List of Indefinite Pronouns

Always Singular

Another	Anybody	Anyone	Anything	Each	Either
Everybody	Everyone	Everything	Little	Much	Neither
Nobody	None	No one	Nothing	One	Other
Somebody	Someone	Something			

Always Plural

Both	Few	Many	Others	Several

Singular or Plural

All	More	Most	Some

Singular Indefinite Pronouns

      S   V

- <u>Each</u> of the poets <u>belongs</u> to a writer's guild.

(The subject of this sentence is the singular indefinite pronoun "each," not the "poets." Remember to cross off prepositional phrases like "of the poets" so that you can identify the correct subject. Because "each" is singular, it takes the singular verb "belongs.")

Plural Indefinite Pronouns:

      S   V

- <u>Few</u> in the audience <u>have heard</u> the guest lecturer's famous speech about soil conservation.

(By crossing off the prepositional phrase "in the audience," you can see that "few" is the subject of the sentence. Because "few" is plural, it takes the plural helping verb "have" before the main verb "heard.")

Singular or Plural Indefinite Pronouns:

The indefinite pronouns in this category are singular when they refer to a singular term and plural when they refer to a plural term. Take, for instance, the indefinite pronoun "most":

         S   V
Singular: <u>Most</u> of the milk <u>has been drunk</u> by the children.

(In this case, "most" refers to the singular word "milk." Therefore, "most" is also singular and requires the singular verb "has been drunk.")
         S   V
Plural: <u>Most</u> of the cookies <u>have been eaten</u> by the children.

(In this case, "most" refers to the plural word "cookies." Therefore, "most" is also plural and requires the plural verb "have been eaten.")

Now that you have reviewed subject-verb agreement, try a practice exercise to test your understanding of the material.

Exercise: Subject-Verb Agreement

Directions: In each of the following questions, choose the option that corrects an error in the underlined portion(s). If no error exists, choose "no change is necessary."

1. The five-year-old girl sometimes <u>falls</u> off her bike since it no longer <u>have</u> training
                                        A   B
    wheels, but she bravely <u>tries</u> to ride it again.
                              C

    A.   fall
    B.   has
    C.   try
    D.   No change is necessary.

2. Langston Hughes <u>was</u> a famous poet, playwright, and novelist whose works
                      A
    <u>appeals</u> to many readers; in fact, one of his most popular pieces <u>is</u> a poem called
      B   C
    "Mother to Son."

    A.   were
    B.   appeal
    C.   are
    D.   No change is necessary.

3. When you <u>visit</u> the dentist for help with a tooth that <u>have been aching</u>, you <u>hope</u>
         A   B   C

   that the treatment will be as painless as possible.

   A. visits
   B. has been aching
   C. hopes
   D. No change is necessary.

4. One of the trees in Uncle Johnny's apple orchard <u>was planted</u> over one hundred
                                                            A

   and fifty years ago when my great-great grandparents <u>were</u> alive; most of the
                                                               B

   other apples trees, though, <u>are</u> only fifty years old.
                                          C

   A. were planted
   B. was
   C. is
   D. No change is necessary.

5. Alligators, which <u>are</u> large, dangerous reptiles that <u>live</u> in swampy areas,
                           A   B

   <u>resembles</u> logs when they are at rest.
       C

   A. is
   B. lives
   C. resemble
   D. No change is necessary.

6. The little boy with the blond curls <u>love</u> to read dinosaur books; his favorite
                                             A

   dinosaur <u>is</u> Tyrannosaurus Rex, which experts <u>believe</u> was the king of the
               B   C

   dinosaurs.

   A. loves
   B. are
   C. believes
   D. No change is necessary.

7. Neither the directors nor the producer of the record company <u>have heard</u> of the
   A

   young jazz artist who <u>has been dazzling</u> local fans every time he <u>plays</u> the
   B   C

   saxophone.

   A. has heard
   B. have been dazzling
   C. play
   D. No change is necessary.

8. There <u>was</u> a baby blanket and a pacifier in the crib where the twins <u>were sleeping</u>
   A   B

   peacefully until their nap <u>was interrupted</u> by a loud noise.
   C

   A. were
   B. was sleeping
   C. were interrupted
   D. No change is necessary.

9. Everyone who <u>sees</u> the one-hundred-year-old house <u>marvels</u> at the condition in
   A   B

   which the owners <u>have maintained</u> it.
   C

   A. see
   B. marvel
   C. has maintained
   D. No change is necessary.

10. Either the DVD or the VHS tapes <u>have been rented</u> for the evening; most of the
    A

    store's customers <u>seems</u> to own a VCR, but many <u>wish</u> to purchase a DVD player in
    B   C

    the near future.

    A. has been rented
    B. seem
    C. wishes
    D. No change is necessary.

Chapter 16: Pronoun-Antecedent Agreement

In Chapter 15 on subject-verb agreement, you learned that subjects and verbs must agree in number. Singular subjects require singular verbs; plural subjects require plural verbs. Similarly, pronouns must agree in number with the words to which they refer. The words that pronouns refer to are called antecedents. To understand how pronoun-antecedent agreement works, you might find it helpful to review a few key terms.

Pronouns

A pronoun is a word that replaces a noun. As you probably recall, a noun is a person, place, or object. Writers use pronouns to stand in place of a noun and to avoid overusing a particular noun. Pronouns come in a variety of forms but can be categorized according to person. In this case, the term "person" does not necessarily refer to a human being but rather to the point of view from which you are writing. In English, three points of view exist: first, second, and third. Each point of view includes both singular pronouns (those that refer to one individual) and plural pronouns (those that refer to two or more individuals).

The first person point of view refers to the self with the pronouns that follow.

First Person Pronouns

Singular	Plural
I, me, my, mine, myself	we, us, our, ours, ourselves

The second person point of view refers to an individual to whom you are directly talking. Notice that the second person pronouns are almost the same in the plural category as they are in the singular one.

Second Person Pronouns

Singular	Plural
you, your, yours, yourself	you, your, yours, yourselves

The third person point of view refers to an individual or individuals about whom you are talking. In this case, the person is not directly in front of you but is a third party about whom you speak to others.

Third Person Pronouns

Singular	Plural
he, him, his, himself she, her, hers, herself it, its, itself	they, them, their, theirs, themselves

Antecedents

An antecedent is the word that a pronoun refers to; an antecedent is usually a noun, but it may be another pronoun. <u>Pronouns must agree in number with their antecedents</u>. Study the following models.

- <u>Danny</u> and <u>Kelly</u> ordered <u>their</u> wedding cake from a family-run bakery on Edgewood Avenue.

(In this sentence, the pronoun "their" refers to the antecedents "Danny" and "Kelly.")

- Itching uncomfortably from fleas, the <u>cat</u> scratched <u>its</u> neck.

(In this sentence, the pronoun "its" refers to the antecedent "cat.")

Most of the time, pronoun-antecedent agreement will occur as naturally in your writing as it did in the above examples. However, you should be aware of <u>a few challenging situations</u> that may arise with pronoun-antecedent agreement.

Indefinite Pronouns

Pronoun-antecedent agreement with indefinite pronouns can be somewhat confusing. Indefinite pronouns that are always singular, such as *anyone, anybody, everyone, everybody, no one, nobody, one, someone, somebody,* etc., can be especially troublesome. For a complete list of these pronouns, please review Chapter 15 on subject-verb agreement.

Note the following examples.

Incorrect: <u>One</u> of the employees left <u>their</u> sunglasses in the women's restroom.

(In this sentence, the plural pronoun "their" incorrectly refers to the singular antecedent "one.")

Correct: <u>One</u> of the employees left <u>her</u> sunglasses in the women's restroom.

(The singular pronoun "her" agrees in number with its antecedent "one.")

!!TEST TAKING TIP!! *In order to match the pronoun and antecedent, be sure to cross off any prepositional phrases that you see in the sentence. If you cross off "of the employees" and "in the women's restroom," you will see that the remaining words are "One left their sunglasses." Clearly, "they," which is plural, does not agree in number with "one," which is singular.*

Below is another set of examples.

Incorrect: <u>Everyone</u> who finishes the 5K River Run is a winner, regardless of how <u>they</u> place in the race.

(In this sentence, the pronoun "they" refers to the antecedent "everyone." However, "they" is plural, whereas "everyone" is a singular indefinite pronoun. The pronoun and antecedent do not agree.)

Correct: <u>Everyone</u> who finishes the 5K River Run is a winner, regardless of how <u>he</u> or <u>she</u> places in the race.

(The singular pronouns "he" and "she" agree in number with "everyone.")

    <u>Although the majority of indefinite pronouns are singular, some can be either singular or plural depending on how they are used in a sentence</u>. These pronouns include *any, all, more, most,* and *some.* Look at the following examples.

Singular: <u>All</u> of the nation proudly displayed <u>its</u> patriotism.

Plural: <u>All</u> of the states proudly displayed <u>their</u> patriotism.

(In the first sentence, "all" refers to one nation, so it is singular. Therefore, the singular pronoun "its" agrees in number with the antecedent "all." In the second sentence, "all" refers to many states, so "all" is plural. Therefore, the plural pronoun "their" agrees in number with the plural antecedent "all.")

Antecedents Joined by "And"

<u>Use a plural pronoun with antecedents joined by "and</u>."

- The <u>employee and the supervisor</u> left <u>their</u> day planners in the office.

- The <u>circus and the carnival</u> always delight <u>their</u> audiences.

    An <u>exception to this rule</u> involves plural antecedents that act as a unit, which is often the case with food dishes.

- <u>Spaghetti and meatballs</u> is especially tasty if <u>it</u> is seasoned with extra garlic.

(In this sentence, the singular pronoun "it" agrees in number with the singular antecedent "spaghetti and meatballs.")

Antecedents Joined by "Or" or "Nor"

When you studied subject-verb agreement with the word groups "either . . . or" and "neither . . .nor," you learned that the verb always agrees in number with the closer of the two subjects. Pronoun-antecedent agreement with these word groups works in the same way. <u>The pronoun always agrees in number with the closer of the two antecedents</u>.

- <u>Either</u> the <u>employees</u> <u>or</u> the <u>supervisor</u> left <u>her</u> day planner in the office.

(Although this sentence may sound very odd to you, it is grammatically correct. Sometimes written English does not sound right because it differs so much from spoken English. Nevertheless, the pronoun in an "either . . . or" expression must agree in number with the nearer of the two subjects. In this case, "supervisor" is closer to the pronoun in question than the word "employees" is. Therefore, the correct pronoun choice is "her," which agrees in number with "supervisor.")

- <u>Neither</u> the <u>ocean</u> <u>nor</u> sandy <u>beaches</u> will ever lose <u>their</u> appeal for college students on spring break.

(In this sentence, the plural antecedent "beaches" is closer to the pronoun in question, making "their" the correct choice.)

Now that you have reviewed pronoun-antecedent agreement, try the following practice exercise.

Exercise: Pronoun-Antecedent Agreement

Directions: For each of the following questions, choose the option that corrects an error in the underlined portion(s). If no error exists, then choose "no change is necessary."

1. Everyone who had tea and cookies for dessert placed <u>their</u> dirty dishes in the sink.

    A. her
    B. its
    C. our
    D. No change is necessary.

2. Either the cocker spaniel puppies or the Siamese kitten rests <u>their</u> head in my lap every night as I am doing homework.

    A. its
    B. her
    C. his
    D. No change is necessary.

3. The tourists love visiting Germany because of <u>its</u> rich history and fascinating
   A
   attractions. <u>They</u> particularly enjoy visiting the old, majestic castles, each of
   B
   which has an interesting story behind <u>it</u>.
   C

   A. their
   B. he
   C. them
   D. No change is necessary.

4. Neither the mother nor the daughters could find <u>her</u> keys anywhere in the house.

   A. its
   B. his
   C. their
   D. No change is necessary.

5. Anyone who works hard can improve <u>their</u> writing, but many students feel as if
   A
   <u>they</u> do not have enough time to dedicate to <u>their</u> papers.
   B   C

   A. his/her
   B. he
   C. his
   D. No change is necessary.

6. The couple walked hand in hand on the beach behind <u>their</u> house; the ocean
   A
   waves lazily lapped up against <u>their</u> feet. <u>They</u> watched in wonder as the rain
   B   C
   clouds disappeared, leaving behind a rainbow whose brilliant colors painted the

   morning sky.

   A. his
   B. her
   C. it
   D. No change is necessary.

7. Samantha enjoys wearing <u>her</u> old, well-worn blue jeans because <u>it</u> are so
   A   B
   much more comfortable than <u>her</u> new pair.
   C

   A. their
   B. they
   C. his
   D. No change is necessary.

130

8. The little boy eagerly mounted <u>his</u> rocking horse; <u>it</u> is black and white with a
                                           A   B

   wide, toothy grin on <u>its</u> face.
                        C

   A. their
   B. they
   C. her
   D. No change is necessary.

9. The political demonstration will be held in the downtown plaza near the house

   where Carl lives. <u>He</u> plans on attending the demonstration even though <u>he</u> does
                          A   B

   not know what <u>they</u> will address.
                          C

   A. they
   B. she
   C. it
   D. No change is necessary.

10. The antique store has <u>their</u> own policy about returning and exchanging items.

   A. his
   B. her
   C. its
   D. No change is necessary.

Chapter 17: Clear Pronoun Reference

A pronoun must refer clearly to a specific antecedent. Study the following sentences for a brief review of pronouns and antecedents:

- The <u>lawyer</u> left <u>her</u> briefcase in the courtroom.

(In this sentence, the pronoun "her" refers to the antecedent "lawyer.")

- The <u>minister</u> inspired many people with <u>his</u> message about peace and love.

(In this sentence, the pronoun "his" refers to the antecedent "minister.")

<u>Two problems</u>, however, <u>may occur with pronoun reference</u>. First, the antecedent may be unclear in a sentence. Second, the antecedent may be missing in a sentence.

Unclear Antecedents

A pronoun should refer clearly to its antecedent. In addition, a pronoun can refer to only one antecedent and should do so without causing confusion. Sometimes, though, <u>sentences with several nouns and pronouns can cause problems with pronoun reference</u>. When readers cannot tell which word a pronoun is referring to, the whole sentence becomes confusing. Consider the examples below.

UNCLEAR: The computer sat on the desk next to the filing cabinet. After Karen put her book bag on <u>it</u>, she began to type her essay.

(Pronoun reference is unclear in this sentence. Did Karen put her book bag on the desk or on the filing cabinet? The pronoun "it" could refer to either noun.)

The following examples model two correct alternatives to the above sentence. In each correction, the word "it" has been replaced with a specific noun.

CLEAR: The computer sat on the desk next to the filing cabinet. After Karen put her book bag on the <u>desk</u>, she began to type her essay.

CLEAR: The computer sat on the desk next to the filing cabinet. After Karen put her book bag on the <u>filing cabinet</u>, she began to type her essay.

Examine the sentence below for pronoun reference problems. It too has an unclear antecedent.

UNCLEAR: Brendon told Connor that <u>he</u> should invite Ciara to the prom.

(The pronoun "he" could refer to either Brendon or Connor. While one reader may think that "he" refers to Brendon, another may conclude that "he" refers to Connor. To avoid confusion, a pronoun should have only one antecedent.)

The sentences below avoid problems with pronoun reference.

CLEAR: Brendon told Connor that <u>he, Brendon</u>, should invite Ciara to the prom.

(Although it may seem a bit repetitious to use the name "Brendon" twice, your sentence will have clear pronoun reference if you do so.)

CLEAR: Brendon told Connor that <u>he, Connor</u>, should invite Ciara to the prom.

(In this sentence, the pronoun "he" clearly refers to Connor.)

Missing Antecedents

In addition to proofreading sentences carefully for unclear antecedents, you should look for problems with pronoun reference that can occur when a pronoun is missing an antecedent. Remember that every pronoun must have a clear antecedent—that is, the word or phrase to which it refers. <u>When the antecedent is missing altogether, the sentence might confuse readers</u>.

!!GRAMMAR ALERT!! Words that frequently result in missing antecedents include the following: "it," "this," and "they."

Study the following examples:

MISSING: In the course syllabus, <u>it</u> states that the exam will cover four chapters from the textbook.

(In this example, the word "it" is missing a clear antecedent, or word to which it refers.)

CLEAR: <u>The course syllabus</u> states that the exam will cover four chapters from the textbook.

(This sentence clearly indicates that the syllabus states information about the exam.)

MISSING: Pat and Judy love going to the movies on the weekends. <u>This</u> has created a special bond between them for the past thirty-five years.

(In this sentence, the word "this" is missing an antecedent. Readers do not know what "this" refers to.)

Now consider the following correction.

CLEAR: Pat and Judy love going to the movies on the weekend. <u>This pastime</u> has created a special bond between them for the past thirty-five years.

(The word "pastime" clarifies what "this" refers to.)

MISSING: <u>They</u> say that people should maintain a well-balanced diet low in fats and carbohydrates.

(Who says that people should maintain a well-balanced diet? The word "they" is missing an antecedent.)

CLEAR: <u>Nutritionists</u> say that people should maintain a well-balanced diet low in fats and carbohydrates.

(The subject "nutritionists" offers a clear and specific alternative to the vague word "they.")

Finally, the word "which" may also result in a missing antecedent.

MISSING: The well-groomed poodles barked loudly at the pedestrian, <u>which</u> made him angry.

(In this sentence, the word "which" is missing a clear antecedent. A pronoun can refer to only one specific word or phrase. A pronoun, however, cannot refer to an idea. The word "which" incorrectly refers to the idea expressed before it. Try one of the alternatives below.)

CLEAR: The well-groomed poodles barked loudly at the pedestrian. <u>The barking</u> made him angry.

CLEAR: The well-groomed poodles barked loudly at the pedestrian. <u>The loud noise</u> made him angry.

(Both of these alternatives replace the vague word "which" with clear antecedents.)
After reviewing pronoun reference, you are ready to try a practice exercise.

Exercise: Pronoun Reference

Directions: For each of the following questions, choose the option that corrects an error in the underlined portion(s). If no error exists, then choose "no change is necessary."

1. Dr. Van Hook told Nancy, her teacher's aide, that <u>she</u> needed to tutor several students after class.

    A.   she, Nancy,
    B.   he
    C.   it
    D.   No change is necessary.

2. Bill, the foreman of the construction company, is concerned about safety in

    the large building. <u>They have had</u> three accidents in the past week.

    A. It has had
    B. She has had
    C. Members of his crew have had
    D. No change is necessary.

3. Jessica saw <u>her</u> friend Megan at the mall while <u>she</u> was eating pizza at the food
             A   B

    court; the food smelled and tasted delicious, but <u>it</u> seemed rather costly.
                                                  C

    A. their
    B. she, Megan,
    C. they
    D. No change is necessary.

4. <u>They</u> say that the number of American women working outside <u>their</u> homes has
     A   B

    decreased slightly in recent years. <u>This fact</u> may be due to the high cost of day
                                            C

    care for infants and toddlers.

    A. Sociologists
    B. her
    C. This
    D. No change is necessary.

5. In Chapter 19, <u>it says</u> that more students learn through visual and hands-on

    teaching methods than through auditory ones.

    A. she says
    B. they say
    C. the author says
    D. No change is necessary.

6. The experienced children's writer and the new illustrator produced <u>their</u> book a
                                                          A

    week ahead of schedule, but the editor said that <u>she</u> needed <u>them</u> to make
                                                   B   C

    several small changes before the book could go to press.

    A. her
    B. they
    C. him
    D. No change is necessary.

7. The patient told his nurses that they were the best caretakers it could have.
          A   B   C
   A. their
   B. she
   C. he
   D. No change is necessary.

8. Ted told James that they had been given too much work by their boss and that
                        A   B
   the deadline was tomorrow, which seemed unfair.
                    C
   A. he
   B. his
   C. tomorrow. This demand seemed
   D. No change is necessary.

9. Kathy's grandfather enjoys cherry almond cake with vanilla ice cream; he told
                                                                           A
   her that this is his favorite.
   B   C

   A. they
   B. them
   C. this dessert
   D. No change is necessary.

10. Visiting the theme park and watching the dolphins as they perform tricks always
                                                          A
    delight the little boy and his sister, and they, the children, squeal with laughter.
                                B   C
    A. it
    B. their
    C. they
    D. No change is necessary.

Chapter 18: Pronoun Shifts

In Chapter 17 on pronoun reference, you studied an important rule: pronouns must refer clearly to their antecedents. In this chapter, you will learn that you should use pronouns carefully to maintain a <u>consistent point of view</u> in your writing.

What Is Point of View?

Point of view is the <u>standpoint from which you are writing</u>. Three points of view exist: first person (the person speaking), second person (the person spoken to), and third person (the person spoken about). Each point of view requires a specific pronoun. The chart below illustrates the pronouns used for each point of view.

Chart for Point of View

	Singular	Plural
First	I, me, my	we, us, our
Second	you, your	you, your
Third	he, him, his, she, her, hers it, its	they, them, their

Notice that point of view may refer to singular pronouns like "I" and "she" or to plural pronouns like "we" and "they."

An error occurs when you accidentally shift from one point of view to another. <u>Once you begin writing from one point of view, you should continue using that point of view</u>. For instance, if you begin writing in the first person point of view, you should continue referring to the first person with pronouns such as "I," "me," and "my." Avoid suddenly shifting from the first person to the second person "you" or the third person "he," "she," or "they." Study the following shifts in point of view.

Pronoun Shift: <u>I</u> prefer long walks outside to workouts in the gym because <u>you</u> can save expensive monthly fees.

(Notice the shift from the first person "I" to the second person "you"; remember that once you begin with a specific point of view, you must continue using it.)

Correct: <u>I</u> prefer long walks outside to workouts in the gym because <u>I</u> can save expensive monthly fees.

(The first person point of view "I" is now being maintained.)

Pronoun Shift: When <u>one</u> logs onto the computer during peak business hours, <u>you</u> can expect a long wait for Internet access.

(Note the sudden shift from the third person "one" to the second person "you." Once you start using third person, you must maintain it.)

Correct: When <u>one</u> logs onto the computer during peak business hours, <u>one</u> can expect a long wait for Internet access.

(The third person point of view is now being maintained through the word "one.")

Pronoun Shift: Because <u>tourists</u> want to preserve <u>their</u> memories for many years to come, <u>we</u> often take pictures and film scenes with <u>our</u> video cameras.

(Notice the shift from the third person "tourists" and "their" to the first person "we" and "our." To maintain a consistent point of view, continue using the third person.)

Correct: Because <u>tourists</u> want to preserve <u>their</u> memories for many years to come, <u>they</u> often take pictures and film scenes with <u>their</u> video cameras.

(In this sentence, the third person point of view is being consistently used with the pronouns "they" and "their.")

Indeed, consistency is the key to maintaining point of view. Stay with one point of view at a time.

Test your understanding of point of view by completing the following exercise.

Exercise: Pronoun Shifts

Directions: For each of the following questions, choose the option that corrects an error in the underlined portion(s). If no error exists, then choose "no change is necessary."

1. As the newlywed couple cut coupons from the Sunday newspaper, <u>they</u>
    A

    anticipated how much money <u>you</u> would save at the grocery store located next to
    B

    <u>their</u> house.
      C
    A. we
    B. they
    C. our
    D. No change is necessary.

138

2. Charles and I enjoy walking through <u>your</u> neighbor's flower garden and trying to
                                         A

name all the different flowers even though <u>we</u> are both allergic to <u>their</u> pollen.
                                        B   C

    A. our
    B. they
    C. your
    D. No change is necessary.

3. After <u>one</u> finishes Victor Hugo's novel <u>Les Miserables</u>, <u>she</u> will want the story to
         A   B

continue even though it is already very long and may have taken <u>her</u> a while to
                                                          C

read.

    A. we
    B. you
    C. me
    D. No change is necessary.

4. <u>You</u> should follow the advice of your teacher when you take multiple choice
    A

exams: keep <u>your</u> first guess on a given item because it is more likely to be
               B

correct than <u>your</u> second guess.
             C
    A. He
    B. our
    C. my
    D. No change is necessary.

5. The senior citizens in the nursing home welcome visits from <u>their</u> family and
                                                        A

friends because <u>you</u> often feel lonely when <u>they</u> are no longer living at home.
                  B   C
    A. our
    B. they
    C. you
    D. No change is necessary.

6. <u>You</u> should drive cautiously on the busy city expressway, for <u>he</u> never knows
    A   B

when another driver may swerve out in front of <u>him</u>.
                                           C
    A. One
    B. you
    C. us
    D. No change is necessary.

7. The local pet store attracts many visitors because of <u>its</u> window display of
   A

   puppies. Delighted to have an audience, a greyhound puppy chases <u>its</u> tail as
                                                                      B

   several children clap <u>their</u> hands.
                         C
   A. our
   B. your
   C. my
   D. No change is necessary.

8. Many of <u>us</u> were surprised to hear hip hop music playing in the elevator that <u>we</u>
          A   B

   took to <u>their</u> hotel rooms.
           C
   A. them
   B. you
   C. our
   D. No change is necessary.

9. The elegant star graciously signed <u>our</u> fans' autograph books even though <u>she</u>
                                       A   B

   was in a hurry to get to <u>her</u> rehearsal.
                            C
   A. her
   B. I
   C. your
   D. No change is necessary.

10. Many young men and women who want to serve <u>their</u> country enlist in the Army
                                               A

    Reserves; by doing so, <u>we</u> make a valuable contribution to <u>their</u> nation.
                           B   C
    A. your
    B. they
    C. our
    D. No change is necessary.

Chapter 19: Pronoun Case

In previous chapters, you learned that pronouns are words that stand in for nouns. By using pronouns, you can avoid repeating nouns. Sometimes, though, errors can occur with pronouns in terms of pronoun-antecedent agreement, pronoun reference, and pronoun shifts. Yet another area to become aware of is pronoun case. <u>Pronoun case refers to the role that a pronoun performs in a sentence.</u> This role depends on the way that the pronoun is being used. In English, three major pronoun cases exist: the subjective case (pronouns as subjects); the objective case (pronouns as objects), and the possessive case (pronouns that show ownership). Study the chart below.

A Chart of Pronoun Case

Subject Pronouns

	Singular	Plural
First Person	I	we
Second Person	you	you
Third Person	he, she, it	they

Object Pronouns

	Singular	Plural
First Person	me	us
Second Person	you	you
Third Person	him, her, it	them

Possessive Pronouns

	Singular	Plural
First Person	my, mine	our, ours
Second Person	your, yours	your, yours
Third Person	his, her, hers	their, theirs

Let's examine pronoun case more closely.

Subject Pronouns

Subject pronouns, as the name suggests, act as the subject of a sentence. Study the models below.

- We moved to Green Cove Springs, Florida, to experience the countryside.

(In this sentence, "we" is the subject; therefore, "we" is a subject pronoun.)

- She brushed her silky black hair into a sophisticated upsweep.

("She" is the subject of this sentence; therefore, "she" is a subject pronoun.)

Subject Pronouns and Compound Subjects

One subject pronoun generally does not cause any problems in your writing. You would not write, for instance, "Us moved to Green Cove Springs, Florida, to experience the countryside" or "Her brushed her silky black hair into a sophisticated upsweep." However, problems with pronoun case may occur in sentences with a compound subject in which one or both of the subjects happen to be a pronoun.

Circle the correct pronoun in the sentences below.

- My boyfriend and (I / me) went to the beach to celebrate his twentieth birthday.
- The neighbors and (we / us) ate a delicious hot dog lunch at Manny's Doghouse.
- The boys and (she / her) celebrated the softball championship with the coach.

Perhaps you felt as if you were guessing when you tried to select the correct pronouns above. Try the following test taking tip to choose the correct form of the pronoun in compound subjects.

!!TEST TAKING TIP!! *Place your finger over the noun in the compound subject. For example, in the first sentence above, you should put your finger over "my boyfriend." Then, try each pronoun by itself. Would you say, "I went to the beach to celebrate his twentieth birthday" or "Me went to the beach to celebrate his twentieth birthday"? You would no doubt say "I"; therefore, "I" is the correct pronoun in the compound subject of this sentence.*

Applying this test taking tip to the other two sentences, you would say, "We ate a delicious hot dog lunch at Manny's Doghouse"; thus, the compound subject is "The neighbors and we." Further, you would say "She celebrated the softball championship with the coach"; hence, the compound subject is "The boys and she."

Subject Pronouns After Linking Verbs

Yet another rule to apply regarding subject pronouns is the following: Use a subject pronoun after a linking verb (am, is, are, was, were). Study the examples below.

INCORRECT: It was <u>me</u> who snatched the last chocolate chip cookie from the jar.

CORRECT: It was <u>I</u> who snatched the last chocolate chip cookie from the jar.

(The subject pronoun "I" should follow the linking verb "was.")

INCORRECT: It is <u>him</u> who drives the red convertible Mercedes.

CORRECT: It is <u>he</u> who drives the red convertible Mercedes.

(The subject pronoun "he" should follow the linking verb "is.")

Object Pronouns

In addition, <u>object pronouns</u>—as their name suggests—<u>act as the object of a sentence</u>. An object pronoun may follow a verb or a preposition.

Object Pronouns That Follow Verbs

In the sentences below, the object pronouns follow verbs.

- My mother bought <u>me</u> a lovely pink and white dress for Easter.

(In this sentence, the object pronoun "me" follows the action verb "bought.")

- The CEO sent <u>them</u> an exciting email about their holiday bonuses.

(In this sentence, the object pronoun "them" follows the action verb "sent.")

Object Pronouns That Follow Prepositions

In the sentences below, the object pronouns follow prepositions.

- The nurse was surprised when Mr. Johnson, her patient, said that the flowers were for <u>her</u>.

(In this sentence, the object pronoun "her" follows the preposition "for.")

- Dr. Samuels loaned the lap top computer to <u>me</u> after he finished his report.

(In this sentence, the object pronoun "me" follows the preposition "to.")

143

Just as errors in pronoun case can occur with compound subjects, so too can errors occur with compound objects. To make the correct choice with compound objects, try the following strategy: place your finger over the noun that comes before the pronoun in question. Then, decide which pronoun you would use if it were by itself in the sentence.

Applying this strategy, circle the correct pronoun in the examples below.

- The conference chairperson invited Rosalyn and (he / him) to discuss instructional technology.
- The police officer asked Fred and (she / her) if they had seen the car accident.
- The talented, young pianist played a Gershwin composition for the Smiths and (we / us).

(In the first sentence, you would write, "The conference chairperson invited <u>him</u> to discuss the instructional technology"; therefore, the object pronoun "him" is the appropriate choice. Similarly, you would state, "The police officer asked <u>her</u> if [she] had seen the car accident"; thus, the object pronoun "her" is the correct choice. Lastly, you would write, "The talented, young pianist played a Gershwin composition for <u>us</u>," making the object pronoun "us" the right response.)

Possessive Pronouns

The last form of pronoun case for you to review concerns possessive pronouns. <u>Possessive pronouns show ownership</u>, for example, <u>my</u> dog, <u>your</u> pickup truck, <u>her</u> baby blanket.

While possessive pronouns are fairly straightforward in their usage compared to subject and object pronouns, keep in mind that <u>possessive pronouns never take an apostrophe</u>. This rule can be somewhat confusing because you are used to using apostrophes to show ownership with nouns, for example, the <u>man's</u> wallet, the <u>students'</u> science teacher, the <u>house's</u> air conditioner. However, possessive pronouns do not require the apostrophe to show ownership. (For a review of the apostrophe, please study Chapter 21 on standard punctuation.) Examine the models below.

INCORRECT: The black cat with the loud purr is <u>our's</u>.

CORRECT: The black cat with the loud purr is <u>ours</u>.

INCORRECT: <u>Your's</u> is the next pizza to be delivered.

CORRECT: <u>Yours</u> is the next pizza to be delivered.

Now that you have reviewed pronoun case, try the following exercise.

Exercise: Pronoun Case

Directions: For each of the following questions, choose the option that corrects an error in the underlined portion(s). If no error exists, then choose "no change is necessary."

1. Although the humanities professor gave James and <u>I</u> tickets to the symphony, <u>we</u>

                                       A   B

   could not go because <u>our</u> baby was feverish.

                        C

   A. me
   B. us
   C. we
   D. No change is necessary.

2. Mrs. DelMarco teaches science at the high school. The students and <u>she</u> took a

                                                                       A

   trip to the Museum of Natural History and Science where the curator showed

   <u>them</u> a dinosaur exhibit that <u>they</u> found fascinating.

  B   C

   A. her
   B. they
   C. them
   D. No change is necessary.

3. Florida voters expressed a great deal of concern about the public education

   system. According to <u>them</u>, education is more important to <u>they</u> than any other

                                A   B

   social issue that <u>they</u> have listened to the politicians discuss.

                    C

   A. they
   B. them
   C. their
   D. No change is necessary.

4. Katlin and <u>me</u> are driving to St. Augustine to shop at the Outlet Mall; <u>we</u> like

              A   B

   shopping there because the stores offer valuable discounts to customers like <u>us</u>.

                                                                              C

   A. I
   B. us
   C. ours
   D. No change is necessary.

5. Kneeling at Kara's feet, Chris asked if <u>she</u> would marry him, and then <u>he</u> gave
                                           A   B

   <u>hers</u> a princess-cut diamond ring.
    C
   A. her
   B. him
   C. her
   D. No change is necessary.

6. It is <u>they</u> who sold <u>we</u> the property that <u>we</u> recently rented to another family.
            A   B   C
   A. them
   B. us
   C. our
   D. No change is necessary.

7. Sitting on <u>her</u> father's shoulders, the little girl watched the Mardi Gras parade in
                 A

   awe. <u>She</u> held out her hand to catch beads, and much to her surprise, the king
         B

   of the parade gave <u>she</u> an enormous teddy bear.
                     C
   A. she
   B. Her
   C. her
   D. No change is necessary.

8. Between you and <u>I</u>, this math class is more difficult than <u>I</u> expected; <u>we</u> should
                     A   B   C

   visit the Learning Lab for one-on-one assistance.

   A. me
   B. my
   C. us
   D. No change is necessary.

9. The teenager promised <u>his</u> parents that his brother and <u>him</u> would be home by
                             A   B

   11:00 p.m.; their mother told <u>them</u> that to arrive home punctually.
                                   C
   A. him
   B. he
   C. they
   D. No change is necessary.

10. Terrell has been urging Stacey and <u>me</u> to buy a new office computer; <u>he</u> believes
                                            A   B

    that it will increase <u>our</u> office productivity.
                            C

    A. I
    B. him
    C. us
    D. No change is necessary.

Chapter 20: Standard Spelling

Computers have changed the way the world operates today and nowhere is that more evident than in college classrooms. However, even with the advent of these marvelous machines, and the fact that most word processing programs on the market today come equipped with a handy tool known as spell check, you will not be able to use that convenient feature on the writing portion of the exit exam. Acquiring a good basic knowledge of spelling will lead to improved vocabulary skills. Both of these skills are essential in helping you become a more successful college student. One of the best ways to improve in both of these skill areas is to learn how to use a dictionary and thesaurus. While this section of the guide can help you learn and understand the rules for Standard American English spelling and how to correct common spelling errors, knowing how to use a dictionary and a thesaurus can provide you with sources that will prove valuable not only in spelling, but word definition, word usage, pronunciation, and syllabication.

Tips for improving spelling:
* Routinely use a dictionary and a thesaurus.
* Make and keep a list of words you misspell and review them on a regular basis.
* Review the section in this guide on misused and confused words and make it a point to learn how to spell these words and also learn what they mean.
* Become familiar with the spelling guidelines listed in this section of your guide.

Spelling Guidelines

Below are some guidelines that will help you with standard spelling. In addition to the guidelines, understand that all words in the English language are made up of vowels and consonants. Vowels and consonants are letters that represent certain sounds. Vowels consist of the letters *a, e, i, o, u.* All letters that are not vowels are consonants (b, c, d, f, g, h, j, k, l, m, n, p, q, r, s, t, v, w, x, z). The letter *y* can be either a vowel or a consonant.

Guideline 1: *I* before *e* except after *c* or if it sounds like *a.*
Examples: receive (except after *c*)
weight (sounds like *a*)
believe (*I* before *e*)
*Exceptions: **conscience, either, neither, foreign, height, science, seize, society, species, their, weird***

Guideline 2: When adding an ending beginning with a vowel, drop the final silent *e.*
Example: **write + ing = writing**

Guideline 3: When adding an ending beginning with a consonant, keep the final *e.*
Example: **care + less = careless**

Guideline 4: When you add an ending to a word that ends in a consonant plus *y,* change *y* to *i* and add *–es.*
Example: **city + es = cities**

Guideline 5: When a vowel comes before the *y*, do not change *y* to *i*.
Example: **fly + er = flyer**
*Exception: When adding *-ing* to a word ending in *y*, do not drop the *y*, even if the *y* is preceded by a consonant.
Example: **study + ing = studying**

Guideline 6: Double the final consonant when a vowel ending is being added to a root word that ends in a single consonant preceded by a single short vowel sound.
Example: **commit + ed = committed**

Guideline 7: Double the final consonant when the word is one syllable.
Example: **trap + ed = trapped**

Guideline 8: Double the final consonant when the word is accented on the last syllable.
Example: **admit + ed = admitted**

Guideline 9: Most words form their plurals by adding *–s,* including words that end in *o* preceded by a vowel.
Example: **school + s = schools and stereo + s = stereos**
*Exception: If the word ends in *o* and is preceded by a consonant, it will form its plural by adding *–es.*
Examples: **tomato + es = tomatoes; potato + es = potatoes**

Guideline 10: Words that end in *s, ss, sh, ch, or x* most often form their plurals by adding *–es.*
Examples: **class + es = classes, mass + es = masses; wish + es = wishes; clench + es = clenches; tax + es = taxes**

Guideline 11: Some words ending in *f* form their plurals by changing the *f* to v and adding *–es.*
Examples: **life = lives; themselves = themselves**

Guideline 12: Some words form their plurals by changing letters in the word.
Example: **woman = women**

Guideline 13: Words made up of two or more words form their plurals by adding *s* to the key word.
Example: **mother-in-law + s = mothers-in-law**

Guideline 14: Some words that have foreign origins take on plurals that are irregular. If a word takes on an irregular plural, the form of the word will change as shown in the example below.
Example: **The plural of the word medium, from the Latin word *medius* (middle), is media.**

Challenging Words

ability	jewelry
absence	knowledge
accident	language
achieve	loneliness
address	measure
although	mistake
analyze	newspaper
anxious	necessary
argument	occasion
attention	occurrence
beautiful	prejudice
because	psychology
believe	quiet
between	quite
calendar	quick
cereal	rhythm
commitment	recognize
conscious	ridiculous
convenient	sandwich
decide	schedule
describe	separate
different	sophomore
disappoint	succeed
education	truly
entrance	unity
examine	usually
exaggerate	vegetable
exercise	visitor
fascinate	writing
foreign	written
friend	x-ray
government	yearn
grocery	yesterday
harass	yield
height	zany
illegal	zealous
immediate	zebra
intelligence	zest

Exercises: Standard Spelling

In the sentences below, circle the word in the parentheses that is spelled correctly.

1. When she (dropped, droped) her purse, the contents (spilled, spiled) out all over the floor.

2. Toward the end of the school year, Connie's social (calendar, calander) is filled with numerous (commitments, comitments).

3. (Developing, Developeing) good study habits will help you become a (successful, succeedful) college student.

4. I am (hoping, hopping) to get a good grade in my math class.

5. Louis has been (absent, abcent) three days this week.

6. Darla likes peanut butter and jelly (sandwiches, sandwitches).

7. Holly (believes, belives) she is going to get a good grade in English class even though her (attendance, attendence) has been poor.

8. Jack plans on (retiring, retireing) this year.

9. June (studied, studyed) for the test, but she did not pass.

10. Colleen, who was not (confident, confedent) in her driving ability, was (perpared, prepared) to fail the road test.

In the paragraph below, mark through the words that are spelled incorrectly and write the correct spelling above each one.

I always knew I wanted to be a writter. My mother told me that even before I could write, I would make up very creative storyes to tell my friends. Once I learned to put my words down on paper, I found it to be both challenging and excitieing. Waiting for the next thought to pop into my head was like finding the missing peaces of a jigsaw puzle. I got a lot of pleasure from siting down with my pad and pen in hand and pondering how I could develope characters and place them in foriegn lands. I never new where my imagination was going to take me, but I always knew the adventure would be thriling. While I may have tremendous creative abilityies, I have always had dificulty with spelling. My inability to spell corectly has cost me both time and money in my profession. If I had only learned the rules for Standard American English spelling, I could be spending more time creating story ideas and less time being frustrated over my poor spelling habits.

Chapter 21: Standard Punctuation:
End Marks, Commas, Semicolons, Colons, and Apostrophes

Imagine reading a paragraph without any punctuation. Not a period, comma, semicolon, or apostrophe appears in the entire paper. How would you know when one thought ends and another begins? How would you understand the relationship between words and ideas? How would you determine the writer's main point?

Reading a paper without punctuation would be like driving through an unfamiliar city without any traffic signals. Without traffic signs and lights, you would not know when to start and stop or where to turn. You might get lost, or worse still, cause an accident. Similarly, without punctuation in a paper, you would not know when one sentence stops and another starts. When reading, you would no doubt get lost as one thought collides into another.

Punctuation plays a critical role in writing because it allows you to break large thoughts into smaller units that readers can better understand. End marks, commas, semicolons, and apostrophes help make writing clear and orderly.

Let's study the rules of standard punctuation.

End Marks

End marks, such as the period, question mark, and exclamation point, signal the end of a sentence.

A <u>period</u> follows statements, mild commands, and indirect questions.

Statement:	Linda wore an elegant purple pants suit.
Mild Command:	Finish mowing the lawn before dinner.
Indirect Question:	I wonder how many students earn a bachelor's degree each year in the United States.

Secondly, a <u>question mark</u> follows a direct question.

Questions:	Are you going to the Daytona International Speedway to watch the drag race?
	Which seasoning adds more zest to spaghetti, basil or oregano?

Lastly, an <u>exclamation point</u> follows an expression of strong feeling. Use this mark sparingly in your writing, though, because the more it is used, the less powerful it becomes.

Exclamation Points:	What a spectacular display of fireworks!
	She throws an amazing curve ball!

Commas

The comma is the most commonly used punctuation mark in college writing; unfortunately, it is also the most confusing and the most frequently misused mark of punctuation. The comma separates parts of a sentence. When used correctly, the comma helps readers understand sentences. By studying the following rules, you will learn how to use the comma more effectively.

Seven Key Rules of Comma Usage

Rule 1: **Use a comma before a coordinating conjunction (FAN BOYS—FOR, AND, NOR, BUT, OR, YET, SO) that connects two independent clauses. (Remember that an independent clause is just a formal name for a sentence.)**

- The elderly woman ordered a cup of ginger tea, but the waiter forgot to bring it to her.

- The cat curled up against my leg, and she purred happily upon being petted.

!!COMMA ALERT!! *No comma is needed before a coordinating conjunction when you are not joining two sentences, as in the example below.*

- The cat curled up against my leg and purred happily upon being petted.

(Notice that after the coordinating conjunction "and" in this sentence, there is no subject. Because you are no longer joining two complete sentences, no comma is required before the conjunction.)

Rule 2: **Place a comma after an introductory word, phrase, or clause to separate it from the rest of the sentence.**

- **Introductory Word:**

    Sharon has studied diligently to earn her real estate license. Therefore, she should do well on the exam.

    Sure, I would be happy to drive you home.

- **Introductory Phrase (A phrase is a group of words):**

    In truth, Leslie is the most talented computer programmer in the company.

    After reading the mystery novel, Chris locked all the windows and doors in the house.

154

- **Introductory Clause (An introductory clause is a dependent clause containing a subordinating conjunction, a subject, and a verb.** Please review the Chapter 9 for a more thorough discussion of clauses.)

> <u>Before it began to rain,</u> we picked strawberries in the field.

> <u>As the love ballad played softly on the radio,</u> the couple danced in the empty club.

!! COMMA ALERT!! *Place a comma after an introductory dependent clause; avoid placing a comma before a dependent clause that comes at the end of a sentence, as in the following example:*

> We picked strawberries in the field <u>before it began to rain.</u>

Rule 3:　　**Use commas to separate three or more items in a series.**

- At the breakfast buffet, we sampled <u>scrambled eggs, bacon, grits, pancakes, and fresh fruit</u>.

- The sixth-grade choir members <u>memorized the lyrics, rehearsed the song, and then performed</u> before their families in the auditorium.

Rule 4:　　**Use a comma to separate two or more adjectives that describe the same noun when these adjectives are not connected by a coordinating conjunction.**

- The <u>kind, compassionate</u> teacher tutored me before and after algebra class.

(In this sentence, the adjectives "kind" and "compassionate" describe the noun "teacher"; to avoid confusion, they are separated from each other with a comma.)

- The <u>clean, fresh</u> scent of Mrs. Hendrick's laundry fragranced the morning air.

(In this sentence, the adjectives "clean" and "fresh" describe the noun "scent" and are separated by a comma.)

Sometimes, however, a comma is not used between two (or more) adjectives that describe a noun, as in the example below.

- She wore her <u>long black</u> hair in a French braid.

How do you know whether or not to place a comma between adjectives? To make that decision, try the following sentence tests:

Test 1: **Place the word "and" between the two adjectives. If the sentence reads clearly with the word "and," you can correctly use a comma in its place.**

Let's try Test 1 on the following sentences.

- The <u>clean and fresh</u> scent of Mrs. Hendrick's laundry fragranced the morning air.

(This sentence reads clearly; therefore, you can put a comma between "clean" and "fresh.")

Now examine the sentence below.

- She wore her <u>long, and black</u> hair in a French braid.

(This sentence does not flow well; therefore, you should omit the comma between "long" and "black.")

Test 2: **Rearrange the adjectives, putting the second before the first. If the sentence reads clearly after this switch, you can correctly place a comma between the two adjectives.**

- The <u>fresh, clean</u> scent of Mrs. Hendrick's laundry fragranced the morning air.

(This sentence reads clearly; thus, you can place a comma between "clean" and "fresh.")

Now apply the test to the sentence below.

- She wore her <u>black, long</u> hair in a French braid.

(This sentence reads awkwardly; thus, you should leave out the comma between "long" and "black.")

Rule 5: **Place a comma before and after an interrupter—that is, a word, phrase, or clause that interrupts a sentence's flow. Interrupters provide extra information that is helpful but not necessary for the sentence to make sense. By setting off interrupters with commas, you help readers understand the main idea of your sentence.**

Word Interrupters:

- The phone rang several times. Matt could not answer it, <u>however,</u> because he was taking a shower.

- The high school graduate wore his gift, <u>a watch,</u> with pride.

156

Phrase Interrupters:

- The mother cooks her toddler's favorite dish, <u>spaghetti with meatballs,</u> at least once a week.

- Thousands of Florida public school teachers, <u>according to a recent study,</u> will be either retiring or resigning each year over the next decade.

Clause Interrupters:

- St. Catherine's Episcopal Day Care, <u>which is located in Jacksonville, Florida,</u> provides preschoolers with many valuable learning experiences.

(In the above sentence, the underlined clause interrupter adds information that is interesting but not necessary for the sentence to make sense.)

- Travis Jones, <u>who practices family law,</u> often provides free legal services to the underprivileged in his community.

(In this sentence, the underlined clause interrupter offers information that is helpful but not necessary for the sentence to make sense.)

!!COMMA ALERT!! *Avoid using commas around who, whose, when, where, and which clauses when they express information that is essential to the sentence.*

- The man <u>who practices family law</u> often provides free legal services to the underprivileged in his community.

(In this sentence, the information in the clause "who practices family law" is necessary for readers to understand the sentence. Without the "who clause," we would not know which man provides free legal services. Therefore, you should avoid placing commas around the "who clause.")

!!COMMA ALERT!! *Avoid using commas with "that" clauses.*

- The man <u>that practices family law</u> often provides free legal services to the underprivileged in his community.

(Notice that no comma comes before or after the "that clause.")

Rule 6: **Use commas to set off direct quotations. A quotation represents a speaker's exact words. Set off a direct quotation with commas that separate it from the rest of the sentence and make your point clear.**

- My father once told me, "Improvise, adapt, and overcome when you encounter life's obstacles." (Use a comma before the quotation.)

- "Improvise, adapt, and overcome when you encounter life's obstacles," my father once told me. (Use a comma after the quotation.)

- "Improvise, adapt, and overcome," my father once told me, "when you encounter life's obstacles." (Place commas before and after the quotation.)

Rule 7: **Use commas for miscellaneous reasons, including numbers, dates, addresses, and letters.**

Numbers: Use commas to clarify numbers.

- I won $1,500.00 in the Florida State Lottery.

Dates: Use commas within dates, specifically after days and years.

- My brother was born on November 24, 1970, in a taxicab as our parents were rushing to the hospital.

Addresses: Use commas to separate streets from cities; cities from states; and states from the remainder of a sentence.

- Grandma Irene lived at 3753 North Richmond Street, Chicago, Illinois, for over fifty years.

Letters: Use a comma after the opening and closing lines of a social letter.

- Dear Mr. and Mrs. Williams,
- Yours truly,

Semicolons

The semicolon (;) is a relatively sophisticated mark of punctuation. By learning how to use it, you can enhance the quality of your writing.

The semicolon can be used in three ways, each of which is explained below.

Rule 1: **Use a semicolon to join two related independent clauses that are roughly the same length. Your sentence will have the following pattern:**

Independent Clause (IC)   ;   Independent Clause (IC)

                                    IC   IC
- Tommy ordered a jumbo hot dog from the hot dog vendor; Sara ordered a Polish sausage sandwich with sauerkraut.

                            IC   IC
- Toni likes to listen to country music; her husband William prefers to listen to rock.

158

(In the sentences above, the semicolon is used to join two closely related independent clauses that are about the same length.)

Rule 2:   **Use a semicolon to connect two independent clauses that are also joined with an adverbial conjunction—that is, a transition. (Be sure to place a comma after the transition.) Your sentence will have the following pattern:**

Independent Clause (IC)   **; transition,**   **Independent Clause (IC)**

Please see Chapter 6 for a list of transitions.

                                  IC   IC
- We love eating outside at the café; **however,** sometimes we cannot eat

  outdoors because of the bothersome flies.

                                  IC
- Most Florida residents run their air conditioners all day long during the
                                  IC
  summer; **consequently,** their utilities bills are quite high.

(In the sentences above, two related independent clauses are joined with a semicolon, a transition, and a comma.)

Rule 3:   **Use a semicolon to separate items in a series that already has a number of commas. In this situation, the semicolon can help you avoid confusion. Your sentence will have the following pattern:**

           Item A;   **Item B;**   **Item C**

Confusing: Tracey needed many supplies for her classes. She bought paint, brushes, and canvas paper for art, a computer disk, a loose leaf notebook, and pens for English, and goggles, gloves, and a lab manual for biology.

(All the commas in this sentence may confuse the reader.)

Clear: Tracey needed many supplies for her classes. She bought paint, brushes, and canvas paper for art; a computer disk, a loose leaf notebook, and pens for English; and goggles, gloves, and a lab manual for biology.

(The semicolons help the reader to understand the main idea by clearly separating the three classes.)

Colons

The colon (:) is used to call attention to some part of a sentence. Because it brings about a sudden stop in a sentence, it has the same effect as a period. To use colons correctly, you must make sure that they follow independent clauses that either introduce a list or provide an explanation about something that has been written.

- Once I get to the store, I need to buy the following items: hairspray, deodorant, and mouthwash.
- While I was out shopping, I picked up something I had been wanting for a long time: the most recent U2 CD.

Colons are also used to introduce quotations, separate hours and minutes, separate titles and subtitles, separate the volume number from the page number in a publication, follow a salutation in a formal letter, and follow standard heading lines in a memorandum.

- I told Susan: "Review the section in your textbook on colons so you will be prepared for tomorrow's quiz."
- I leave work every day at 5:00 p.m.
- John Donne's poem, "A Valediction: Forbidding Mourning," is required reading in my literature class.
- There is a great article on stress survival in <u>Redbook</u> 198 (Feb. 2002): 30-36.
- Dear Mr. Lopez:
- To: Betsy Griffey
  From: Patti Levine-Brown

One of the most common misuses of the colon is placing it after a phrase instead of an independent clause.

Incorrect
- My mother has several health problems. Such as: high blood pressure, high cholesterol, and diabetes.

Correct
- My mother has several health problems: high blood pressure, high cholesterol, and diabetes.

Apostrophes

The apostrophe, which looks like an upside down comma, is a small mark of punctuation that causes a large amount of confusion. It has two uses that, with some study, you can master in your writing. First, it represents the omission of certain letters. Secondly, it shows ownership.

Apostrophes for Contractions

You are probably familiar with the first use of the apostrophe—to represent a contraction, that is, a shortening of a word caused by the omission of one or more letters. English has many contractions, including those illustrated below.

I am	=	I'm
There is	=	There's
Would not	=	Wouldn't
It is	=	It's
You are	=	You're

In contractions, the apostrophe goes where the omitted letter was. In "there's," for instance, the apostrophe replaces the letter "i."

One contraction that causes a great deal of confusion is "it's." How do you know whether to spell this word as "it's" or "its"? "It's" is a contraction for "it is" or "it has." "Its" is a possessive pronoun, like his, hers, and yours. To decide how to spell this confusing word, try the following test: Take the contraction "it's" and replace it with the words "it is" or "it has." If the sentence makes sense, you should spell the word as "it's." If, however, the sentence does not make sense, you should spell the word as "its." Let's apply this test.

- <u>It's</u> challenging to begin a new job in an unfamiliar city.

("<u>It is</u> challenging to begin a new job in an unfamiliar city" makes sense; therefore, you should use the contraction "it's.")

- The dog gnawed on <u>its</u> juicy steak bone.

("The dog gnawed on <u>it is</u> or <u>it has</u> juicy steak bone" does not make sense; thus, you should write "its" with no apostrophe.)

!!NOTE: "It's" and "its" are the only two spellings of this word; the word " its' " does not exist and is always incorrect.

Apostrophes for Possession

Apostrophes that show ownership can be very confusing. Why do some words have an apostrophe before the –s, and others have the apostrophe after the –s? Why do some words that end in –s have no apostrophe? The following guidelines will help you answer these questions.

161

Rule 1:   Place the apostrophe before the –s if the word that shows ownership is singular. Remember that the term "singular" refers to one item.

Singular Word	Singular Word Showing Ownership
the supervisor	the supervisor**'s** leadership
the dolphin	the dolphin**'s** audience
the gardener	the gardener**'s** tools
the boy	the boy**'s** father

When a singular word takes ownership over another term, you place an apostrophe followed by –s at the end of the singular word. **The placement of the apostrophe is determined by the word that takes possession over another, not by how many items are owned.** For instance, the gardener could own one tool or many tools, but because there is just one gardener, the apostrophe is placed before the –s: the gardener**'s tool** or the gardener**'s tools**.

Rule 2:   Place the apostrophe after the –s if the word that shows ownership is plural. Remember that the term "plural" refers to two or more items.

Plural Word	Plural Word Showing Ownership
the supervisors	the supervisor**s'** leadership
the dolphins	the dolphin**s'** audience
the gardeners	the gardener**s'** tools
the boys	the boy**s'** father

!!PUNCTUATION ALERT!! *Not every word that ends in –s requires an apostrophe; only those words that show ownership take the apostrophe. Avoid placing an apostrophe after a plural word that does not show ownership.*

Incorrect: Carolyn picked a bouquet of <u>wildflowers'</u> for her mother.

Correct: Carolyn picked a bouquet of <u>wildflowers</u> for her mother.

("Wildflowers" is a plural word that ends in –s. Because it does not show ownership over another term, it does not need an apostrophe.)

Rule 3:   Place the apostrophe before the –s in collective nouns that are already plural.

the men's locker room
the women's club
the children's teacher
the people's government

After studying the rules of standard punctuation, you are ready to try an exercise.

Exercise: Standard Punctuation

Directions: For each of the following questions, choose the option that corrects an error in the underlined portion(s). If no error exists, choose "no change is necessary."

1. <u>As the</u> sun settled into the <u>horizon Elizabeth</u> listened to the <u>crickets</u> chirping and
     A   B   C

   creating their own symphony of sounds.

   A. As, the
   B. horizon, Elizabeth
   C. crickets'
   D. No change is necessary.

2. In the Yucatan Peninsula of <u>Mexico, many</u> people do not have air conditioning in
                                              A

   their <u>homes, therefore,</u> these individuals often sleep in hammocks during the
                       B

   <u>hot, humid</u> summers.
          C

   A. Mexico many
   B. homes; therefore,
   C. hot humid
   D. No change is necessary.

3. Have you heard that because <u>there's</u> a shortage of teachers in public <u>schools,</u>
                                    A   B

   <u>some</u> community colleges in Florida will be offering a four-year degree in

   education in the hopes of attracting more people to the <u>profession.</u>
                                                      C

   A. theres
   B. schools some
   C. profession?
   D. No change is necessary.

4. The black puppy chased its <u>tail batted</u> its paw at a fly, and nibbled on a
                                    A

   <u>bone; meanwhile,</u> the puppy was unaware of the <u>children who</u> were giggling
          B   C

   while watching it.

   A. tail, batted
   B. bone, meanwhile,
   C. children, who
   D. No change is necessary.

5. Jack likes to send all his friends <u>email and</u> enjoys the convenience of electronic
                                              A
<u>communication, but</u> Walt prefers to send his friends <u>hand-written letters</u> through
                   B   C
the postal system.

   A. email, and
   B. communication but
   C. hand-written, letters
   D. No change is necessary.

Directions: For each of the following questions, choose the sentence that is correctly punctuated.

6.
   A. The mens World Cup Soccer Game attracted fans from around the world.

   B. The mens' World Cup Soccer Game attracted fans from around the world.

   C. The men's World Cup Soccer Game attracted fans' from around the world.

   D. The men's World Cup Soccer Game attracted fans from around the world.

7.
   A. The down comforter is warm cozy, and comfortable on cold winter nights so Bethany always sleeps with it.

   B. The down comforter is warm, cozy, and comfortable on cold winter nights so Bethany always sleeps with it.

   C. The down comforter is warm, cozy, and comfortable on cold winter nights, so Bethany always sleeps with it.

   D. The down comforter is warm cozy and comfortable on cold winter nights, so Bethany always sleeps with it.

8.
   A. Although Fred has owned his moccasins for years, he still wears them because they fit so well.

   B. Although Fred has owned his moccasins for years', he still wears them because they fit so well.

   C. Although Fred has owned his moccasins for years he still wears them because they fit so well.

   D. Although Fred has owned his moccasins for years, he still wears them, because they fit so well.

164

9.

    A. Would you like to plant a pink purple, or white crepe myrtle tree in your backyard.

    B. Would you like to plant a pink, purple, or white crepe myrtle tree in your backyard.

    C. Would you like to plant a pink, purple, or white crepe myrtle tree in you're backyard?

    D. Would you like to plant a pink, purple, or white crepe myrtle tree in your backyard?

10.

    A. Nicholas, who was running a high fever felt better after his mother gave him grape-flavored medicine.

    B. Nicholas, who was running a high fever, felt better after his mother gave him grape-flavored medicine.

    C. Nicholas who was running a high fever felt better after his mother gave him grape-flavored medicine.

    D. Nicholas, who was running a high fever felt better, after his mother gave him grape-flavored medicine.

Chapter 22: Standard Capitalization

In writing there are several primary uses of capitalization. Capitalization is important because it helps readers understand that some words should stand out, either because of their place in the sentence or who or what is being addressed in the sentence. This chapter of the guide explains the basic rules of capitalization. Capital letters are used with:

1) The first letter of the first word in a sentence
2) The first letter of the first word in a direct quotation
3) The pronoun I
4) Proper nouns, such as:
   Names of people, places, days of the week, months of the year, holidays, commercial products, associations, companies, organizations, political and religious groups.
5) Titles including: books, films, magazines, articles, television programs, poems, essays and songs.
6) Abbreviations and acronyms

Listed below are some examples of how to use capitalization. The letters or words that need to be capitalized are underlined.

First word in a sentence

<u>W</u>e recently bought a new car.

First word in a direct quotation

John said, "<u>S</u>pending a Saturday morning cleaning up the neighborhood park is fine, but it would be nice if people would stop trashing it."

The pronoun I

Mike and <u>I</u> like taking long walks in the morning

Names of people and particular places

After <u>Bonnie</u> quit her job at IBM, she moved to <u>Florida</u> and took a job teaching at the local community college.

Days of the week, months of the year and holidays

I am going to take <u>Friday</u> off because I want to get an early start on the <u>Fourth of July</u> weekend.

Commercial products

There is always at least one container of <u>Breyers</u> ice cream in my freezer.
Notice: Lower case letters are used when naming the type of product.

Associations, companies, organizations, political, and religious groups

My investment portfolio contains stock I purchased from both <u>Charles Schwab</u> and <u>Merrill Lynch</u>.

The <u>National Organization of Women</u> is a strong lobbying group that has acquired a great deal of political power.

My husband's viewpoints on national issues tend to be quite conservative; therefore, it makes sense that he is a registered <u>Republican</u>.

My husband and I never attend church together because I am <u>Methodist</u> and he is Jewish.

Titles, including: books, films, magazines, articles, television programs, poems, essays, and songs

Many of Stephen King's books, such as <u>The Shining</u> and <u>The Green Mile</u>, have been made into successful films.

The article I need for my research paper on breast cancer was in yesterday's edition of <u>The Miami Herald</u>.

Two of my all-time favorite television shows are <u>Crime Story</u> and <u>Unsolved Mysteries</u>.

Abbreviations and acronyms

NASA, YMCA, FBI, IRS, U.S.A., Ave., Blvd., Mrs.

My daughter, who wants to become an astrophysicist, recently attended a program sponsored by <u>NASA</u>.

My husband works out daily at the local <u>YMCA</u>.

A thorough examination of the area led investigators to believe that the fire, that started in the home of <u>Mrs.</u> Karen Jones, 2111 Beach <u>Blvd.</u>, had been set deliberately.

Exercises: Standard capitalization

The sentences below contain errors in capitalization. Choose the option that corrects the errors in the underlined section of the sentences. If there is no error, select "no change is needed."

1. My <u>mother's</u> name is <u>Delema</u>, but she prefers that people call her <u>Dee</u>.

   A. Mother's
   B. delema
   C. dee
   D. No change is needed.

2. My husband and my sister-in-law both have Birthdays in the month of September.

    A. husband
    B. Sister-in-law
    C. birthdays
    D. No change is needed.

3. Florida State University, located in Tallahassee, Florida, is an outstanding Educational institution.

    A. florida state university
    B. tallahassee, florida
    C. educational
    D. No change is needed.

4. Even though I am a Florida Native, I have never been to Key West.

    A. florida
    B. native
    C. key west
    D. No change is needed.

5. Suzanne and I have known each other since our days together at Paxon High school.

    A. paxon
    B. high
    C. School
    D. No change is needed.

6. Kathleen is a graduate of Ball state University in Muncie, Indiana.

    A. Graduate
    B. State
    C. muncie
    D. No change is needed.

7. Even though I don't particularly care for the Summers in Florida, I enjoy living near the ocean.

    A. summers
    B. florida
    C. Ocean
    D. No change is needed.

8. I am doing well in my english and biology classes, but I am struggling in algebra.

    A. English
    B. Biology
    C. Algebra
    D. No change is needed.

9. I sent Josh to the Learning Resource <u>center</u> to find a <u>tutor</u> who could help him with <u>math</u>.

    A. Center
    B. Tutor
    C. Math
    D. No change is needed.

10. I subscribe to our local <u>Newspaper</u>, but on <u>Sundays</u> I enjoy reading the <u>New York Times.</u>

    A. newspaper
    B. sundays
    C. new york times
    D. No change is needed.

In the story below there are 15 errors in capitalization. Circle the errors and then write the words as they should appear in the spaces provided.

Research in the field of Gene therapy may be the answer to a prayer for people who suffer from a rare and deadly inherited liver and Metabolic disease known as Crigler-Najjar syndrome, a disease that can cause jaundice -- a yellowing of the skin and whites of the eyes—and chronic fatigue, and interferes with the body's production of an important liver enzyme. Without this enzyme, the liver cannot process bilirubin, a waste product that is produced from the destruction of blood cells. The lack of this enzyme means bilirubin, produced continually in the human body, can't be excreted and remains in the blood. Additionally, bilirubin levels rise during illness or after injury, making life for a crigler's patient fretful because he or she must be on guard constantly.

People with this condition take numerous medications and sleep under special blue lights. This process, called Phototherapy, helps break down bilirubin, which can become toxic to the brain if levels get too high, causing damage much like a stroke. In those with Crigler's, the bilirubin cannot be excreted from the body. Crigler's does not always strike every child in a family. Some youngsters with the syndrome have brothers and sisters who do not have the disease. Studying families with children who had the disease in the 1940s, Physicians John Crigler and Victor Najjar found that parents could be healthy carriers of a Recessive gene that causes the disease, and that their children would have a one-in-four chance of inheriting the syndrome.

Most of the studies have centered on families in the amish and Mennonite communities. These descendants of Swiss and German Anabaptists who settled in Pennsylvania in the 1700s have suffered from numerous Genetic disorders because members of the communities are forbidden to marry outside their religion.

As a result, many of the people in the groups are related, which increases their chances of carrying hereditary diseases that do not affect them, but show up in their children.

Physicians agree that it would be a revolution for the following generation if medical research could discover which Amino acids in the genes cause problems and plug in new genes that can replace the defective ones.

"If gene therapy in the treatment of Crigler's works, it could lead to advances in the treatment of other diseases like Multiple Sclerosis and Muscular Dystrophy," said Alvin Colar, a Pediatrician with a hospital in Jacksonville, Fla. He has a 2-year-old patient who has been diagnosed with the disease.

"The people doing this research are brilliant. The fact that they can now separate amino acids and localize the genes that are causing the problems is amazing. It will be interesting to see what happens with gene therapy over the next 20 years."

Note: This is a revised version of an article written by Patti Levine-Brown that appeared in the River City News section of the <u>Florida Times Union</u> on January 3, 2001.

1. _____

2. _____

3. _____

4. _____

5. _____

6. _____

7. _____

8. _____

9. _____

10. _____

11. _____

12. _____

13. _____

14. _____

15. _____

Word Choice Skills

Chapter 23: Appropriate Expressions

When someone is asked what he or she likes about a particular poem, short story, or novel, many will make reference to the way the author expresses himself or crafts his words. Knowing how to express yourself in words is an important skill to possess in both the college classroom and in the work place. Whether you are composing a memo, outlining a set of directions for a project that the employees in your department must follow, or completing a research paper for one of your classes, your command of the English language is essential for communicating effectively. When choosing appropriate language in your writing, try to avoid jargon, clichés, and slang. Consider both your purpose and audience and then choose your words carefully and craft your writing accordingly.

Jargon

Jargon is language that is used by a group of people that belong to a special field or vocational community. Technical language used by computer technicians or engineers would be a good example of jargon, although there are other areas such as science and education that also use specialized vocabulary. Most words considered to be jargon are unfamiliar words, but familiar words can also be used in an unfamiliar manner. People outside the field would have difficulty understanding what is written. It is appropriate to use the specialized vocabulary (jargon) if you are writing for people in that specialized area, but it should not be used when people outside of the area will be reading the material.

Examples:

pedagogy	collateral	hypertext	cookie	parameters
contingency	Boolean logic	imperative	methodology	case sensitive

Clichés

A cliché is a phrase that has been overused. It may have produced a vivid image the first time it was used, but now it is no longer viewed as interesting. Using clichés limits the information in your writing and makes it seem unimaginative.

Examples:

dirt cheap	off your rocker	pain in the neck	over the hill
washed up	watch your mouth	chip on your shoulder	a deer in the headlights
dark horse	as easy as pie	easy as 1,2,3	darkest before the storm

Slang

Slang is nonstandard language that is usually used in conversations within a community of people in an informal setting. It is difficult for people outside of the group to understand the meaning of slang. It is not considered proper to use for formal papers.

Examples:

the bomb	rankin'	babe	big house	copper
cruising	chick	axle grease	crack up	ain't

The best way to improve word choice and appropriate expressions in your writing is to build your vocabulary skills. Dictionary skills, context clues, and prefixes, suffixes, and roots are some of the best ways to strengthen and build vocabulary skills. Improving your skills in these areas can help you learn how to choose more effective words and appropriate expressions

Dictionary Usage

A dictionary is a valuable tool that does more than just define words. In addition to word meaning, a dictionary provides information on syllabication, pronunciation, spelling, parts of speech, and word origin.

Word Meaning:

The dictionary gives you the denotative meaning (literal meaning) of words. It also lists any multiple (more than one) meanings the word may have. For example, the word deposit has several meanings:

1. to place or entrust, as for safekeeping; 2. to give as a pledge or partial payment; 3. to put or set down; 4. something left lying; 5. sand, clay, minerals, etc., deposited by natural forces.

Syllabication:

The dictionary shows how words are divided into syllables. Dots or spaces are used to separate the syllables in each word. For example, the word deposit is shown as having three syllables – **de.pos.it**.

Pronunciation:

The dictionary provides pronunciation keys to help you understand how words are divided into sounds. Accent marks are used to show the stress on each syllable. A heavy mark (') indicates that more stress is placed on that syllable when the word is pronounced. A light mark (') indicates that less stress is placed on that particular syllable when the word is pronounced. For example, the word deposit is shown as having a heavy stress mark on the second syllable - **di-poz' it**.

Spelling:

The dictionary gives the spelling for each word, its plural, and any special form the word may take on when adding or dropping letters to create new words.
For example, the word deposit forms its plural (*pl.*) by adding an **s**: The miner discovered several large <u>deposits</u> of gold along the riverbank.

Parts of Speech:

The dictionary uses abbreviations to indicate the part of speech for each word meaning. The word deposit has multiple meanings, so you will see the abbreviation *v*, for verb, next to the dictionary entry of one meaning of the word. For example: Angela deposited $500 on a car. You will also see the abbreviation *n*, for noun, next to another meaning of the word. For example: Juan went to the bank this morning to make a deposit.

Word Origin:

The dictionary provides you with the origin (the language from which the word is derived) of many words. Usually, this information is enclosed in brackets such as: [L] - Latin, [Fr] – French, and [Gk] - Greek.

Context Clues

Another way to strengthen your vocabulary is to pay attention to the clues you may be given about certain words in a sentence. These clues, known as context clues, can help you understand the meaning of unfamiliar words, but they are not guaranteed to give you a clear and exact definition of every word that you do not know. There are several types of context clues, but some of the most common are: definition, examples, antonyms, synonyms, and general meaning of the passage.

Definition: An author may decide to define a word in the sentence for the reader. The definition will follow a word and be set off by commas, dashes, or parentheses.
Sentence: Osteoporosis, a medical condition that arises from a decrease in bone mass, takes place when old bone breaks down faster than new bone can be produced.
Note: The definition of osteoporosis immediately follows the word and is set off by commas.

Examples:
An author may decide that a reader will better understand the meaning of a sentence if he includes examples. Examples describe and illustrate words in a sentence.
Sentence: I love all kinds of pasta including: angel hair, fettuccine, and linguine.
Note: angel hair, fettuccine, and linguine are examples of pasta.

Antonyms:
An author may decide that a reader will better understand the meaning of a sentence if he includes contrasting words. Contrasting words, also known as antonyms, are words that have opposite meaning.
Sentence: Regardless of my student's pessimistic views concerning their exits examinations, I continue to be optimistic that they will all pass.
Note: pessimistic and optimistic are antonyms.

Synonyms:
An author may decide that a reader will better understand the meaning of a sentence if he includes similar words. Similar words, also known as synonyms, are words that have the same meaning.
Sentence: The sad look on her face told her friends how unhappy she was about not having won first place in the contest.
Note: Sad and unhappy are synonyms.

General meaning of the passage:

When reading you must often depend on your ability to understand the details in a passage to determine the meaning of unfamiliar words. Words in the passage may also have implied or suggestive meanings, referred to as connotative meanings. You will have to pay particular attention to the information surrounding a word, or words, in a sentence or passage to understand what is being implied.

Human <u>societies</u> tend to come together where **water** exists. In places where it is plentiful, **water** seems less like a substance than an <u>environment</u>: People <u>drink it, cook in it, bathe in it, wash wastes away in it, harness it for power, and swim in it</u>. Some 71 percent of the <u>Earth's surface</u> is ocean **water**, and <u>human bodies</u> are about 66 percent **water** <u>by weight</u>, so if we have, say, <u>a 128-pound person, about 85 pounds of him or her will be</u> **water.** If Earth amounts to a **watery** environment flecked by the <u>landmasses we call continents</u>, the <u>human body</u> amounts to a **watery** <u>mass with significant proportions of other materials immersed in it</u>. (Krogh, David. 2002, *Biology, A Guide to the Natural World*, 2nd ed. p. 37).

Note: This passage gives the reader several clues to its overall meaning. Water is used several times indicating that the author wants the reader to know something important about water. In the first and second sentences, the author links the synonyms societies and environment to water so the reader can see that they have something in common. In the third sentence, he gives the reader examples of what people do with water. In the fourth sentence, he makes a direct comparison between the amount of water that makes up the Earth's surface and the amount of water that makes up the human body. This comparison is followed by an example of the number of pounds of water that make up a human body. In the fifth sentence the word landmasses is defined in relation to continents and the term human body is defined in relation to watery mass. The words landmass and watery mass are used in contrast to one another to show a connection between the Earth and human life; therefore, the general sense of this passage is that water is important to life.

Prefixes, Roots, and Suffixes

Another way to improve your vocabulary skills and become a more effective writer is to understand word parts or prefixes, roots, and suffixes. Knowing how to break down a word, and analyze its parts, can make a big difference in the number of words you come to know. A prefix is a word part that comes before a word that can change its meaning. A suffix is a word part that comes after a word that can change its meaning. The root of a word is its essential part or base.

Example: The prefixes *non* and *un* both mean not.
The word nonessential means not essential or not necessary.
The word unhappy means not happy.

Example: The suffix *or* refers to "one who"
Adding the ending *or* to the word advise (advisor) changes its meaning from offering advice or counsel to <u>one</u> <u>who</u> gives advice or counsel.
Example: Photo means *light*.
Words such as photocopy or photoactive both refer to something that is done with light. When you photocopy something you reproduce it by using light. If something is photoactive it can respond to light.

174

Below is a list of some common prefixes, roots and suffixes

Prefixes

Prefix	Meaning	Examples
a, ab	away, from; away from	abnormal
a, an	not, without	anemia
a	on, in, at	aboard
ad	to, toward	administer
ante	before	antemeridian
anti	against	antiwar
bi	two, twice	biannual
co	together	coworker
con, con	together, with	connect
de	from, away; down from	decrease
dis	apart from; opposite	disagree
ex	out of, beyond	exhale
hyper	excessive	hyperactive
in, il, ir	into, not	inactive, illegal, irrational
inter	among, between	intersect
intra	within, inside	intramural
mis	wrong; bad	mistake; misfortune
mono	one	monopoly
multi	many, much	multilateral, multiplex
non	not	noncommittal
per	throughout	peruse
poly	many	polygamy
post	after	postgraduate
pre	before	preview
pro	before, forward	prologue, propel
re	again; back	review; recall
sub	under, below	submerge
super	over, above	superimpose
tri	three	trilogy
un	not	unequal

Roots

Root Word	Meaning	Example
act	do	actor
ann; enn	year	annually
alter	other	alternate
anthrop	man	anthropogenesis
aqua	water	aquatic
audio	hear	auditory
auto	self	autocracy
belli	war	bellicose
bio	life	biology
cap; capit	head	capital
cardi	heart	cardiac
cede; ceed	yield	concede
cred	belief	credence
cycl	circle	cyclone
derm	skin	dermatology
dic	speak	diction
fac	make	faction
flex	bend	flexible
geo	earth	geography
gram; graph	write	graphology
hetero	different	heterogeneous
homo	same	homograph
ject	throw	eject
junct	join	conjunction
loc	place	location
loqu, log	speak	eloquent
ment	mind	mentality
micro	small	microscopic
mis; mit	send	transmit
mot; mov	move	movable
neo	new	neologism
ord	row	orderly
orig	beginning	origin
path	feeling	sympathy
ped; pod	foot	pedal
photo	light	photography
port	carry	export
pos	place	deposit
quer; ques	to ask	query; question
rupt	break	bankrupt
scrib; script	write	transcribe; transcript
tact	touch	contact
vac	empty	evacuate
ver	truth; turn	verdict; divert
vict	conquer	victory
voc	voice	vocalize

Suffixes

Suffix	Meaning	Example
-able, ible	capable of being	touchable; edible
-al	relating to	theatrical
-an	belonging to	Italian
-ance, -ancy, -ence	act of, state of being	appearance
-ant	state of being	reliant
-ard	one who	steward
-dom	state of being	freedom
-ee	one who is	employee
-er	one who; action or process	teacher; murder
-ful	full of	joyful
-fy	to make	satisfy
-hood	state of being	brotherhood
-c	pertaining to	classic
-ier; -yer	one who	designer; lawyer
-ical	relating to	comical
-ion, -sion, -tion	state of being	tension; contention
-ism	state or quality of	plagiarism
-st	a person who	botanist
-ity	state or quality of	necessity
-ive	having the quality of	passive
-less	without	hopeless
-ment	state or quality of	puzzlement
-ness	state of being	sadness
-ology	study of	pathology
-or	one who	doctor
-ous	full of	joyous
-phobia	fear of	agoraphobia
-ship	state or quality of	friendship
-tude	state of being	gratitude
-ward	in the direction of	eastward

After reviewing the prefix, root, and suffix meanings above, choose the appropriate word to fit the sentences below

1. After the doctor _____ the medication, Carol was finally able to get out of bed without feeling so nauseated.

   A. addicted
   B. administered
   C. adapted

2. The teacher admitted that she made a _____ when she calculated my final grade.

   A. misfortune
   B. misconduct
   C. mistake

3. I did not do very well on the _____ that we were given on the first day of class.

   A. pretest
   B. preface
   C. prefix

4. I am going to ask my teacher to let me _____ the test.

   A. rewrite
   B. review
   C. retake

5. I am going to _____ myself in this _____ because I do not want to fail the exit examination.

   A. submerse; subject
   B. subjugate; subject;
   C. submit; subject

6. Because he continually spent more money than he made, Jeff found himself in a real

   _____ .

   A. embarrassment
   B. embezzlement
   D. predicament

7. As I grew into _____, I retained many fond memories of my _____ that I have enjoyed sharing with my children.

   A. sisterhood; adulthood
   B. adulthood; childhood
   C. childhood; adulthood

8. In light of the _____ acts that occurred on September 11, _____ has been the focus of many television programs.

    A. terrorist; heroism
    B. loyalist; capitalism
    C. communist; Nazism

9. Nina's _____ is very important to all of her friends.

    A. goodness
    B. kindness
    C. happiness

10. The toddler began walking _____ his mother, but once he caught sight of the colorful flags posted at the end of the store aisles, he changed direction and headed straight for the toy department.

    A. toward
    B. afterward
    C. forward

Exercises: Appropriate Expressions

In the exercises below, choose the best word to fit the context of the sentence

1. Disease and hunger are_____ in the war-torn countries of the Middle East.
    A. rampant
    B. around
    C. present

2. The meeting was such a _____ one, not even those involved knew exactly what was going to be discussed until they arrived.

    A. big
    B. clandestine
    C. undercover

3. Campbell was so _____ by the speaker, she could barely bring herself to look at him.

    A. rushed
    B. challenged
    C. intimidated

4. Arnold was _____ into believing that the investment he made in Matt's business would make him a wealthy man.

    A. talked
    B. duped
    C. led

5. The angry driver leaned out the window and made several _____ remarks to the woman who nearly ran him off the road.

    A. upsetting
    B. caustic
    C. loud

6. Cindy tried to provide some _____ to Joel who was very upset over the breakup with his girlfriend.

    A. happiness
    B. advice
    C. solace

7. Alice's _____ attitude toward her coworkers eventually caused her to lose her job.
    A. frantic
    B. belligerent
    C. mundane

8. The _____ employees threatened to walk out if their demands for improved working conditions were not met.

    A. disgruntled
    B. compatible
    C. revered

9. By her own _____, Mandy passed up a piece of chocolate cake and stuck to her diet.

    A. power
    B. admission
    C. volition

10. The noisy students became _____ once the teacher started the movie.

    A. subdued
    B. talkative
    C. stigmatized

Chapter 24: Correct Use of Easily Confused and Misused Words

Many words that sound alike, such as blue (the color) and blew (the past tense of blow) are easily confused. These words, known as homonyms, may sound the same but they have different meanings and spellings. Additionally, people frequently confuse words like whose and who's: Whose shows possession and who's is the contraction for who is. Also, words that are misspelled are often misused. This chapter of the guide will help you distinguish between commonly confused and misused words.

Below is a list of some commonly confused and misused words and their definitions. After reviewing the list, complete the exercises in this section.

accept – to receive
except – all but

affect – to influence
effect – result

all right – correct; certainly
alright – a substandard spelling

advice – an opinion
advise – to counsel

all ready – totally prepared
already – previously

a lot – much or many
allot – to assign

brake – to stop
break – to fall apart

capital – money or property owned by a business; top part of a column
capitol – the building in which the U.S. Congress meets

compliment –praise
complement – go together

counsel – to give advice
council – elected officials
consul – foreign representative

course – a direction; school subject; part of a meal
coarse –rough

cite – to quote
site – a place
sight – to see

hear – listen to
here – at this time

hole – a hollow place
whole – all or entire

its – belonging to
it's – contraction for it is

knew – recognize; understand
new – latest; inexperienced

know – be aware of; acquainted with
no –not

lain – past tense of lie
lane – narrow country road or city street

loose – not secured or fastened tightly
lose – misplaced; not winning

pair – a set of two
pear – a fruit

passed – to go by or hand to
past – something done before

peace – calm
piece – a part of

plain – simple; natural
plane – aircraft; flat surface

181

principal – chief; head
principle – ultimate source; fundamental truth

right –correct
rite – a system of ceremonial procedure
write – to form words

their – belonging to
there – at or in a place; toward
they're – contraction for they are

to – toward
too – also
two – the number

thorough – complete; careful
threw – past tense of throw
through – finished; in one side and out the other

whether – alternative; in either case
weather – atmospheric conditions

where – a place or location
wear – to have on

whose – belonging to someone
who's – contraction for who is

you're – contraction for you are
your – something belonging to you

Exercises: Easily Confused and Misused Words

Fill in the blanks with the word(s) that best fit the context (meaning) of the following sentences.
*Note: if you need help, use the word list on the previous page.

1. The _____ (cite, sight, site) of the accident was still littered with debris when I drove _____ (threw, through) the area.

2. My _____ (advise, advice) to you would be not to sign the contract.

3. You may not believe me, but the name of the _____ (principal, principle) of my high school is Andrew Jackson.

4. _____ (Your, You're) outlook on life will never improve unless you learn to let go of the hurt that caused you pain in the _____ (passed, past).

5. Because I have lost weight, my new dress is _____ (to, too, two) _____ (lose, loose) and I have no idea what to _____ (where, wear) to the party.

6. Larry is having difficulty deciding on which scholarship to _____ (accept, except) because he is not sure which college he wants to attend.

7. I was late getting to George's house and found out that he had _____ (already, all ready) left to go to the play.

8. If you change your negative attitude, you might be surprised at the _____ (affect, effect) it will have on the people around you.

9. Sela's parents would not let her go to the concert because they did not _____ (no, know) the people she wanted to ride with.

10. Laney Barr, who was recently elected president of our city _____ (council, counsel), is an old friend of mine.

182

Part Four: Posttests

Writing Posttest

Directions: Choose the most effective word or phrase within the context suggested by the sentence(s).

1. The mystery novel held its readers in _____.

    A.   suspension
    B.   suspicion
    C.   suspense

2. The lab assistant _____through the microscope at the biological specimen.

    A.   scanned
    B.   peered
    C.   gawked

Directions: Choose the option that corrects an error in an underlined portion. If no error exists, choose "no change is necessary."

3. It's a common occurrence for college students to loose their keys on campus.
  A   B   C

    A.   Its
    B.   lose
    C.   there
    D.   No change is necessary.

Directions: Choose the sentence in which the modifiers are correctly placed.

4.
    A.   Leaping from tree to tree in our backyard, the squirrel searched busily for food.

    B.   The squirrel searched busily for food leaping from tree to tree in our backyard.

    C.   The squirrel searched busily for food in our backyard leaping from tree to tree.

5.
    A.   Rowing the canoe across the lake, our oars made a gentle, swooshing sound in the water.

    B.   Our oars made a gentle, swooshing sound in the water rowing the canoe across the lake.

    C.   As Derrick and I rowed the canoe across the lake, our oars made a gentle, swooshing sound in the water.

Directions: Choose the most effective word or phrase within the context suggested by the sentence(s).

6. Many drivers travel with a cell phone; _____, they no longer need to stop to use a pay phone at a telephone booth.

      A.   consequently
      B.   next
      C.   however
      D.   likewise

Directions: Choose the sentence that most clearly expresses the thought without errors in structure.

7.
      A.   If Veronica received three job offers this week, she did not accept any of them because she loves her current position.

      B.   Although Veronica received three job offers this week, she did not accept any of them because she loves her current position.

      C.   Provided that Veronica received three job offers this week, she did not accept any of them because she loves her current position.

Directions: Choose the sentence that has no errors in structure.

8.
      A.   The president wrote and to deliver an inspirational State of the Union address.

      B.   The president wrote and delivering an inspirational State of the Union address.

      C.   The president wrote and delivered an inspirational State of the Union address.

Directions: Choose the correct word or phrase within the context suggested by the sentence.

9. At the popular club, strobe lights flicker in the smoky room, hip hop music lures people onto the dance floor, and dancers _____ in time to the music.

      A.   move
      B.   they move
      C.   to move
      D.   are moving

Directions: Choose the option that corrects an error in the underlined portion(s). If no error exists, choose "no change is necessary."

10. If the light turns yellow at the busy <u>intersection. Then</u> drivers should stop as a safety precaution.

      A.   intersection then
      B.   intersection, then
      C.   intersection; then
      D.   No change is necessary.

11. In the public <u>library, which</u> is located in downtown <u>Jacksonville, children</u>
                        A   B

sit at Miss Roberta's <u>feet as</u> she reads a story about a mischievous monkey
                              C

in an ice cream shop.

      A.   library. Which
      B.   Jacksonville. Children
      C.   feet; as
      D.   No change is necessary.

12. When Renata opened her mailbox, she discovered an envelope from her former college <u>roommate, the envelope</u> contained a wedding invitation.

      A.   roommate and the envelope
      B.   roommate and, the envelope
      C.   roommate; the envelope
      D.   No change is necessary.

13. As the fire fighters drove the hook and ladder truck in the <u>parade, they</u>
                                                          A

waved at a little boy who watched them in <u>awe; suddenly,</u> they turned on the
                                                B

truck's <u>siren and</u> they rushed off in an emergency.
             C
      A.   parade; they
      B.   awe, suddenly,
      C.   siren, and
      D.   No change is necessary.

14. Jordan <u>seen</u> an affordable motorcycle on the showroom floor and <u>bought</u> the
          A   B

bike so that she <u>could ride</u> it to work.
                  C
      A.   saw
      B.   had boughten
      C.   could rode
      D.   No change is necessary.

15. I <u>should have wore</u> a sweater to the theatre because I felt quite cold there.

    A.   should wore
    B.   should had worn
    C.   should have worn
    D.   No change is necessary.

16. In past decades, people <u>used</u> typewriters to prepare reports. Nowadays,
                         A

most individuals <u>preferred</u> to type on a computer because they <u>can save</u> so
              B   C

much time.

    A.   use
    B.   prefer
    C.   could save
    D.   No change is necessary.

17. Since the local museum opened its dinosaur exhibit last month, many parents <u>took</u> their children to see the fossils and skeletons on display.

    A.   take
    B.   were taking
    C.   have taken
    D.   No change is necessary.

18. Neither the cookies nor the candy <u>interest</u> the determined dieter who prefers to snack on carrots and celery.

    A.   interests
    B.   are interesting
    C.   have interested
    D.   No change is necessary.

19. Each of the blues musicians <u>perform</u> a thirty-minute set and <u>moves</u> the fans
                                  A   B

with soulful guitar playing that <u>fills</u> the entire amphitheatre.
                                      C
    A.   performs
    B.   move
    C.   fill
    D.   No change is necessary.

20. The superintendent of the schools <u>has exclaimed</u> that each school <u>is</u>
    A   B

    responsible for making an "A" or a "B"; everybody <u>is working</u> hard to achieve
    C

    this goal.

     A.   have exclaimed
     B.   are
     C.   are working
     D.   No change is necessary.

21. The sleeping dog awoke when <u>his</u> owners returned home; <u>she</u> patted
    A   B

    <u>him</u> on the head.
    C

     A.   their
     B.   they
     C.   them
     D.   No change is necessary.

22. When Mrs. McBride's students read a short story by Edgar Allen Poe short story, <u>they</u>
    A

    asked <u>her</u> about <u>his</u> intriguing life.
              B   C

     A.   you
     B.   me
     C.   our
     D.   No change is necessary.

23. The manager of the clothing department told <u>us</u> to display the sundress that
    A

    had just arrived, so <u>we</u> placed <u>it</u> on a mannequin in the window.
                   B   C

     A.   you
     B.   they
     C.   you
     D.   No change is necessary.

24. The photographer told Steve, <u>his</u> assistant, that <u>he</u> needed to use a wide
                           A   B

    lens camera to film the zebras in <u>their</u> natural habitat.
    C

     A.   their
     B.   he, Steve,
     C.   its
     D.   No change is necessary.

25. Between you and <u>me</u>, Paul and <u>her</u> have been dating for several

                      A   B

years, but <u>they</u> do not plan on marrying.

                 C

    A.   I
    B.   she
    C.   them
    D.   No change is necessary.

26. Ashley's suit looked <u>tasteful</u> on her; it was <u>carefully</u> sewn by a <u>skillful</u> tailor.

                           A   B   C

    A.   tastefully
    B.   careful
    C.   skillfully
    D.   No change is necessary.

27. Gabriel is the _____ of the two brothers.

    A.   younger
    B.   youngest
    C.   more young
    D.   most young

28. I just <u>received</u> an email from my sister who is a <u>sophomore</u> in <u>collage</u>.

              A   B   C

    A.   recieved
    B.   sophmore
    C.   college
    D.   No change is necessary.

29. Bess works for a <u>cable company</u> in the <u>southwest</u> where she frequently

                          A   B

speaks <u>Spanish</u> with her customers.

               C

    A.   Cable Company
    B.   Southwest
    C.   spanish
    D.   No change is necessary.

30. Have you gotten <u>your</u> beauty sleep after a hard <u>weeks</u> <u>labor</u>?

    A.   you're
    B.   week's
    C.   labor.
    D.   No change is necessary.

31. <u>Because the</u> Smiths and Jones have been close neighbors for over twenty
              A

<u>years they</u> occasionally baby sit each <u>other's</u> grandchildren.
      B   C

    A.   Because, the
    B.   years, they
    C.   others
    D.   No change is necessary.

Directions: Choose the sentence that is correctly punctuated.

32.
    A.   Russell enjoys golf baseball, and tennis but he does not participate in contact sports like football.

    B.   Russell enjoys golf baseball, and tennis, but he does not participate in contact sports like football.

    C.   Russell enjoys golf, baseball, and tennis but he does not participate in contact sports like football.

    D.   Russell enjoys golf, baseball, and tennis, but he does not participate in contact sports like football.

Directions: Read the following passage carefully and then answer the questions. (Note: Intentional errors may have been included in this passage.)

    1. _____. 2. Job candidates are tested in a variety of areas, including their appearance, qualifications, and interpersonal skills. 3. The moment a candidate enters the waiting room, she is being evaluated. 4. To create a favorable first impression, she should arrive ten or more minutes early and wait patiently for the interview. 5. Ideally, the job seeker will have dressed in formal business attire, for doing so establishes a confident, professional image. 6. Unfortunately, casual clothes, such as blue jeans and tennis shoes, may suggest an indifferent attitude on the part of the interviewee. 7. Formal attire, like a tailored suit, shows that the candidate takes the position seriously. 8. Establishing a positive image through professional dress prepares the job seeker for the question and answer session of the interview. 9. During this stage, applicants should anticipate two types of questions: behavioral and ambition ones. 10. _____, behavioral questions assess one's teamwork skills and ability to deal with job conflicts. 11. Secondly, ambition questions focus on one's career plans. 12. By answering these questions honestly and sincerely, a candidate will favorably impress the interviewer. 13. Interviews can be nerve-wrecking experiences. 14. In brief, an interview is like a test for which job applicants must carefully prepare.
Information in this paragraph has been paraphrased from the following source: Bacon, Su. "Expect Interviewers to Assess Everything." Florida Times Union 2 June 2002: H13

33. Which of the following sentences, when inserted in the blank labeled number 1, is the **best** main idea or topic sentence for the passage?

    A.   Business attire demonstrates that the candidate takes the interview seriously.

    B.   Applicants should arrive at least ten minutes early to the interview.

    C.   A job interview is like an exam for which applicants must carefully prepare.

    D.   Candidates can expect to be asked behavioral and ambition questions.

34. Which sentence provides the specific support for sentence 3 in the passage?

    A.   To create a favorable first impression, she should arrive ten or more minutes early and wait patiently for the interview (sentence 4).

    B.   During this stage, applicants should anticipate two types of questions: behavioral and ambition ones (sentence 9).

    C.   Secondly, ambition questions focus on one's career plans (sentence 11).

    D.   By answering these questions honestly and sincerely, a candidate will favorably impress the interviewer (sentence 12).

35. Which numbered sentence is **least** relevant to the passage?

    A.   sentence 2
    B.   sentence 6
    C.   sentence 10
    D.   sentence 13

36. Which word or phrase, if inserted in the blank in sentence 10, would make the relationship of the ideas in sentences 9 and 10 clearer?

    A.   Conversely
    B.   First
    C.   Therefore
    D.   Also

Directions: Read the following passage carefully and then answer the questions. (Note: Intentional errors may have been included in the passage.)

1. _____. 2. According to Bill Watterson, the creator of *Calvin and Hobbes*, engaging comic strips reflect their creators' curiosity and enthusiasm for learning. 3. In just a few panels, these cartoonists express readers' unspoken thoughts and feelings. 4. In addition, some comic strips, such as Charles Schulz's *Peanuts*, portray life from the point of view of children, inviting readers to look

more innocently at the world. 5. Interestingly, comics are frequently referred to as the "funnies."
6. In fact, most comics contain humor, which involves the element of surprise. 7. Readers find humor in comics that not only surprise their expectations but also reveal a truth about life. 8.
For instance, in a *Dilbert* comic strip by Scott Adams, Dilbert claims, "I have become one with my computer." 9. He then announces that he has achieved "a perfect blend of logic and emotion." 10. Just when Dilbert is about to say that he has reached a state of "Nirvana," his friend Dogbert exclaims, "Nerdvana." 11. Readers laugh at this surprisingly clever pun as they reflect on how difficult it is to achieve balance in their own lives. 12. _____, comic strips are a form of popular art that gives insight into life while entertaining audiences.
Information in this passage has been paraphrased from the following sources: Watterson, Bill. The Calvin and Hobbes Tenth Anniversary Book. Kansas City, Missouri: Andrews and McMeel, a Universal Press Syndicate Company, 1995. Adams, Scott. It's Obvious You Won't Survive by Your Wits Alone: A Dilbert Book. Kansas City, Missouri: Andrews and McMeel, a Universal Press Syndicate Company, 1995.

37. Which sentence, if inserted in the blank labeled number 1, is the **best** main
     idea or topic sentence of the passage?

       A.   The comics are found in the funnies section of the local newspaper.

       B.   In some comic strips, characters become one with their computers.

       C.   Comic strips are a form of popular art that both entertains audiences and offers
             insight into life.

       D.   A few comics portray life from a child's point of view.

38.   Which sentence provides the specific support for sentence 5 in the passage?

       A.   According to Bill Watterson, the creator of *Calvin and Hobbes*, engaging comic
             strips reflect their creators' curiosity and enthusiasm for learning (sentence 2).

       B.   In just a few panels, these cartoonists express readers' unspoken thoughts and
             feelings (sentence 3).

       C.   In addition, some comic strips, such as Charles Schulz's
             Peanuts, portray life from the point of view of children, inviting readers to look
             more innocently at the world (sentence 4).

       D.   In fact, most comics contain humor, which involves the element of
             surprise (sentence 6).

39. Select the arrangement of sentences 8, 9, and 10 that provides the most logical sequence of ideas and supporting details in the paragraph. If no change is necessary, select Option A.

A. For instance, in a *Dilbert* comic strip by Scott Adams, Dilbert claims, "I have become one with my computer." He then announces that he has achieved "a perfect blend of logic and emotion." Just when Dilbert is about to say that he has reached a state of "Nirvana," his friend Dogbert exclaims, "Nerdvana."

B. He then announces that he has achieved "a perfect blend of logic and emotion." Just when Dilbert is about to say that he has reached a state of "Nirvana," his friend Dogbert exclaims, "Nerdvana." For instance, in a *Dilbert* comic strip by Scott Adams, Dilbert claims, "I have become one with my computer."

C. Just when Dilbert is about to say that he has reached a state of "Nirvana," his friend Dogbert exclaims, "Nerdvana." For instance, in a *Dilbert* comic strip by Scott Adams, Dilbert claims, "I have become one with my computer." He then announces that he has achieved "a perfect blend of logic and emotion."

D. Just when Dilbert is about to say that he has reached a state of "Nirvana," his friend Dogbert exclaims, "Nerdvana." He then announces that he has achieved "a perfect blend of logic and emotion." For instance, in a *Dilbert* comic strip by Scott Adams, Dilbert claims, "I have become one with my computer."

40. Which word or phrase, if inserted in the blank in sentence 12, would make the relationship of the ideas in sentences 11 and 12 clearer?

A. On the other hand
B. Indeed
C. For instance
D. Next

Paragraph Posttest

Directions: On a separate sheet of paper or on the computer, write a practice paragraph according to the guidelines below. When you have completed the paragraph, submit it to your teacher for feedback.

You will have 50 minutes to plan, write, and proofread a paragraph on one of the topics below.

TOPIC 1   A valuable lesson you learned outside of school

TOPIC 2   A little-known place that people should visit

In your writing, you should do the following:

- Establish your main idea clearly.
- Develop your main idea with adequate and relevant support.
- Organize your ideas logically and coherently.
- Make effective choices in vocabulary and sentence structure.
- Observe the conventions of standard American English grammar, spelling, capitalization, and punctuation.

Take a few minutes to think about what you want to say before you start writing. Leave yourself a few minutes at the end of the period to proofread and make corrections.

You may cross out or add information as necessary, but you should write or type as legibly as possible so that your teacher can easily read your paragraph.

Part Five: Answer Keys

Answer Keys

Chapter 1: The Topic Sentence

1. D
2. D
3. C
4. B
5. D

Chapter 2: Supporting Details

1. D
2. B
3. C
4. A
5. B
6. A

Chapter 3: Logical Patterns

1. B
2. B
3. B
4. C
5. C
6. B

Chapter 4: Relevance of Details

1. C
2. A
3. C
4. A
5. B

Chapter 5: Transitional Devices

1. B
2. D
3. B
4. D
5. C

Chapter 6: Putting the Parts Together

Passage 1

1. C
2. D
3. A
4. C
5. D

Passage 2

1. B
2. B
3. B
4. D
5. A

Passage 3

1. B
2. A
3. D
4. C
5. D

Passage 4

1. D
2. D
3. B
4. A
5. C

Passage 5

1. B
2. C
3. B
4. D
5. A

Passage 6

1. C
2. B
3. D
4. C
5. B

Passage 7

1. D
2. C
3. A
4. A
5. D

Passage 8

1. A
2. C
3. B
4. B
5. C

Passage 9

1. B
2. B
3. D
4. C
5. A

Passage 10

1. C
2. A
3. A
4. B
5. B

Chapter 7: Modifiers

1. C
2. B
3. A
4. C
5. B
6. C
7. C
8. A
9. C
10. A

Chapter 8: Parallel Structure

1. B
2. A
3. C
4. B
5. A
6. C
7. A
8. D
9. B
10. D

Chapter 9: Coordination and Subordination

1. A
2. D
3. B
4. C
5. A
6. B
7. C
8. A
9. C
10. A

Chapter 10: Fragments

1. A
2. B
3. A
4. C
5. B
6. D
7. B
8. D
9. C
10. C

Chapter 11: Run-ons

1. C
2. B
3. C
4. A
5. B
6. C
7. D
8. C
9. D
10. C

Chapter 12: Adjectives versus Adverbs and Degree Forms of Adjectives and Adverbs

1. B
2. D
3. C
4. D
5. D
6. C
7. C
8. D
9. A
10. D

Chapter 13: Verb Forms

Past Tense Endings Exercise

1. jumped
2. talked
3. played
4. learned
5. seated
6. called
7. camped
8. walked
9. stared
10. raced

Chapter 13: Verb Forms

Verb Forms Exercise

1. B
2. B
3. B
4. B
5. A
6. D
7. B
8. C
9. D
10. A

Chapter 14: Verb Tense

1. D
2. A
3. D
4. A
5. B
6. A
7. D
8. C
9. C
10. B

Chapter 15: Subject and Verb Agreement

1. B
2. B
3. B
4. D
5. C
6. A
7. A
8. A
9. D
10. B

Chapter 16: Pronoun Antecedent Agreement

1. A
2. A
3. D
4. C
5. A
6. D
7. B
8. D
9. C
10. C

Chapter 17: Clear Pronoun Reference

1. A
2. C
3. B
4. A
5. C
6. D
7. C
8. C
9. C
10. D

Chapter 18: Pronoun Shifts

1. B
2. A
3. D
4. D
5. B
6. A
7. D
8. C
9. A
10. B

Chapter 19: Pronoun Case

1. A
2. D
3. B
4. A
5. C
6. B
7. C
8. A
9. B
10. D

Chapter 20: Standard Spelling

Sentence exercise

1. dropped
2. calendar; commitments
3. developing; successful
4. hoping
5. absent
6. sandwiches
7. believes; attendance
8. retiring
9. studied
10. confident; prepared

Chapter 20: Standard Spelling

Paragraph exercise

writer, stories, exciting, pieces, puzzle, sitting, develop, foreign, knew, thrilling, abilities, difficulty, correctly.

Chapter 21: Standard Punctuation

1. B
2. B
3. C
4. A
5. D
6. D
7. C
8. A
9. D
10. B

Chapter 22: Standard Capitalization

Sentence exercise

1. D
2. C
3. C
4. B
5. C
6. B
7. A
8. A
9. A
10. A

Chapter 22: Standard Capitalization

Story exercise

gene, metabolic, Syndrome, Crigler's, phototherapy, physicians, recessive, Amish, genetic, amino, multiple sclerosis, muscular dystrophy, pediatrician

Chapter 23: Appropriate Expressions

Prefix, root, suffix exercise

1. B
2. C
3. A
4. C
5. A
6. C
7. B
8. A
9. C
10. A

Chapter 23: Appropriate Expressions

Sentence exercise

1. A
2. B
3. C
4. B
5. B
6. C
7. B
8. A
9. C
10. A

Chapter 24: Correct Use of Easily Confused and Misused Words

1. site, through
2. advice
3. principal
4. your past
5. too, loose, wear
6. accept
7. already
8. effect
9. know
10. council

Answer Key for the Writing Pretest

1.	B		21.	D
2.	C		22.	C
3.	D		23.	B
4.	A		24.	B
5.	C		25.	A
6.	D		26.	C
7.	B		27.	B
8.	C		28.	D
9.	B		29.	B
10.	B		30.	C
11.	C		31.	B
12.	C		32.	C
13.	B		33.	A
14.	D		34.	B
15.	A		35.	A
16.	C		36.	D
17.	A		37.	D
18.	C		38.	A
19.	A		39.	C
20.	B		40.	D

Answer Key for the Writing Posttest

1.	C		21.	B
2.	B		22.	D
3.	B		23.	D
4.	A		24.	B
5.	C		25.	B
6.	A		26.	D
7.	B		27.	A
8.	C		28.	C
9.	A		29.	B
10.	B		30.	B
11.	D		31.	B
12.	C		32.	D
13.	C		33.	C
14.	A		34.	A
15.	C		35.	D
16.	B		36.	B
17.	C		37.	C
18.	A		38.	D
19.	A		39.	A
20.	D		40.	B

Part Six: Explanation Answer Keys

Explanatory Answer Key for Chapter 1 – The Topic Sentence

1.1 D This is broad enough to cover the people listed in the paragraph, yet it does not cover a wider scope.

Incorrect choices
- A This only mentions two of the examples from the paragraph. It would not cover Mother Teresa, Gandhi, or Martin Luther King.
- B This is incorrect because charismatics, according to the paragraph, are people with followers.
- C This is too specific because it only mentions one of the examples.

1.2 D This statement includes all the ideas presented in the paragraph.

Incorrect choices
- A This is incorrect because the paragraph states that readers should preview before they read.
- B This is too specific. It only mentions one stage of the reading method.
- C This is too specific because it mentions the result of the reading method without mentioning any of the steps involved.

1.3 C This paragraph lists many methods to use to draw the observer's eye to a particular section of an artwork.

Incorrect choices
- A This is too specific. It only lists one method.
- B This is too specific; it lists one of many methods.
- D This is too broad. It includes numerous techniques and does not limit the reason why artists use these techniques.

1.4 B This statement tells about the changing view of heroes throughout the past century, and it includes the two limiting factors, the United States and the past century, used in the paragraph.

Incorrect choices
- A This is too specific because it mentions some of the heroes, but it doesn't mention all the types of heroes included in the paragraph.
- C This is too broad because it includes all the countries and all the centuries.
- D This is too specific because it only mentions one of the types of heroes named in the paragraph.

1.5 D This is correct because it is general enough to include the ideas in the paragraph, and it includes the limiting time factor.

Incorrect choices
    A   This includes only a small part of the ideas presented in the paragraph.
    B   This is too limited; it only presents a part of the ideas presented.
    C   This is not correct because it says all networks.

Explanatory Answer Key for Chapter 2 – Supporting Details

2.1 D Sentence 11 tells how Mother Teresa used her charisma, but specifics were not mentioned.

Incorrect choices
    A   Sentence 3 is supported by many of the sentences that follow it. The sentences explain how charismatics used their talents to tempt people to follow them and to change the existing rules.
    B   Sentence 7 is supported by sentence 8 which tells how King used his charisma to have people protest nonviolently.
    C   Sentence 8 is supported by sentence 10 which states the result of King's actions.

2.2 B Sentence 6 states one of the results of using the previewing methods in sentence 5.

Incorrect choices
    A   Sentence 4 supports the topic sentence by listing one of the steps necessary to efficient reading.
    C   Sentence 7 supports the topic sentence by listing one of the steps necessary to read efficiently.
    D   Sentence 8 supports the topic sentence by listing one of the steps necessary to read efficiently.

2.3 C Sentence 6 gives a minor detail that tells how the symmetry of the lines can be used.

Incorrect choices
    A   Sentence 2 supports the topic sentence by naming one way artists draw a viewer's eye to a part of the painting.
    B   Sentence 5 supports the topic sentence by naming one method artists use to draw the viewer's eye to a part of a painting.
    D   Sentence 8 supports the method mentioned in sentence 5 by telling how color can be used to draw the viewer's eye to a part of the painting.

2.4 A   Sentence 3 tells us that military men were viewed as heroes, but examples or explanations were not provided.

Incorrect choices
  B   Sentence 4 is supported by sentences 5 and 6 because the sentences give examples of the ideas presented in sentence 4.
  C   Sentence 6 is supported by sentence 7 which gives examples of the characters mentioned in sentence 6.
  D   Sentence 8 is supported by sentence 9 which tells how the view of heroes changed.

2.5 B   Sentence 4 is not supported by any explanation or example.

Incorrect choices
  A   Sentence 2 is supported by sentence 3 which lists examples of the types of shows mentioned in sentence 2.
  C   Sentence 5 is supported in the second half of the sentence which lists examples of animals who are stereotyped.
  D   Sentence 6 is supported by sentence 7 which names network shows in which minorities are rarely seen.

2.6 A   Sentence 3 states what weather is important to the maple farmers and why.

Incorrect choices
  B.   Sentence 4 supports sentence 5 by telling about the sap that comes out of the tree.
  C   Sentence 5 supports the topic sentence by naming one of the steps necessary to get maple sap out of the trees.
  D   Sentence 6 supports the topic sentence because it names a step in the process of making maple syrup.

Explanatory Answer Key for Chapter 3 – Logical Patterns

3.1 B   This gives details about Gandhi, so it would logically follow sentence 6 which states how Gandhi used his charisma. It states how Gandhi would use passive resistance methods.

3.2 B   This arrangement is the most logical. All three sentences are about previewing and the transitions first and after lead us to the proper sequence.

3.3 B   This arrangement is the most logical because it puts the two sentences about the symmetry of the lines together with the sentence introducing the concept first. Then it tells how the lines can be used to draw the eye. The third sentence introduces a new method of drawing the eye to a part of a painting. The minor details for using color are found in sentences 7 and 8 which follow the given sentences.

3.4 C   This sentence gives details about American military leaders in World War II who became government leaders. Their election to the office helps us to understand that these men were viewed as heroes, so this sentence should be placed before sentence 4. The remainder of the sentences deal with other types of people as heroes.

3.5 C The show, *Will and Grace*, is an example of the idea stated in sentence 4 because it was a show which portrayed homosexuals stereotypically.

3.6 B This arrangement is the most logical because the maple tree owners have to first put the taps into the trees, the sap has to be taken out of the tree, and then it must be processed. The steps of the process have to be in that sequence in order to make sense.

Explanatory Answer Key for Chapter 4 – Relevance of Details

To judge if an idea is relevant, you should consider the main idea or topic sentence, so the topic sentence is included before the answer.

4.1 Charisma improves the standing of a recognized leader and makes the influence of a challenger more powerful.

4.1 C Martin Luther King's first job does not have a strong relationship to his use of charisma to succeed as a challenger. The other sentences tell about people who were leaders and challengers and state how they were able to achieve their goals by using their charisma.

Incorrect choices
- A Sentence 4 names a good example of a leader who used charisma to achieve his goals.
- B Sentence 6 explains how Gandhi used his charisma to persuade people to follow his cause.
- C Sentence 11 states that Mother Teresa was able to persuade people to help the poor.

4.2 Many people feel that reading quickly will make understanding more difficult, but if you are taught the proper methods, reading efficiently usually leads to better comprehension.

4.2 A This paragraph is about reading efficiently and understanding. The main point is not about whether people find reading enjoyable.

Incorrect choices
- B Sentence 3 names a step in the reading method that helps people read efficiently.
- C Sentence 4 names one of the steps to reading efficiently.
- D Sentence 5 explains how to preview which is one of the steps to reading efficiently.

4.3   There are various methods that artists use to draw the viewer's eye to the part of the painting they want to emphasize.

4.3 C   This paragraph is about the use of various techniques to draw the viewer's eye to a particular spot in a painting. It is not about wheels. This sentence is about wheels.

Incorrect choices
A   Sentence 5 names a method to pull someone's eye to a spot in a painting.
B   Sentence 4 states a method to use to draw a viewer's eye to a spot in a painting.
D   Sentence 2 names a technique to use to draw the viewer's eye to a part of a painting.

4.4   The public's view of heroes in the United States has changed throughout the last century.

4.4 A   This sentence is about heroes, but it is not about the heroes in the United States or about heroes in the last century. Although the subject is similar, the limiting factors are different in this sentence.

Incorrect choices
B   Sentence 3 is related to the topic sentence because it names the group thought to be heroes in the United States during the world wars that took place within the last 100 years.
C   Sentence 4 is related to the topic sentence because it names another group that people in the United States within the last century considered heroic.
D   Sentence 5 is related to the topic sentence because it names examples of people that some of the public in the United States viewed as heroes. It also addresses people in the past century.

4.5   Until 2002 major television networks in the United States either portrayed minorities in a stereotypical manner or rarely included them in shows and movies, and this needed to be changed.

4.5 B   Sentence 5 addresses animals, not people, and the group named is not considered to be a minority in the animal world.

Incorrect choices
A   Sentence 7 is related to the topic sentence because it gives a result of the practice of portraying minorities stereotypically, or not including them in shows.
C   Sentence 3 gives examples of shows that do have minorities as characters, but the minorities are not weekly given a majority of airtime.
D   Sentence 2 supports the topic sentence by stating that some shows are using minorities, but the minorities are not given a majority of airtime weekly.

Explanatory Answer Key for Chapter 5 – Transitional Devices

5.1 B For example is appropriate here because sentence 3 gives an example of a person who is charismatic. The first two sentences of the paragraph introduce the concept and the remainder of the sentences address examples of people who have used charisma to make their ability to be a leader or challenger stronger.

Incorrect choices
A   Therefore is used in a cause and effect relationship.
C   Similarly is used when comparisons are made.
D   Because is used in a cause and effect paragraph, not an illustration and example paragraph.

5.2 D Finally should be used in this sentence because the paragraph lists steps to be an efficient reader, and the sentence without the transition is the last step of the process.

Incorrect choices
A   In front of is usually used as a part of a spatial paragraph.
B   In contrast is used in a paragraph that states how ideas or items are different.
C   Likewise is used in a paragraph that states similarities of objects or ideas.

5.3 B Because does show a cause and effect. The first part of the sentence is the cause and the second part is the effect.

Incorrect choices
A   To summarize would not be appropriate because this is not a summary paragraph. The ideas are not concisely written.
C   Despite is used when there is a contrast, not a list of causes and an effect.
D   Similarly indicates a comparison, not a list of causes and an effect.

5.4 D However should be used in this sentence because it introduces a contrast from beliefs in an earlier time and the beliefs in 2001.

Incorrect choices
A   Similarly is used when a likeness is shown, not a contrast.
B   For instance is used to introduce an example of a concept or an idea, not to show contrast.
C   Finally is used in addition, process, or time order sentences. It does not show contrast.

5.5 C The factors in this paragraph are all causes for people believing a change should be made. As a result tells the reader that an effect will be named in sentence 7.

Incorrect choices
A   In the same way is a phrase that indicates a likeness will be stated, not a result.
B   Specifically is used when examples are being stated, not an effect.
D   Yet is used to signify that a contrast is going to be stated, not an effect.

Explanatory Answer Key for Chapter 6 – Putting the Parts Together

Passage 1

1 C The topic deals with men's and women's different standards for marriage and casual dates, so this would be the best topic sentence.

Incorrect choices
- A This is only a small part of the paragraph. It is too specific.
- B This sentence has the word all in it. This study did not test all women and men so it cannot be the topic sentence.
- D This only mentions the women so it cannot be the topic sentence.

2 D This statement has no examples or statistics to support it.

Incorrect choices
- A This sentence is supported by sentence 3.
- B This sentence is supported by sentence 5.
- C This sentence is supported by sentence 6.

3 A This arrangement makes the most sense because the first sentence supports sentence 2 and the next one states that a difference existed between the men's criteria for marriage partners and dates. The third sentence addresses the size of the difference so it would logically follow the sentence introducing the difference.

4 C This transition signals that a contrast will be stated in the sentence. The contrast is between the men's and women's attitudes.

Incorrect choices
- A For example signals an example, not a contrast.
- B Presently designates a current time, not a contrast.
- D Similarly indicates that a comparison will occur, not a contrast.

5 D This sentence is not relevant because it addresses an amount of dating, not choosing a partner for a casual date or marriage.

Incorrect choices
- A This sentence is about the study.
- B This sentence is about the study.
- C This sentence is about the study.

Passage 2

1 B This topic sentence states that people have different feelings about this "walking catfish". Some people like it and some people do not like it.

Incorrect choices

   A This statement is not related to whether people like the fish. It just states how it moves.

   C This statement is too specific because it only mentions how one group feels about this catfish.

   D This statement is too specific. It only mentions how two groups feel. It does not mention the third group.

2 B This statement explains how this fish would be cooked.

Incorrect choices

   A Sentence 4 supports the topic by naming one way people feel about this catfish.

   C Sentence 6 supports the topic by naming another way people feel about the "walking catfish."

   D Sentence 8 supports the topic by stating why this catfish is disliked.

3 B This arrangement of sentences is correct because it first states that people dislike this fish. The second sentence tells about the fish's unique ability to crawl across land and about its huge appetite. The third sentence lets you know that the fish's abilities make it disliked because it eats all the fish in ponds and lakes.

4 D Unlike signals a contrast with the material that came before this statement. This sentence tells about people that feel negatively about this fish which is different from the other people mentioned in the paragraph.

Incorrect choices

   A Therefore indicates a cause and effect, not a contrast.

   B Presently designates a current time, not a contrast.

   C Finally either signals the end of a list or the last step or event. The transition in this sentence has to designate a contrast will occur.

5 A Sentence 9 is about fish farms, not about feelings about the "walking catfish."

Incorrect choices

   B Sentence 8 is about people's feelings about the catfish.

   C Sentence 7 is about the reasons why the catfish is disliked.

   D Sentence 6 is about why the catfish is disliked.

Passage 3

1 B This sentence states information about the changes in college attendance that took place at the end of the twentieth century. It includes both the men and the women.

Incorrect choices
- A This statement is too specific because it only includes the men.
- C This statement is too specific because it only includes the women.
- D This statement is too broad.

2 A Sentence 1 does not have any statistics or examples to support it.

Incorrect choices
- B Sentence 5 is supported by sentences 6-10.
- C Sentence 6 is supported by sentence 7.
- D Sentence 9 is supported by sentence 10.

3 D There were songs and television shows about the problems caused to young men because they were intellectual.

4 C As a result indicates an effect will be stated. Men may have taken jobs instead of continuing schooling because many salaries were above minimum wage.

Incorrect choices
- A While signals two events happening at the same time, not a cause and effect.
- B On the contrary signals a contrast, not a cause and effect.
- D Likewise indicates a similarity will be stated, not a cause and effect.

5 D Sentence 3 is about a need for childcare, not a need to go to college.

Incorrect choices
- A Sentence 7 relates to the topic because it gives information about why men's attendance has dropped.
- B Sentence 6 relates to the topic because it gives information about why men's attendance has dropped.
- C Sentence 4 relates to the topic because it introduces the idea that there are many theories about why some men are not attending college.

Passage 4

1 D This statement covers the ideas in the paragraph. It states information about offering children choices and tells you why it is important.

Incorrect choices
- A This statement is too specific. It only tells how to limit choices.
- B This is misstated because it states adults should allow children to choose anything, unlike the paragraph which names what type of items children should choose.
- C This statement is too specific because it deals with only one aspect of allowing a child to make choices.

213

2 D   Sentence 9 provides support for sentence 8 in the paragraph. It tells why you should use the method stated in sentence 8.

Incorrect choices
  A   Sentence 3 does not provide support for sentence 8.
  B   Sentence 4 does not provide support for any sentence in the paragraph. It is about work, not about working with children.
  C   Sentence 7 supports sentence 6.

3 B   This arrangement is the best because the first two sentences relate to the power struggles adults go through with children. The first sentence introduces the idea of using directives and the second sentence tells why it may not be a good idea. The third sentence relates to the choices you should offer children. The sentence that follows the selection gives an example of how to word the choice.

4 A   For example is appropriate for this sentence because the sentence states an example of how to limit a child's choices.

Incorrect choices
  B   Whereas shows a contrast, not an example.
  C   Equally indicates a comparison, not an example.
  D   Because signals a cause and effect, not an example.

5 C   Sentence 4 deals with a power struggle with adults, not children.

Incorrect choices
  A   Sentence 2 relates to the topic because it tells about some choices that children can make.
  B   Sentence 3 relates to the topic because it also relates to giving children choices.
  D   Sentence 5 relates to the topic because it is about limiting choices.

Passage 5

1 B   This sentence names the types of diseases named in the paragraph and states how they are caused, spread, and treated.

Incorrect choices
  A   This sentence is not true. The word all makes it untrue because some sexually transmitted diseases can be cured.
  C   This statement is too specific because it only mentions one characteristic of a sexually transmitted disease.
  D   This statement is too specific because it only mentions a few of the sexually transmitted diseases.

2 C   Sentence 4 is not supported with any examples or statistics.

Incorrect choices
  A   Sentence 8 is supported by sentence 9.
  B   Sentence 5 is supported by sentences 6 and 7.
  D   Sentence 3 is supported by the sentences that follow it.

3   B   This statement names two types of sexually transmitted diseases that are caused by bacterium. The statement before introduces the idea that bacteria can be a cause of these diseases.

4   D   Although signals the contrast between the results of the treatment and a cure.

Incorrect choices
    A   Because indicates a cause and effect, not a contrast.
    B   Meanwhile signals a time order paragraph or sentence.
    C   For example indicates that an example of the idea previously presented will be given, not a contrast.

5   A   Sentence 10 is related to the method ministers recommend for avoiding sexually transmitted diseases. It is not related to what causes, spreads, and treats sexually transmitted diseases.

Incorrect choices
    B   Sentence 9 is related to the topic because it tells that a sexually transmitted disease can be cured under certain conditions.
    C   Sentence 8 relates to the topic because it mentions a type of sexually transmitted disease.
    D   Sentence 7 relates to the topic because it tells about treatment for a sexually transmitted disease.

Passage 6

1   C   This statement states general information about a method used in art and names an example. It is written in spatial order which means the paragraph should create a picture of the window in order to show the reader how radial balance is used.

Incorrect choices
    A   This statement is about Gothic art which is an idea not developed in the paragraph.
    B   This statement is too specific. It only mentions one feature of the window.
    D   This statement is too specific. It only mentions one feature of the window.

2   B   Sentence 4 tells about the seraphim mentioned in sentence 5.

Incorrect choices
    A   Sentence 2 supports the topic sentence.
    C   Sentence 6 relates to creating a picture of this window and the window's use of radial balance.
    D   Sentence 8 sums up the reasons for certain objects being placed in specific spots on the window.

3   D   The arrangement in this group helps the reader to see the window and the placement of its circles around the center. The picture should help the reader see how radial balance is employed in this window.

4 C   The outer are the appropriate words to use in this sentence because they should tell where something is placed. The placement of the pictures is important to an understanding of radial balance.

Incorrect choices

    A   In the future would not be appropriate to signal a placement of an object in a picture.
    B   Likewise signals a similarity, not a placement of a picture.
    D   Inversely indicates a contrast would be stated, not a placement.

5 B   Sentence 3 is not relevant because it describes the beauty of the window, whereas the remainder of the paragraph tells about the placement of pictures in this window as an example of radial symmetry.

Incorrect choices

    A   Sentence 2 is related to the topic because it describes the window as having a flower-like form that helps develop the concept of the use of symmetry.
    C   Sentence 5 is related to the topic because it describes how the pictures in the window illustrate symmetry.
    D   Sentence 6 is related to the topic because it describes how the pictures in the window illustrate symmetry.

Passage 7

1 D   This statement states why people use Ecstasy and how it affects their body and mind.

Incorrect choices

    A   This statement is too broad because it is about all drugs, not just Ecstasy.
    B   This statement is too specific because it does not state the results to the user's mind and body.
    C   This statement is too broad because it mentions illegal drugs, not just Ecstasy.

2 C   Sentence 4 is not supported. The paragraph does not state how or why environmental factors make the side effects of Ecstasy worse.

Incorrect choices

    A   Sentence 6 is supported by sentence 7.
    B   Sentence 5 is supported by sentence 6.
    D   Sentence 3 is supported by sentence 4.

3 A   This is the best placement for this sentence because it tells what the serotonin, mentioned in sentence 5, does for the body.

4 A   While signals two events happening at the same time; in this case the two actions are the ecstasy euphoria taking place and the physical effects happening.

Incorrect choices

    B   After signals time but the two events would have to follow one another.
    C   Before indicates time, but the events would have to come at separate times instead of at the same time.
    D   For example indicates a model should follow, but in this case two events happening at the same time are given.

5 D Sentence 2 is the least relevant because it states what the students use while on Ecstasy, but it does not state an effect on their body or mind.

Incorrect choices
    A Sentence 8 is related because it restates most of the topic sentence.
    B Sentence 6 is related because it states damage that can occur because of the use of Ecstasy.
    C Sentence 4 is related because it states damage that can occur because of the use of Ecstasy.

Passage 8

1 A This statement is general enough to include the events that are listed in this paragraph.

Incorrect choices
    B This statement is too specific because it only mentions one event.
    C This statement is too specific because it only mentions one event.
    D This statement is too specific because it only mentions one event.

2 C Sentence 4 tells one of the changes people made after the fire.

Incorrect choices
    A Sentence 6 supports sentence 5 by telling how Cleveland's changes have changed the area.
    B Sentence 5 supports sentence 4 by stating what happened after the fire.
    D Sentence 3 supports the topic sentence by telling how extensive the pollution was.

3 B This arrangement is appropriate because the fire has to happen before the scientists investigate the effects of the fire, and the effects of the scientists' study has to come after the investigation.

4 B Meanwhile is the most appropriate because this sentence states what was happening at the same time as the events in the previous sentence.

Incorrect choices
    A Consequently indicates an effect will be stated; it does not denote time.
    C For example signals an example or a model of a concept.
    D Similarly signals a comparison, not time.

5 C Sentence 6 states that Cleveland's river area is a tourist area, but it does not relate to the specific changes that occurred due to the pollution.

Incorrect choices
    A Sentence 4 relates to the problem stated in sentences 2 and 3.
    B Sentence 5 is related to the changes the city made due to the pollution.
    D Sentence 7 is related to the topic because it relates to the effect of the pollution.

Passage 9

1 **B** This statement is a general statement that tells how stem cells might be used.

Incorrect choices
- A This statement is too specific because it mentions only one way stem cells might help people.
- C This statement is too specific because it only mentions one effect of the use of stem cells.
- D This statement is too specific because it only mentions one possible effect of the use of stem cells.

2 **B** Sentence 6 specifically supports the information in sentence 5 by telling how diabetes affects diabetics' bodies.

Incorrect choices
- A Sentence 2 does not support the topic sentence or sentence 5.
- C Sentence 7 supports the ideas in sentence 6.
- D Sentence 9 supports the ideas in sentence 8.

3 **D** This statement should be placed after the sentence that states that diabetics suffer from afflictions caused by the condition.

4 **C** For instance is appropriate in this sentence because diabetes is used as an example.

Incorrect choices
- A Similarly signals a comparison, not an example.
- B Meanwhile indicates time, not an example.
- D As a result signals a cause and effect, not an example.

5 **A** Sentence 2 is the least relevant because it relates to how people feel about research with mice, not how research with diabetic mice can help doctors know what will happen to people who use stem cells to help their disease.

Incorrect choices
- B Sentence 5 relates to a condition that might be helped by stem cells.
- C Sentence 6 relates to research done with diabetes.
- D Sentence 9 relates to the research done with stem cells.

Passage 10

1 **C** This statement has a general statement that covers the events that occurred at Fort Clinch during the Civil War and some of the effects.

Incorrect choices
- A This statement is too specific because it only mentions one event.
- B This statement is too specific because it only mentions one event.
- D This statement is too broad because it mentions forts, not just Fort Clinch.

2 A Sentence 2 does not have any explanation, statistics, or examples to support it.

Incorrect choices
   B Sentence 3 is supported by sentence 5.
   C Sentence 5 is supported by sentence 6.
   D Sentence 7 is supported by sentence 8.

3 A This placement is appropriate because this statement tells why the location of the fort made it a useful place to control during the Northern blockade.

4 B But is appropriate because it indicates that a contrast will be made between the good and bad points of occupying Fort Clinch during the Civil War.

Incorrect choices
   A Similarly indicates a comparison, not a contrast.
   C For example signals a model or example, not a contrast.
   D Therefore indicated an effect will be named, not a contrast.

5 B Sentence 2 is related to the present, not to the use of the fort during the Civil War.

Incorrect choices
   A Sentence 1 is related to the use of the fort during the Civil War.
   C Sentence 3 is related to the use of the fort during the Civil War.
   D Sentence 4 is related to the use of the fort during the Civil War.

Explanatory Answer Key for the Writing Pretest

Skill Being Tested	**Explanation**

Word Choice

1. (B) This item measures your understanding of word choice. Option A is incorrect because Tyler cannot "revisit" mail. Further, Option C is invalid because the word "redeemed," which has either a spiritual or financial meaning, does not fit the context of the sentence about mail. Finally, Option B is accurate because it expresses what happens with the process of mail—one person sends it and another *receives* it.

Word Choice

2. (C) To understand this question, you must study the context of the sentence. Because the award-winning author *humbly* thanked his fans, you can conclude that he showed much modesty. Choice A is incorrect because the word "vanity" contradicts the author's sense of humility. Additionally, Choice B is false because the term "uncertainty" suggests doubt; however, the sentence does not indicate that he is uncertain but rather humble. In Choice C, the word "modesty" complements the term "humbly" and is the correct response.

Confused Words

3. (D) This sentence quizzes you on easily confused words. Choice A is inaccurate because the word "whether" is used to express an either-or situation—for example, "whether you come to the party or stay home." However, this item calls for the meteorological spelling—"weather." Choice C, moreover, is false because the word "idea" is a noun that expresses a thought or concept. Yet in this sentence, the term needed is "ideal" which means desirable. Lastly, Choice B is invalid because when you refer to a geographical region that is a "capitol," you spell it with an – o. Choice D is correct because the sentence contains no error.

Modifiers

4. (A) This item tests your awareness of misplaced modifiers. A modifier is a descriptive word or group of words that should be placed next to the noun or pronoun it modifies. When modifiers are misplaced, readers feel confused. In this group of sentences, choice B is incorrect because the modifier – "grilled on Grandpa's stove" – has been misplaced before the subject Desmond, creating the misreading that Desmond was grilled. Additionally choice C is false because the modifier has been incorrectly placed next to Desmond, again suggesting that he was grilled. Choice A, though, is correct because the modifier logically follows the noun "steak."

Modifiers

5. (C) This problem challenges you to correct a dangling modifier—that is, an error in which the sentence lacks a specific noun or pronoun being modified. The modifier in question is "struggling to fly." Choice A is invalid because the modifier has been placed before "gust of wind" and therefore suggests that the gust of wind struggled to fly the kite. Choice B, furthermore, is inaccurate because the modifier has been placed after "tree," implying that the tree attempted to fly the kite. Only Choice C corrects the dangling modifier by revealing who was struggling to fly the kite—two young boys.

Coordination

6. (D) One of the ways in which you can achieve coordination is to join two sentences with a transition that has a semicolon before it and a comma after it. This item invites you to choose the appropriate transition based on the context of the sentence. Look at the relationship between the two sentences: The swimmer trained thoroughly; as a result, she felt confident. Option A is invalid because "nevertheless" suggests a contrast, not a result. Option B, furthermore, is false because "besides" implies addition, not result. Option C is also incorrect because "similarly" suggests a relationship based on likeness, not result. Only Option D, "consequently," correctly expresses the relationship of result.

Subordination

7. (B) This question requires you to use subordination effectively by selecting the appropriate subordinating conjunction. Subordination occurs when you join a dependent clause (one that cannot stand alone) and an independent clause (one that can stand alone). Examine the relationship between the clauses in each choice. Choice A, with the subordinating conjunction "in order that," does not make sense and is therefore false. Choice C, with the subordinating conjunction "even though," conveys an illogical contrast. However, Choice B, with the subordinating conjunction "because," logically expresses a cause and effect relationship: *Because we love to read, we visit the library.*

Parallelism

8. (C) This problem quizzes you on parallelism (or sentence balance). Two or more items in a series must share the same grammatical structure to be parallel. Option A is incorrect because the verb "sell" is not parallel with the verb phrase "to volunteer." Option B, moreover, is false because the verb "sell" and the word "volunteering" are not parallel. Option C, though, is accurate because the verbs "sell" and "volunteer" are parallel.

Parallelism

9. (B) In this item, you are looking for a word that is parallel with the key terms in the series: "running" and "diving," both of which end in –ing. Option A is false because "play" is not parallel with "running" and "diving." Option C is also incorrect because "to play" does not parallel "running" and "diving." In addition, Option D is invalid because "and they play" is not consistent with "running" and "diving." Only Option B, "playing," parallels "running" and "diving."

Fragments

10. (B) This item challenges you to recognize fragments. Choice A is incorrect because if you place a period after "falling" and before "the," you will create a fragment. Choice C is inaccurate because if you separate "appeared" from "and" with a period, you will produce a fragment. Choice B, however, is appropriate because a comma, not a period, should follow the introductory clause "When the rain stopped falling and the sun once again emerged." By replacing the period with a comma in this item, you correct the fragment. Lastly, Choice D does not apply because a change is necessary.

Fragments

11. (C) Examine this statement carefully for fragments. Choice A is false because if you were to place a period between "old" and "he," you would create a fragment. Furthermore, Choice B is not applicable because putting a period between "deal" and "by" results in a fragment. However, Choice C works well because by adding the pronoun "he" before "also," you correct the missing subject fragment. A mistake has been made; therefore, Choice D does not apply.

Comma Splices

12. (C) This sentence tests your ability to recognize and correct the comma splice—that is, an error that occurs when you join two sentences with a comma. In fact, a comma splice has occurred between "day" and "they." Option A is inaccurate because the absence of punctuation between "day" and "they" results in a fused sentence (an error that occurs when you join two sentences with no punctuation). Option B is false because a comma has been misplaced after the coordinating conjunction "so." Remember that if you use a coordinating conjunction (for, and, nor, but, or, yet, so) to connect two sentences, you should place a comma *before* the conjunction. Option C, however, corrects the comma splice by placing a semicolon between the two complete sentences. Recall that you can use a semicolon to link two sentences that express a related idea and that are approximately the same length. Clearly, a mistake has been made; thus, Choice D is invalid.

Fused Sentences

13. (B) This problem quizzes you on fused sentences. Please review Item # 12 for a definition of this error. Choice A is incorrect because if you were to place a period between "request" and "Ian," you would create a fragment. Choice C is not accurate because the lack of punctuation between "hour" and "so" creates a fused sentence. Remember to place a comma before a coordinating conjunction like "so" when you are joining two sentences. Choice B, though, uses a semicolon to correct the fused sentence that occurs between "scooter" and "it." Because an error exists, Choice D is inapplicable.

Standard Verb Forms

14. (D) This sentence measures your understanding of standard verb forms. Verbs come in three forms: the present, the past, and the past participle. To make regular present tense verbs such as "type" and "earn" past tense, you add a "d" or an "ed" to them, for example, "typed" and "earned." However, irregular verbs such as those that have been underlined in this item do follow such clear-cut rules. Interestingly, this sentence discusses a past tense action, one that happened "yesterday." Each verb has been correctly used, so Option D is the right response. In Item A, "ran" is the correct past tense form of the present tense verb "run." In Item B, "had broken" is the appropriate past participle form. Lastly, in Item C, the verb "get" is the correct choice after the helping verb "did."

Standard Verb Forms

15. (A) This sentence portrays past tense actions. Option B is not accurate because "run" is a present tense verb. Further, Option C is invalid because "given" is the past participle form of "give"; "given" is used incorrectly because a past participle must always be accompanied by a helper like "has," "have," or "had." Only Option A contains the correct answer: the verb "came" is the appropriate past tense form of "come." An error exists, thus eliminating Option D.

Shifts in Verb Tense

16. (C) This item prompts you to look for shifts in verb tense. The word "since" at the beginning of the sentence implies that an action has begun in the past and continues to the present. In fact, ever since 1936, *Gone with the Wind* has intrigued audiences. The appropriate verb tense to use in this situation is the present perfect—that is, "has" or "have" plus the past participle. Choice A is false because the present tense verb "captivates" does not express the appropriate time relationship. Choice B, moreover, is incorrect because the past progressive verb "was captivating" does not convey the necessary time relationship. Only Choice C, "has captivated," offers the present perfect form of the verb necessary to the meaning of this sentence. Lastly, Choice D is false because the past tense verb "captivated" does not suggest the proper time relationship.

Shifts in Verb Tense

17. (A) Study the verb tenses in this sentence. Notice that the statement about the 1980s rock bands concerns a past tense event. By contrast, the statement about what is happening "these days" addresses the present tense. Option B is inapplicable because the past tense verb "called" does not fit the present tense context; similarly, Option C does not work because the past tense verb "were experiencing" does not match the present tense situation. However, Option A is accurate because the past tense verb "played" is appropriate for events that happened in the 1980s. This sentence contains a mistake; therefore, Option D is invalid.

Subject-Verb Agreement

18. (C) To master this item, you might find it helpful to review the subject-verb agreement rule regarding the word groups "either . . . or" and "neither . . . nor." The verb always agrees in number with the closer of the two subjects in these word groups—that is, with the subject following "or" or "nor." In this item, both the tortoise and the hare are singular; however, the verb agrees with only the closer of the two subjects. Because the "hare" is the closer subject, the verb must agree with it, making Option C, the singular verb "wins," the correct response. By contrast, Option A is incorrect because the plural verb "are winning" does not agree with "hare." Similarly, Option B is not accurate because the plural verb "were winning" does not agree with "hare." Lastly, Option D is false because the plural verb "win" does not agree with "hare."

Subject-Verb Agreement

19. (A) This question prompts you to proofread for subject-verb agreement. Choice B is inapplicable because the plural verb "have" does not agree in number with the singular subject "litter." (Remember that while the word "every," which occurs before "litter," may appear to suggest a plural context, "every" actually refers to a singular item.) Additionally, Choice C is incorrect because the plural verb "capture" does not agree with the singular subject "runt." However, Choice A is valid because the singular verb "looks" agrees with the subject "one." If you missed this item, try the following test strategy: Cross off any prepositional phrases that occur in the sentence, such as "of the puppies." After doing so, you will prevent yourself from thinking a prepositional phrase contains the subject of the sentence, and you are more likely to make the correct subject-verb agreement choice.

Subject-Verb Agreement

20. (B) This item tests your understanding of subject-verb agreement. Remember to cross off any prepositional phrases that you see. Once you eliminate the prepositional phrase between "each" and the verb, you will see that "each" is in fact the subject. Therefore, Choice A is false because the plural verb "appear" does not agree with the singular subject "each." Furthermore, Choice C is incorrect because the plural verb "portray" does not agree with the singular subject "painting." By contrast, Choice B is accurate, but to understand why, you might find it helpful to review inverted sentences that begin with vague sentence starters like "here" and "there." Recall that such words can never be the subject of a sentence. In fact, the subject in an inverted sentence follows the verb. For instance, "dragonfly" and "butterflies" form a compound subject in this sentence; therefore, they require a plural verb, making Choice B—"are"—correct. Because a mistake has been made, Choice D is false.

Pronoun-Antecedent Agreement

21. (D) Pronouns must agree in number (singular or plural) with their antecedents (the nouns or pronouns to which they refer). In this sentence, no change is necessary, making Option D correct. In Item A, the pronoun "he" agrees with the antecedent "boy." In Item B, the pronoun "they" agrees with the antecedent "elephants." Lastly, in Item C, the pronoun "he" agrees with the antecedent "boy."

Pronoun Shifts

22. (C) Try to avoid shifting from one point of view to another when you write. In English, three points of view exist: first, second, and third. Notice that Item A, "us," and Item B, "we," in the underlined areas are both first person plural pronouns. However, a sudden shift occurs in Item C with the third person pronoun "their." Thus, Option C, "our," is the appropriate response because it provides a first person pronoun that is consistent with the rest of the sentence. Because a mistake has been made, Choice D does not work.

Pronoun Shifts

23. (B) This question tests your recognition of pronoun shifts. Choice A is invalid because the first person pronoun "my" does not correctly refer to the third person "Darla." Additionally, Choice C is false because the first person pronoun "us" incorrectly refers to the third person "brothers." However, Choice B, the third person pronoun "she," is appropriate because it is consistent with "Darla." An error has occurred, eliminating Choice D.

Pronoun Reference

24. (B) This item tests your comprehension of pronoun reference. Pronouns should refer clearly to one antecedent. Option A, "their," is incorrect because it lacks a clear antecedent. In addition, Option C, "they," is not valid because it does not clearly refer to an antecedent. However, the pronoun "he" in Item B could refer to either "Mr. Avery" or "Devin." To clarify the pronoun reference, you should select Option B—"he, Devin." Indeed, Option D does not apply.

Pronoun Case

25. (A) Examine this sentence for correct use of pronoun case, which refers to the function a pronoun performs in a sentence. A pronoun may serve as a subject, an object, or a possessive word. Choice B is incorrect because "them" is an object pronoun; however, a subject pronoun is needed before the verb "enjoy." Choice C is also invalid because "they" is a subject pronoun; in this sentence area, an object pronoun is needed after the preposition "for." Choice A, though, is correct because the subject pronoun "she" is needed before the verb "love." Because an error exists, Choice D is ineffective.

Adjectives and Adverbs

26. (C) This sentence challenges you to distinguish adjectives from adverbs. Adjectives describe nouns or pronouns, whereas adverbs describe verbs, adjectives, or other adverbs. Choice A, the adjective "quiet," is invalid because the adverb form of this word—"quietly"—is needed to modify the adjective "elegant." Further, Choice B, the adverb "elegantly," is inapplicable because the adjective "elegant" is the appropriate form before the noun "essay." However, Choice C, the adverb "profoundly," correctly modifies the verb "touched." A mistake has occurred, so Choice D is false.

Degrees of Adjectives and Adverbs

27. (B) In English, adjectives come in three degree forms: basic (standard), comparative (used for two items), and superlative (used for three or more items). In this item, Josh is one member on a team; therefore, the sentence calls for the superlative form of the adjective "powerful." Option A, "more powerful," is incorrect because it is the comparative form. Option C, "most powerfullest," is false because it uses two superlative words—"most" and the grammatically incorrect "powerfullest." Yet Option B, "most powerful," provides the appropriate superlative form. Clearly, an error has occurred; thus, Option D is invalid.

Standard Spelling

28. (D) This question tests your spelling. Commonly misspelled words are those that have several consonants, such as the underlined words in this question: "committee," "succeeded," and "different." Each word, though, has been spelled correctly, making Option D the right response. Options A, B, and C all present incorrect spellings.

Standard Punctuation

29. (B) This problem assesses your mastery over punctuation. Choice A—"Although, Heather"—is invalid because a comma should not follow a subordinating conjunction like "although." Rather, a comma should follow the entire dependent clause that "although" begins; thus, Choice B—"shower, she"—is accurate. By contrast, Choice C—"so, because"—illustrates an error: a comma should not come before a subordinating conjunction like "because." Clearly, a mistake has been made, thereby eliminating Choice D.

Standard Punctuation

30. (C) This item challenges you to use punctuation effectively. Remember to place a comma before a coordinating conjunction when you are joining two sentences but to omit the comma before the conjunction when you are connecting a compound subject, object, or verb. In Item A, you are joining the compound object "programs" and "music" with "and"; therefore, no comma is needed, eliminating Choice A. In Item B, however, you are connecting two complete sentences, so you need to place a comma before the coordinating conjunction "so." Choice B, therefore, is false. Item C tests your recall of the rule for comma usage between adjectives: you should place a comma between adjectives that you could join with "and" and that you could logically switch the order of. It would not make sense to write "next and fund-raising," nor would it be appropriate to write "fund-raising, next." Thus, Choice C—"next fund-raising"—offers a much needed correction. Choice D is inapplicable because a change is necessary.

Standard Punctuation

31. (B) Examine the punctuation in this sentence carefully. Option A is invalid because commas must be used to separate "sweet" from "cold" and "juicy" in this three-item series. Furthermore, Option C is false because a comma is rarely used before the word "that." Option B, though, is correct because a semicolon should be placed before the transitional word "surprisingly" and a comma after it. Indeed, Option D is incorrect because a change is necessary.

Capitalization

32. (C) This item prompts you to capitalize effectively. Choice A is inaccurate because countries like the "Philippines" should always be capitalized. Choice B is false because languages like "English" should always be capitalized. Choice C, though, is valid because seasons such as "fall" should be lowercased. Choice D, then, is inapplicable because a change is necessary.

Main Idea

33. (A) This item measures your ability to find the main idea in a passage. Choice B is inaccurate because it focuses on one aspect of the mermaids—their attempt to lure sailors—but does not capture the overall idea of the reading. Additionally, Choice C is false because it offers one specific detail about Lorelei but does not provide a general overview of the passage. Choice D is also inapplicable because it concentrates on a historical detail, not a central idea. Only Choice A expresses the main point that the myth of mermaids has fascinated humankind for a long time.

Supporting Details

34. (B) This question asks you to identify specific support for the general statement that mermaids have conflicting inner qualities. Option A is invalid because it provides historical information but does not clarify the mermaids' dual nature. Option C is inapplicable because it provides a general statement, not specific support for sentence 6. Option D is false because it mentions a mermaid film but does not develop the point about inner characteristics. Only Choice B, which immediately follows sentence 6, develops the statement about the mermaids' inner traits.

Sequence of Ideas

35. (A) This test item prompts you to find the correct sequence of ideas for three sentences. Option A is correct because it presents historical information about sailors telling stories of mermaids; this option then presents an analysis of the syllables within "mermaid" and concludes by translating what those syllables mean. The translation of "mermaid" should immediately follow the syllable analysis. By contrast, Option B is inaccurate because the sentence offering a translation of the word "mermaid" follows the general statement about history, not the specific analysis of the word. Further, Option C is false because the translation illogically comes before the syllable analysis, which is then followed by historical information. Lastly, Choice D is confusing because the historical information is illogically sandwiched between the translation of "mermaid" and the syllable analysis of this word.

Relevant Ideas

36. (D) This problem challenges you to find the least relevant idea in the passage. Choice A is inaccurate because sentence 2 provides valuable historical information. Choice B is erroneous because sentence 5 contains an important translation of the term "mermaid." Additionally, Choice C is inappropriate because sentence 9 gives a helpful specific example of mermaids. Choice D, though, is valid because it provides an irrelevant detail about the film *The Little Mermaid*, which does not support the main ideas in the paragraph.

Main Idea

37. (D) You are looking for the main idea of this passage. Option A is incorrect because it discusses one quality of impressionism—the portrayal of everyday subjects—but does not offer an overview of the entire passage. Option B is false because it discusses a specific aspect of impressionism—namely, the use of light colors—but does summarize the main idea. Option C is also inaccurate because it mentions four features of impressionism without providing a general overview of the paragraph. Only Option D discusses the main focus of the passage—the impact of impressionism on the art world; therefore, this option is correct.

Sequence of Ideas

38. (A) This item challenges you to arrange the sequence of ideas logically. Option A is correct because it begins with a distinction between traditional and impressionistic-artists. This option goes on to list four key elements of impression. It then provides an explanation of the first element, themes. The transition "to begin" starts a series of sentences in which explanations of all four elements are provided. Option B, though, is incorrect. This option begins logically with a distinction between traditionalists and impressionists. The second and third sentences, however, are out of order. The key elements of impressionism should be mentioned before specific themes, which are an example of one of the elements. Option C is tricky because it opens with the transition "to begin." Yet before specific themes can be explained, you should discuss what the key elements of impressionism are. Additionally, the distinction between traditionalists and impressionists comes illogically at the end of the sequence. Lastly, Option D is incorrect because the sentence about traditionalists versus impressionists is illogically sandwiched between the other two statements.

Relevant Ideas

39. (C) Look for the least relevant detail in the passage. Choice A does not work because sentence 6 provides an important detail about colors. Choice B, moreover, is inaccurate because sentence 8 names specific impressionists whose common goal you learn more about in sentence 9. Choice D is false because sentence 11 offers a necessary conclusion to the passage. However, Choice C is the right response because sentence 10 provides irrelevant information about hotels.

Transitional Devices

40. (D) This item requires you to find the best transition for joining sentences 4 and 5. Remember to focus on the relationship between sentences 4 and 5, not on the two types of artists discussed in sentence 5. Option A, "however," inaccurately suggests that a contrast exists between the sentences. Option B, "finally," is false because it offers closure to a paragraph that is still being developed. Option C, "on the other hand," is incorrect because it expresses a contrast between the sentences. Only Option D, "in addition," correctly conveys a relationship of addition: In addition to portraying everyday themes, impressionism depicts nature realistically.

Explanatory Answer Key for the Writing Posttest

Skill Being Tested	Explanation

Word Choice

1. (C) This item measures your understanding of word choice. Option A is incorrect because a mystery novel cannot hold someone in "suspension," a word that means to delay. Further, Option B is invalid because the word "suspicion," which indicates mistrust or disbelief, does not fit the context of the sentence about the mystery novel. Finally, Option C is accurate because the word "suspense" expresses expectation or anticipation which is what occurs when someone is held in suspense.

Word Choice

2. (B) To understand this question, you must study the context of the sentence. Choice A is incorrect because the word "scanned" means to examine quickly. Most likely a lab assistant would be carefully examining the specimen not scanning or glancing at it quickly. Additionally, Choice C is false because the term "gawked" suggests that someone stares at something in a stupid way. Hopefully, a lab assistant would not look at a specimen in a stupid way. In Choice B, the word "peered" means to examine or look closely which is what a lab assistant does when he or she looks through a microscope and studies a specimen. Choice B is the correct response.

Confused Words

3. (B) This sentence quizzes you on easily confused words. Choice A is inaccurate because the word "it's" is the contraction for it is which you would use to say, "It is a common occurrence." Choice C is incorrect because the word "their" indicates possession and the sentence clearly states that the keys belong to college students. Note that the word "there" is something that is here or nearby. Choice D, moreover, is false because the sentence is not correct as it is written and a change is needed. Lastly, Choice B is valid because the word "lose" means to misplace an object. A college student would misplace (lose) their keys not loose them. The word "loose" refers to something that is not tied down and does not fit the meaning of the sentence.

Modifiers

4. (A) This question tests your awareness of misplaced modifiers. A modifier is a descriptive word or group of words that should be placed next to the noun or pronoun it modifies. When modifiers are misplaced, readers feel confused. In this question, the modifier is "the squirrel searched busily for food." In Choice B, the modifier has been incorrectly placed before "food," thereby implying that the food was leaping from tree to tree. In Choice C, indicates that the backyard was leaping from tree to tree. However, in Choice A, the modifier is placed correctly indicating the squirrel leaped from tree to tree searching for food.

Modifiers

5. (C) This problem challenges you to correct a dangling modifier—that is, an error in which the sentence lacks a specific noun or pronoun being modified. The modifier in question is "struggling to fly." Choice A is invalid because it does not tell us who rowed the canoe across the lake. The way the sentence reads suggests that the oars actually rowed the canoe by themselves. Choice B, furthermore, is inaccurate because the modifier has been placed after "water," implying that the water attempted to row the canoe. Only Choice C corrects the dangling modifier by explaining who rowed across the lake and the sound that the oars made in the water.

Coordination

6. (A) One of the ways in which you can achieve coordination is to join two sentences with a transition that has a semicolon before it and a comma after it. This item invites you to choose the appropriate transition based on the context of the sentence. Look at the relationship between the two sentences: The drivers travel with cell phones; as a result, they no longer need to stop to use pay phones. Option B is invalid because "next" implies that something follows and is not a result. Option C is also incorrect because "however" suggests a contrasting relationship between the two sentences, not a result. Option D, "likewise," is also incorrect because it suggests that the two sentences are referring to something similar and that does not show a relationship of result. Only Option A, "consequently," correctly expresses the relationship of result.

Subordination

7. (B) This question requires you to use subordination effectively by selecting the appropriate subordinating conjunction. Subordination occurs when you join a dependent clause (one that cannot stand alone) and an independent clause (one that can stand alone). Examine the relationship between the clauses in each choice. Choice A is incorrect because it does not make sense. Using the subordinating conjunction "if Veronica received," indicates that we are not sure if she received any job offers: however, we are saying that she did not accept what she received. Choice C, with the subordinating conjunction "provided that," conveys an illogical contrast because it indicates that we know what Veronica is going to do before she actually does it. The word "provided" says that we know the positions will be made available to Veronica, but she will not accept any of them. However, Choice B, with the subordinating conjunction "although," logically expresses a contrast relationship: *Although* Veronica received three job offers, she did not accept.

Parallelism

8. (C) This problem quizzes you on parallelism (or sentence balance). Two or more items in a series must share the same grammatical structure to be parallel. Option A is incorrect because the verb "wrote" is not parallel with the verb phrase "to deliver." Option B, moreover, is false because the verb "wrote" and the word "delivering" are not parallel. Option C, though, is accurate because the verbs "wrote" and "delivered" both indicate past tense and are parallel.

Parallelism

9. (A) In this item, you are looking for a word that is parallel with the key terms in the series: "lights flicker," "music lures," and "dancers ____." Option B is false because "they move" does not fit the context of the sentence and is not parallel "flicker" and "lures." Option C is also incorrect because "to move" does not parallel "flicker" and "lures." In addition, Option D is invalid because "are moving" is not consistent with "flicker" and "lures." Only Option A, "move," parallels "flicker" and "lures."

Fragments

10. (B) This item challenges you to recognize fragments. Choice A is incorrect because if you have no punctuation between "intersection" and "then," you will create a run-on sentence. Choice C is not correct because placing a semicolon after the introductory clause "If the light turns yellow at the busy intersection," does not correct the fragment. A mistake has been made; therefore, Choice D is not appropriate. Choice B is accurate because placing a comma between "intersection" and "then" makes the statement a complete sentence.

Fragments

11. (D) Examine this statement carefully for fragments. Choice A is false because if you were to place a period between "library" and "which," you would create a fragment. Furthermore, Choice B is not applicable because putting a period between "Jacksonville" and "children" results in a fragment. Choice C is also incorrect because placing the semicolon after "feet" and before "as" also creates a fragment. However, Choice D works well because the sentence is correct as it is written and needs no change.

Comma Splices

12. (C) This sentence tests your ability to recognize and correct the comma splice—that is, an error that occurs when you join two sentences with a comma. In fact, a comma splice has occurred between "roommate" and "the envelope." Option A is inaccurate because the absence of punctuation between "roommate" and "the envelope" results in a fused sentence (an error that occurs when you join two sentences with no punctuation). Option B is false because a comma has been misplaced after the coordinating conjunction "and." Remember that if you use a coordinating conjunction (for, and, nor, but, or, yet, so) to connect two sentences, you should place a comma *before* the conjunction. Clearly, a mistake has been made; thus, Choice D is invalid. Option C, however, corrects the comma splice by placing a semicolon between the two complete sentences. Recall that you can use a semicolon to link two sentences that express a related idea and that are approximately the same length.

Fused Sentences

13. (C) This problem quizzes you on fused sentences. Choice A is incorrect because if you were to place a semicolon between "parade" and "they," you would create a fragment. Choice B is not accurate because placing only a comma after "awe" would make this a run-on sentence. Because an error exists, Choice D is inapplicable. Choice C, though, uses a comma between "siren" and "and" to correct the fused sentence. Remember to place a comma before a coordinating conjunction like "and" when you are joining two sentences.

Standard Verb Forms

14. (A) This sentence measures your understanding of standard verb forms. Verbs come in three forms: the present, the past, and the past participle. To make regular present tense verbs such as "type" and "earn" past tense, you add a "d" or an "ed" to them, for example, "typed" and "earned." This sentence, for example, discusses a past tense action, therefore; Option A "saw" is the correct choice for this sentence to show a past tense action. In Item B, "had boughten" makes no sense because boughten is not a word. In item C, "could rode" is not the correct form of the verb to show a past tense action. Lastly, an error exists thus eliminating Option D.

Standard Verb Forms

15. (C) This sentence portrays past tense actions. Option A is not accurate because "should wore" is the past participle form and must be accompanied by a helper like "has," "have," or "had." Further, Option B is invalid because "should had worn" is the incorrect form of the verb. Only Option C contains the correct answer: the verb "should have worn" is the appropriate past tense form. An error exists, thus eliminating Option D.

Shifts in Verb Tense

16. (B) This item prompts you to look for shifts in verb tense. The phrase "In past decades" at the beginning of the sentence implies that an action has begun in the past and continues to the present. Choice A is false because the present tense verb "use" does not express the appropriate time relationship. Choice C, "could save," is not the correct form of the verb necessary to convey the meaning of this sentence. Choice D is false because a change must be made in order for the sentence to show the correct time relationship. Only choice B is correct because the past tense form of the verb "preferred" shows the necessary time relationship.

Shifts in Verb Tense

17. (C) Study the verb tenses in this sentence. Notice that the opening of the dinosaur exhibit last month concerns a past tense event that is still continuing. Option A is inapplicable because the present tense verb "take" does not fit the past tense context; similarly, Option B does not work because the past tense verb "were taking" does not match the present tense situation. However, Option C is accurate because the past participle form "have taken" is appropriate for events that happened in the past and are continuing today. This sentence contains a mistake; therefore, Option D is invalid.

Subject-Verb Agreement

18. (A) To master this item, you might find it helpful to review the subject-verb agreement rule regarding the word groups "either . . . or" and "neither . . . nor." The verb always agrees in number with the closer of the two subjects in these word groups—that is, with the subject following "or" or "nor." In this item, the verb must agree with the closer of the two subjects. Because "candy" is the closer subject, the verb must agree with it, making Option A, the singular verb "interests," the correct response. By contrast, Option B is incorrect because the plural verb "are interesting" does not agree with "candy." Similarly, Option C is not accurate because "have interest" does not agree with "candy." Lastly, Option D is false because a change is necessary for the sentence to read correctly.

Subject-Verb Agreement

19. (A) This question prompts you to proofread for subject-verb agreement. Choice B is inapplicable because the plural verb "move" does not agree in number with the singular subject "musicians." (Remember that while the word "each," which occurs before "musicians," may appear to suggest a plural context, "each" actually refers to a singular item.) Additionally, Choice C is incorrect because the plural verb "fill" does not agree with the singular verb "moves." Option D is false because a change is necessary for the sentence to be correct. However, Choice A is valid because the singular verb "performs" agrees with singular subject "musicians" and the singular verbs "moves" and "fills."

Subject-Verb Agreement

20. (D) This item tests your understanding of subject-verb agreement. If you don't understand why D is the correct choice, try the following test strategy: Cross off any prepositional phrases that occur in the sentence, such as "of the schools." The subject, "superintendent" is singular, so the singular verb forms "has exclaimed," "is," and "is working" all agree with the singular subject. Removing prepositional phrases will prevent you from thinking a prepositional phrase contains the subject of the sentence, and you are more likely to make the correct subject-verb agreement choice.

Pronoun-Antecedent Agreement

21. (B) Pronouns must agree in number (singular or plural) with their antecedents (the nouns or pronouns to which they refer). In this sentence, option A is incorrect because the singular subject "dog" does not agree with the possessive pronoun "their." Option C is incorrect because the singular subject "dog" does not agree in number with "them," a plural pronoun that would indicate there is more than one dog. Option D is incorrect because there is a mistake in the sentence. Option B is correct because the plural pronoun "they" before the word patted agrees with the pronoun antecedent "his" owners by explaining to the reader that there is more than one owner.

Pronoun Shifts   22. (D) This item quizzes you on needless pronoun shifts. Option A is invalid because the second person "you" incorrectly refers to the students. Option B is also inaccurate because the first person pronoun "me" inaccurately refers to the third person Mrs. McBride. Similarly, Option C represents a needless shift from the third person "her" to the first person "our." Only Option D, no change is necessary, offers a valid choice.

Pronoun Shifts   23. (D) In English, three points of view exist: first, second, and third. Notice that Item A, "us," and Item B, "we," in the underlined areas are both first person plural pronouns. In item C "it" refers to the sundress and is also used correctly. Replacing the underlined words in the sentence with "you," "they," or "you," as listed in options A, B, or C would cause pronoun shift to occur. Thus, Option D is the appropriate response because no change is necessary.

Pronoun Reference   24. (B) This item tests your comprehension of pronoun reference. Pronouns should refer clearly to one antecedent. Option A, "their," is incorrect because it lacks a clear antecedent. In addition, Option C, "its," is not valid because it does not clearly refer to an antecedent. Option D does not apply because it is necessary to make a change in the sentence in order for it to read correctly. However, option B "he, Steve" makes it clear to the reader that Steve told his assistant which kind of camera lens he needed to use.

Pronoun Case   25. (B) Examine this sentence for correct use of pronoun case, which refers to the function a pronoun performs in a sentence. A pronoun may serve as a subject, an object, or a possessive word. Choice A is invalid because "I" is a subject pronoun; in this sentence area, an object pronoun is needed. Choice C is incorrect because "them" is an object pronoun. Because an error exists, Choice D is ineffective. Choice B, though, is correct because the subject pronoun "she" is needed before the verb phrase "have been dating."

Adjectives and Adverbs   26. (D) This sentence challenges you to distinguish adjectives from adverbs. Adjectives describe nouns or pronouns, whereas adverbs describe verbs, adjectives, or other adverbs. Choice A, the adverb "tastefully," is invalid because the adverb form of this word—"tasteful"—is needed to describe the verb "looked." Further, Choice B, "careful," would be incorrect if used before the verb "sewn." Choice C is inapplicable because the adverb "skillfully" is not appropriate when describing the noun "tailor." No mistake has occurred, so Choice D is correct.

Degrees of Adjectives and Adverbs

27. (A) In English, adjectives come in three degree forms: basic (standard), comparative (used for two items), and superlative (used for three or more items). In this item, Gabriel is one of two brothers; therefore, the sentence requires you to select option A, the comparative form of the adjective "younger." Option B, "youngest," is incorrect because it is the superlative form. Option C, "more young," is false because it uses two superlative words and does not fit the context of the sentence. Clearly, an error has occurred; thus, Option D is invalid.

Standard Spelling

28. (C) This question tests your spelling. When we pronounce a word incorrectly, we do hear certain sounds that would help us spell the word correctly. We may also use the wrong word in a sentence because it has a similar spelling. The word "collage" looks and sounds very much like "college," but the two words mean something very different. A "collage" is a collection of things. The word "college" refers to a university. Your sister is a sophomore in "college," not "collage," making Option C the correct choice. Options A and B present incorrect spellings. Option D would be eliminated because an error does occur.

Standard Spelling

29. (B) In this sentence, Option A would not be valid because it is not necessary to capitalize "cable company" unless the proper name of the company is also used in contraction with cable company. For example, you would capitalize "cable company" only if it were used as part of the company's name such as Jones Cable Company. Option C is not valid because "spanish" is the name of a language and is always capitalized. Option D would be incorrect because a change is necessary. Option B is valid because "Southwest" is the name of a region in the United States and is considered a proper noun.

Standard Punctuation

30. (B) This item challenges you to use punctuation effectively. Option A in this sentence would be incorrect because "you're" is the conjunction for you are and would not fit in the context of the sentence. Option C is not valid because the sentence is asking a question; therefore, you would not use a period after the word labor. Option D would be incorrect because a change is necessary. Option B is the correct choice because the word "weeks" needs to include an apostrophe (to show possession) so the reader knows that the labor occurred within the week.

Standard Punctuation

31. (B) This item also challenges you to use punctuation effectively. Remember to place a comma before a coordinating conjunction when you are joining two sentences but to omit the comma before the conjunction. Option A is incorrect because this sentence begins with a subordinate clause and no comma is needed between the first word "because" and the second word "the." Option C is not valid because the word "others" needs an apostrophe to show that the grandchildren belong to both the Smith and Jones families. Choice D is inapplicable because a change is necessary. Option B is correct because a comma is needed between "years and they" to separate the subordinate clause from the independent clause.

Punctuation

32. (D) This item is another test in using punctuation correctly. Choice A is inaccurate because commas are used to separate items in a series and there is no comma between "golf " and "baseball." Also, commas are used with coordinating conjunctions to separate compound sentences. This is a compound sentence but Choice A does not use a comma before the conjunction "but" which is needed to separate the two sentences correctly. Choice B is false because again there is no comma between "golf " and "baseball." Choice C is not valid because there is no comma before the conjunction "but" which is needed to separate the two sentences correctly. Choice D, then, is correct because commas are used correctly to separate items in a series and with the coordinating conjunction "but" to punctuate the compound sentence correctly.

Main Idea

33. (C) This item measures your ability to find the main idea in a passage. Choice A is inaccurate because it focuses on one aspect of the job interview—business attire--but does not capture the overall idea of the reading. Additionally, Choice B is false because it offers one specific detail about when applicants should arrive for the job interview but does not provide a general overview of the passage. Choice D is also inapplicable because it concentrates on what kind of questions candidates should expect, not a central idea. Only Choice C expresses the main point that the job interview is like an exam for which applicants must carefully prepare.

Supporting Details

34. (A) This question asks you to identify specific support for the general statement that the job interview is like an exam for which applicants should carefully prepare. Option B is invalid because it provides information about two types of questions applicants should expect and does not provide support for sentence three that refers to the candidate immediately being evaluated as she enters the waiting room. Option C is inapplicable because it provides a general statement, not specific support for sentence 3. Option D is false because again it refers to how a candidate should answer questions. Only Choice A, which immediately follows sentence 3, develops the statement about a candidate being evaluated the moment she enters the waiting room.

Relevant Ideas

35. (D) This test item prompts you to find the least relevant idea in the passage. Option A is incorrect because sentence 2 needs to follow the main idea of the passage that supports the fact that applicants should carefully prepare for the job interview in a variety of ways. Option B is inaccurate because the sentence 6 offers the reader a more detailed explanation as to why the applicant's style of dress can make a difference in the way he or she is perceived in the job interview. Further, Option C is false because sentence 10 explains one of the two questions that the applicant can anticipate in the job interview which the reader is introduced to in sentence 9. Choice D is correct because the statement "Interviews can be nerve-wrecking experiences" is an obvious statement and the least relevant sentence in the passage.

Sequence of Ideas

36. (B) This test item prompts you to find the correct word or phrase that could be used to make the relationship of certain sentences in the passage clearer. Choice A is inaccurate because "conversely" indicates a contrasting relationship between the sentences and would not fit the context of the meaning linking sentence 9 to sentence 10. Additionally, Choice C is inappropriate because "therefore" implies a cause/effect relationship which does not exist between these two sentences. Choice D is not valid because "also" means too and this idea would not logically come before the use of the transition, secondly in sentence 11. Option B, "First" is the logical choice to fall in sentence 10 because sentence 11 begins with secondly and introduces the second type of question applicants should anticipate in the job interview.

Main Idea

37. (C) You are looking for the main idea of this passage. Option A is incorrect because it only discusses where comics can be located in a newspaper and does not offer an overview of the entire passage. Option B is false because it discusses a specific aspect of comic strips — namely, what becomes of some characters—but does summarize the main idea. Option D is also inaccurate because it mentions what a few comics portray without providing a general overview of the paragraph. Only Option C discusses the main focus of the passage—that comic strips are a popular form of art that both entertains and offers insight into life; therefore, this option is correct.

Supporting Details

38. (D) This item asks you to look for the sentence that provides specific support for sentence 5 in the passage. Choice A does not work because sentence 2 provides details about how comic strips reflect their creators' curiosity and enthusiasm for learning, not that comics are frequently referred to as "funnies." Choice B, moreover, is inaccurate because sentence 3 lends support to sentence 2 by explaining how cartoonists express readers' unspoken thoughts and feelings. Choice C is false because sentence 4 refers specifically to the comic strip, Peanuts by Charles Schultz. It uses Schultz's work to explain how some comic strips invite readers to look more innocently at the world, but it does not lend support to sentence 5 which states that comic strips are frequently referred to as "funnies." However, Choice D is the right response because sentence 6 states that most comics contain humor which supports sentence 5 that states comic strips are frequently referred to as "funnies."

Sequence of Ideas

39. (A) This item challenges you to arrange the sequence of ideas logically. Option A is correct because in sentence 8 follows a statement about readers finding humor in comics that reveal a truth about life. The sentence, beginning with "For instance" provides the reader with an example that clarifies sentence 7. Option B is incorrect because part of the sentence has been left out and the reader has no idea which comic strip the writer is talking about. Option C is incorrect because the sentences are out of order and don't make sense. Option D is incorrect because the passage is inverted. The last sentence needs to come first for the reader to get a real sense of the sentence's meaning.

Transitional Devices

40. (B) This item requires you to find the best transition for joining sentences 11 and 12. Remember to focus on the relationship between sentences 11 and 12, not on the two types of artists discussed in sentence 5. Option A, "on the other hand," inaccurately suggests that a contrast exists between the sentences. Option C "for instance," is incorrect because it leads the reader to believe an example follows. Option D, "next," incorrectly conveys a relationship of addition. Only option B, "indeed" offers the reader a concluding statement that refers back to the main idea in sentence 1 that comic strips are a popular form of art that gives insight into life and entertains audiences.

Part Seven: Appendix

ORGANIZATIONAL CHART FOR PLANNING A PARAGRAPH

Topic _____

Prewriting strategy _____

In the space below complete a prewriting activity such as brainstorming, free writing, or clustering (mapping).

Are the ideas from your prewriting examples; reasons; steps; activities; characteristics describing an item, place, or person; likenesses; differences; meanings; points in an argument; a restatement of ideas; a list of items in order of value or facts?

_____

Now that you have completed your prewriting, you need to think about the pattern of development you will use in your paragraph. Doing that will help you to write a clear and well-organized paper.

_____

Using the list below underline the pattern of development you plan to use.

Patterns		Suggested words or ideas for topic sentence
Process	lists steps or stages	steps, stages
Time Order	lists activities or events	events, activities
Contrast	lists differences	but, yet, different, unlike, however
Comparison	lists similarities	similarly, alike, also, similar
Descriptive	creates a sensory picture by appealing to the senses	name what is being described and group the characteristics
Illustration/ Example	includes a broad statement and examples	your generalization should be the topic statement
Classification	divides a large group into small groups by specific characteristics	name the large group, how many small groups, and a characteristic used to separate them
Cause/Effect	states reasons or conditions and their effects or consequences	cause, effect, problem, solution, as a result, consequences
Argumentation	emphasizes a particular point or issue	name the point you will support
Summary	restates ideas in brief form	group ideas
Definition	lists meanings or explains a meaning thoroughly	name the word being defined and state how many definitions it has, or that one definition needs to be explained
Enumeration/ Addition	stresses supplementary information	another, an additional, moreover

240

Order of Importance	lists items in order of their value	name a grouping word for the items or people and how they are ranked
Spatial	described in the order the characteristics are placed	name the object or place and group the characteristics

Now that you have determined the pattern of development, use the charts on the following pages to choose the transitions and clue words that you may use when writing your paragraph.

Write the transitions and clue words below.

Transitional and Clue Words

Process *list steps* *stages*	Time Order *include* *activities* *events*	Contrast *state differences*	Comparison *state likenesses* *similarities*	Spatial *include words* *that show* *place order*
after	after	alternatively	also	above
afterward	afterward	although	akin	adjacent to
again	again	but	alike	behind
as	as	can be distinguished from	analogous	below
before	at length	conversely	as well	between
finally	at the same time	despite	as well as	beyond
first	before	differs from	by comparison	closer to
following this	currently	different from	by the same token	down from
fourth	during	distinct	comparable	east
immediately	earlier	distinguished from	correspondingly	elsewhere
next	eventually	distinctive	equal	far
second	finally	diverse	equally	farther
then	first	even so	equivalent	here
third	following this	however	identical	in back
while	formerly	in contrast	in a similar manner	in front of
	from now on	in spite of	in like manner	in the distance
	immediately	instead	in the same way	near
	in the future	inversely	likewise	nearby
	in the meantime	nevertheless	parallel	neighboring on
	in the past	nonetheless	related	north
	later	notwithstanding	same	on top
	meantime	on the contrary	similarly	opposite to
	meanwhile	on the one hand/ on the other hand		south
	next	otherwise		straight ahead
	now	rather		there
	presently	still		to the left
	previously	though		to the right
	second	unlike		west
	shortly	yet		
	simultaneously	whereas		
	sometimes			
	soon			
	subsequently			
	then			
	thereafter			
	third			
	today			
	tomorrow			
	when			
	while			

Illustration Example	Classification	Cause Effect	Argumentation/ Emphasis	Summary
state generalization and examples	*name large group divided into a small group by specific characteristics*	*state reason or condition and effect or consequence*	*make your point give evidence to support your claim*	*give brief explanation of what was said*
as demonstrated	categorized	accordingly	absolutely	as had been stated
for example	category	affect	above all	as has been noted
for instance	characteristics	as a result	always	as I have said
in fact	class	because	best	finally
in general	divided into	cause	by all means	in conclusion
in this case	field	consequently	certainly	in other words
in particular	grouped	effect	extremely	in short
specifically	kind	for that reason	emphatically	in summary
such as	parts	hence	highest	lastly
the following examples	some features	if, then	major	summing up
thus	the first category	may be due to	minor	to recapitulate
to demonstrate	the first group	on account of	most	to rephrase
to illustrate	the first kind	problems	most important	to sum up
	the first type	reasons	never	thus
	the second category	results	positively	to summarize
	the second group	since	primary	
	the second kind	so	surely	
	the second type	solutions	undeniably	
	the third category	therefore	unquestionably	
	the third group	thus	vital	
	the third kind		without a doubt	
	the third type		without reserve	
	types			
	various elements			

Definition	Enumeration/ Addition	Order of Importance	Descriptive
list meanings	*provide supplementary information*	*list items in order of value*	*create a picture of the object or scene-* *use adjectives to describe the sight, sound, smell, taste, and feel of the object or scene*
can be defined as	additionally	first	above
connotation	again	more importantly	adjacent to
definition	also	most	behind
denotation	equally important is	second	below
is called	finally	the least important	between
is defined	further	the most important	beyond
meanings	furthermore	third	closer to
means	in addition		down from
term	last		east
	moreover		elsewhere
	one more thing		far near
	secondly		farther
	thirdly		here
			in back
			in front of
			in the distance
			nearby
			neighboring on
			north
			on top
			opposite to
			south
			straight ahead
			there
			to the left
			to the right
			west

Paragraph Outline

I.   Topic sentence _____

                   _____

                   _____

II.   Major support _____

                   _____

1   _____

    A. Minor detail _____

                   _____

    B. Minor detail _____

                   _____

    C. Minor detail _____

                   _____

III.   Major support _____

                   _____

    A. Minor detail _____

                   _____

    B. Minor detail _____

                   _____

    C. Minor detail _____

                   _____

IV.　Major support　_____

　　　_____

　　　_____

　　A.　Minor detail　_____

　　　_____

　　B.　Minor detail　_____

　　　_____

　　C.　Minor detail　_____

　　　_____

V.　Concluding sentence　_____

　　　_____

　　　_____

　　　_____

The Paper Plan:
A Step-by-Step Approach to Essay Writing

I.   On the computer or in your English journal, begin the writing process by doing a <u>prewriting activity</u> such as brainstorming, free writing, or clustering.

II.   In the space provided, write a <u>creative lead-in and background information</u> for the introduction.

_____

_____

_____

_____

III.   Write a <u>thesis statement</u> for the essay.

_____

_____

_____

_____

_____

IV.   Next, write a <u>topic sentence for each of your body paragraphs</u>. (The average essay will have two to four body paragraphs.)

Topic Sentence for Body Paragraph 1:

_____

_____

_____

Topic Sentence for Body Paragraph 2:

_____

_____

_____

Topic Sentence for Body Paragraph 3:

_____

_____

_____

Topic Sentence for Body Paragraph 4:

_____

_____

_____

247

V.   Provide <u>evidence</u> in the form of <u>general statements</u> (explanations, observations, examples) and <u>specific details</u> (facts, examples, experiences) to support each topic sentence. Complete the outline below by listing evidence that you plan to include in each body paragraph.

    A.   **Body Paragraph 1**

        1.

        2.

        3.

    B.   **Body Paragraph 2**

        1.

        2.

        3.

    C.   **Body Paragraph 3**

        1.

        2.

        3.

    D.   **Body Paragraph 4**

        1.

        2.

        3.

VI.   Use <u>transitions</u> to add a sense of unity to your essay. List at least three transitions you plan to include in the paper.

    _____   _____   _____

VII. In the space provided, <u>summarize the main ideas</u> in your essay and <u>re-state the thesis</u> in fresh, original terms.

    _____

    _____

    _____

    _____